Temperance and Cosmopolitanism

AFRICANA RELIGIONS

Edited by
Sylvester A. Johnson, *Virginia Tech*
Edward E. Curtis IV, *Indiana University–Purdue University, Indianapolis*

ADVISORY BOARD:
Afe Adogame, *Princeton Theological Seminary*
Sylviane Diouf, *Historian of the African Diaspora*
Paul C. Johnson, *University of Michigan*
Elizabeth Pérez, *University of California, Santa Barbara*
Elisha P. Renne, *University of Michigan*
Judith Weisenfeld, *Princeton University*

Adopting a global vision for the study of Black religions, the Africana Religions book series explores the rich diversity of religious history and life among African and African-descended people. It publishes research on African-derived religions of Orisha devotion, Christianity, Islam, and other religious traditions that are part of the Africana world. The series emphasizes the translocal nature of Africana religions across national, regional, and hemispheric boundaries.

Temperance and Cosmopolitanism

African American Reformers in the Atlantic World

CAROLE LYNN STEWART

The Pennsylvania State University Press
University Park, Pennsylvania

This book is freely available in an open access edition with the generous support of The Pennsylvania State University Libraries. Digital copies are available for download through the Pennsylvania State University Press website.

Library of Congress Cataloging-in-Publication Data

Names: Stewart, Carole Lynn, author.
Title: Temperance and cosmopolitanism : African American reformers in the Atlantic world / Carole Lynn Stewart.
Description: University Park, Pennsylvania : The Pennsylvania State University Press, [2018] | Series: Africana religions | Includes bibliographical references and index.
Summary "A study of select nineteenth-century African American authors and reformers who mobilized the discourses of cosmopolitanism and restraint to expand the meaning of freedom"—Provided by publisher.
Identifiers: LCCN 2018023205 | ISBN 9780271082035 (cloth : alk. paper)
Subjects: LCSH: American literature—African American authors—History and criticism. | American literature—19th century—History and criticism. | Cosmopolitanism in literature. | Temperance in literature. | African American social reformers—History—19th century.
Classification: LCC PS153.N5 S754 2018 | DDC 810.9/896073—dc23
LC record available at https://lccn.loc.gov/2018023205

Copyright © 2018 Carole Stewart
All rights reserved
Printed in the United States of America
Published by The Pennsylvania State University Press,
University Park, PA 16802–1003

The Pennsylvania State University Press is a member of the Association of University Presses.

It is the policy of The Pennsylvania State University Press to use acid-free paper. Publications on uncoated stock satisfy the minimum requirements of American National Standard for Information Sciences—Permanence of Paper for Printed Library Material, ANSI Z39.48–1992.

FOR MY TEACHERS.

The world as cosmos, a home, and receptacle for the human mode of being, is based upon this perception of space and the human transversal through it. The sacred as orientation and as those forms perceived from this orientation is defined in this movement.

—CHARLES H. LONG

Contents

Acknowledgments *ix*

Introduction: Slave Travels and the Beginnings of a Temperate Cosmopolitanism *1*

1 | William Wells Brown and Martin Delany: Civil and Geographic Spaces of Temperate Cosmopolitanism *23*

2 | Brown's Temperate Cosmopolitan "Home": Creole Civilization and Temperate Manners *57*

3 | George Moses Horton's Freedom: A Temperate Republicanism and a Critical Cosmopolitanism *85*

4 | Frances E. W. Harper's Black Cosmopolitan Creoles: A Temperate Transnationalism *111*

5 | "The Quintessence of Sanctifying Grace": Amanda Smith's Religious Experience, Freedom, and a Temperate Cosmopolitanism *141*

Epilogue: Tempering and Conjuring the Roots of Cosmopolitan Recovery *169*

Notes *181*
Bibliography *199*
Index *211*

Acknowledgments

This book has been a long time in the making, and many people and sources of support have made it possible. My colleagues in the English department at Brock University have been especially supportive of my work and scholarship, having listened to me present on African American reform, particularly on William Wells Brown, Frances Harper, and temperance, on several occasions. Thank you to Mathew Martin, Lynn Arner, Tim Conley, James Allard, Gregory Betts, Neta Gordon, Natalee Caple, Ronald Cummings, Rob Alexander, Barbara Seeber, Martin Danahay, Leah Knight, Gale Coskan-Johnson, Elizabeth Sauer, Sue Speerey, Andrew Pendakis, and Janet Sackfie. Brock University's former dean Douglass Kneale provided support, and the current dean of humanities, Carol Merriam, supported my work and travel funding to conferences related to my research. Thank you also to associate dean Michael Carter, and to the Humanities Research Associates at Brock University for a grant that helped complete this project.

Students have also assisted with this project. Thank you to Liam Campbell for his perceptive discussions in our 2016 directed reading course on cosmopolitanism that addressed the works of Brown and Delany, among others. Emily Van Haren also completed work as my research assistant in 2016 in proofreading parts of the manuscript. In 2014 and 2017 I also taught a graduate course in Brock University's joint graduate program in Canadian American studies with the University at Buffalo on the mythology of the Underground Railroad in Southern Ontario and the transnational history of black Canadian writings. Thank you to the students in those courses, as well as Marian Bredin, Gregory Betts, and Dean Carol Merriam for supporting the creation of that program.

My colleague Dan Malleck from Health Sciences has also been encouraging of my work on temperance. Before I came to Brock in 2010, a journal he edits, the *Social History of Alcohol and Drugs*, published my first paper related to this project, on George Moses Horton, "Slave to the Bottle and the Plough: The Inner and Outer Worlds of Freedom in George Moses Horton's Poetry," *Social History of Alcohol and Drugs* 22, no. 1 (Fall 2007): 45–64. Chapter 3 draws on and develops that first publication. Selections from chapter 2 also appeared in different form in "A Transnational Temperance Discourse? William Wells Brown, Creole Civilization, and Temperate Manners," *Journal of Transnational American Studies* 3, no. 1 (March 2011): https://escholarship.org/uc/item/8qd1j3m9. Parts of chapter 5 originally appeared as "'The Quintessence of Sanctifying Grace': Amanda Smith's Religious Experience, Freedom, and a Temperate Cosmopolitanism," *Journal of Africana Religions* 1, no. 3 (2013): 348–75.

My research and thinking related to these authors and the project began earlier than my tenure at Brock, when I was an assistant professor at the University of Maryland, Baltimore County (UMBC) (2007–10). The English department supported much of my early research on William Wells Brown and on developing ideas related to temperance, civil society, and cosmopolitanism. Thank you to faculty there, including Raphael Falco, and especially to Jessica Berman, who also made time following my departure from UMBC to comment on selected aspects of the manuscript. I also received the Dean's Summer Faculty Fellowship on my Brown research when at UMBC, and in 2009 I was awarded the Dresher Center for the Humanities fellowship for research on the Woman's Christian Temperance Union (WCTU) and its African American chapters. Thank you to Rebecca Boehling for her support and encouragement of my research at that time. I visited the libraries at Northwestern University and the Frances Willard House for initial research on the *Union Signal* and black chapters in the WCTU. This initial research would influence my decision to focus on Frances Harper and Amanda Berry Smith. In 2009, I also participated in a Folger seminar directed by Anthony Pagden titled "From Empire to Cosmopolis," which contributed to some of my developing thoughts on cosmopolitanism.

The work of and conversations with the historian of religions Charles H. Long has long provided me with intellectual guidance and inspiration. Members of the Canadian Association of American Studies, particularly Jennifer Harris, have been a warm and encouraging audience to present my ideas to over the past several years. Patrick Alexander, the director of Pennsylvania State University Press, helped guide this manuscript to completion. Thank you to Alex Vose for her assistance; to the anonymous reviewers whose comments helped to strengthen the manuscript; and to the series editors, Edward Curtis and Sylvester Johnson, for their support of this project. Finally, Jeremy Rehwaldt provided excellent copyediting of unwieldy and repetitive parts, and Nicholas Taylor copyedited and strengthened the final version. Clearly, any errors are my own.

Introduction
Slave Travels and the Beginnings of a Temperate Cosmopolitanism

> It was Hegel's genius to endow lordship and
> bondage with such a rich resonance of meaning
> that the model could be applied to every form
> of physical and psychological domination....
> Above all, Hegel bequeathed a message that
> would have a profound impact on future thought,
> especially ... Marx and Freud ... : that one can
> expect nothing from the mercy of God or exercise
> worldly lordship in His or other names; that
> man's true emancipation, whether physical or
> spiritual, must always depend on those who have
> endured and overcome some form of slavery.
>
> —DAVID BRION DAVIS, *The Problem of Slavery in
> the Age of Revolution, 1770–1823*

RACE, SLAVERY, AND ADDICTION

On May 1, 1851, the doors of the Great Industrial Exhibition of All Nations opened in the Hyde Park section of London. Under the administration and supervision of Prince Albert, Queen Victoria's German consort, the exhibition had been in its planning stages for more than three years. While other world fairs had been held in Europe, the Great Exhibition—dubbed the "Crystal Palace" by the literary magazine *Punch* in recognition of the large three-tiered glass structure that housed it—emphasized the new technology of the Industrial Revolution and encouraged participation from all countries involved. In addition, the event's organizers hoped to stimulate discussion and enhance the possibilities for free trade among the nations. Free trade would encourage the manufacture and dissemination of the products of industrial technology for worldwide consumption, thereby lessening the tension between nations and providing a basis for peace.

The Great Exhibition, the first international fair to which the United States had been invited, provides a cultural backdrop for this study. Between 1830 and 1860, a relatively large number of freed or formerly enslaved African Americans traveled to England seeking financial and political aid in their abolitionist cause. As a result, several African Americans who were fugitive slaves, or who had once been enslaved persons, were present in England in 1851 and attended the exhibition, one of the most prominent of whom was William Wells Brown.

The aims and goals of the Great Exhibition may be characterized by the hopeful words of Immanuel Kant's "Idea for a Universal History from a Cosmopolitan Perspective."[1] Kant recognizes that human beings will increasingly be in a contest to exploit the earth's resources, and in the treatise he sketches an Enlightenment rationale for a peaceful and cooperative exchange to take place. The concept of cosmopolitanism that Kant develops here may be overused in political and cultural theory but, despite its problems and associations with European colonialism, it is useful as part of the heritage of modernity. It stands to reason that abolitionists would engage with and reimagine the practice and meaning of cosmopolitanism, even if they do not explicitly name it. The term captures the ethical ideal of understanding or empathizing with the perspectives of other cultures and diverse traditions. Versions of "liberal cosmopolitanism" inherited from the Enlightenment have raised the problem of the universalizing tendencies of the liberal subject, with the capacity to distance from and yet sympathize with the sufferings of the other. While the Enlightenment definitions of cosmopolitanism derive mainly from Kant, the idea emerged in ancient Greece with Diogenes the Cynic in the fourth century BCE. In that context, the term meant detaching from local customs and communities in favor of being a "citizen of the world" (or cosmos and city, as the two words were conjoined in ancient Greece).[2] Then, as now, the term could be understood as somewhat of a sneer, particularly because Diogenes had little attachment to the idea of world citizenship or statehood. Some critics currently view the word negatively because of its association with the bourgeoisie, who had the relative luxury to travel and detach from local necessities, communities, and customs.[3] While their experience does not fit that characterization, many escaped American slaves and abolitionist reformers traveled, founded new locations, and sought to reform oppressive communities in the African diaspora.

At the cosmopolitan spectacle of the Crystal Palace in 1851, American mechanical technology, ceramics, and horological skills were not comparable to those of many European nations. Despite this, the Americans requested forty thousand square feet of exhibit space, of which they used only twelve thousand. They were able to distinguish themselves in the areas of gun manufacture and mechanical reapers and in the yacht race. The one unique contribution of the Americans at this stage of the Industrial Revolution was the invention of that "peculiar institution" of human slavery in a modern democratic society—and the transformation of human beings into a peculiar species of property.[4]

Obviously, the official American exhibitors mentioned neither enslaved persons nor the American institution and practice of slavery. The issue did arise, however, in relationship to a sculpture that was a part of the American exhibit. The American sculptor Hiram Powers presented a white marble piece titled "The Greek Slave." When Powers exhibited in the United States from 1847 to 1849, the statue was accepted as the first public artistic display of nudity in the United States. The sculpture was of a nude white woman in the style of a Venus de Milo in chains. This was a negative tour de force, given the controversial topic of human slavery in England and the presence of African Americans and their English colleagues in attendance at the Crystal Palace. While the statue became an "emblem of freedom" for white Americans who romanticized the Greek cause in the Greek War of Independence, many also began to see its connection to the abolitionist cause of freedom in the United States.[5]

William Wells Brown, along with William and Ellen Craft (both temperance reformers), attended the World's Fair at the Crystal Palace. Brown was anything but sympathetic to the abstract display of sympathy for the European woman in chains. In his travel narrative *Three Years in Europe*, Brown describes going to the Crystal Palace with the express purpose of antislavery agitation because of the American slaveholding presence at the exhibit. In fact, he made a special effort to affront the sensibilities of his "Virginian neighbours" by strolling around the exhibit with "an English lady... on [his] arm." Appearing a "gentleman," he claims, "the Americans, as far as appearance goes, are behind every other country in the Exhibition. The 'Greek Slave' is the only production of Art which the United States has sent. And it would have been more to their credit had they kept that at home."[6] Brown brought the cartoon of the "Greek slave" from *Punch* magazine that parodied Powers's statue with a more empirical version, titled the "Virginian Slave." William Famer's letter to William Lloyd Garrison notes that Brown "took 'Punch's Virginia Slave' and

Introduction • 3

deposited it within the enclosure by the 'Greek Slave,' saying audibly, 'As an American fugitive slave, I place this 'Virginia Slave' by the side of the 'Greek slave,' as its most fitting companion.'"[7] Notably, Brown's performance was most offensive to white Americans because, in Farmer's words, "to see the arm of a beautiful English young lady passed through that of a 'nigger,' taking ices and other refreshments with him, upon the terms of the most perfect equality, certainly was enough to 'rile,' and evidently did 'rile' the slaveholders who beheld it."[8]

In addition to Brown's critical performance, he had created a panorama in 1850.[9] Panoramas were popular during this period, and Brown was not the only creator of one depicting slavery; the escaped slave Henry Box Brown had also made use of the panorama as an aid to his abolitionist lectures in England. Upon arriving in England, Wells Brown decided to create a panorama as an aid to his lectures. He hired artists to illustrate his depictions and arranged them on a folded canvas. He also provided a pamphlet explaining each of the panels. Brown's panorama showed the atrocities of slavery, including sale advertisements, attempted escapes, and whipping posts on plantations in Virginia and in the slave markets of New Orleans. The twenty-four panels clarify the international implications of American slavery, which could not be contained as simply a domestic issue.[10] In some respects, the Industrial Revolution intensified slavery and had become part of the international discourse regarding civilization and economic exchange.

To be sure, Brown did not create his panorama for display at the American pavilion at the Crystal Palace. It could, nevertheless, be understood as a critical revision of the display of American art represented by Powers's sculpture. At the first international exhibition to which Americans had been invited, the issue of slavery was expressed through an obfuscating avoidance by appealing to an effete classicism in a forum devoted to the marvels of scientific technology. That several English abolitionists and scores of ex-enslaved and escaped enslaved African Americans attended the exhibition reveals the extent to which the Americans were unprepared for a truly cosmopolitan and international discourse. And it is clear that those who had suffered some form of slavery were most capable of entering into this conversation.

The Crystal Palace Exhibition took place in the middle of the 1800s, at the midpoint of the first full century of the American republic, during which its cultural institutions, modes, customs, and sentiments were being established. One of the institutions was African American slavery, and with it the oppression of African Americans. Ira Berlin distinguishes between "societies with slaves" and "slave societies." Societies with slaves permit human slavery as one of the legitimate institutions of the society, but the institution neither dominates nor has a formative position. In contrast, in slave societies, slavery acquires a pervasive and dominant position. Slavery in such societies permeates all other institutions; it is ubiquitous, influencing all the relationships, exchanges, and modalities of the society—in education, business, family, and all economic relationships. Berlin characterizes the American republic as a perfect example of a "slave society."[11]

Enslaved African Americans in the United States were enmeshed within the interstices brought into being by the Industrial Revolution, which determined the actualities and possibilities, styles, and discourses of the Western world during this period. Just as the Crystal Palace symbolized a cosmopolitan international achievement, the problematic nature of this era was well represented in the discourses of the moral philosopher and economist Adam Smith, the historian and economist Karl Marx, and, later, the sociologist Max Weber, in his classic discussion of the relationship between Protestantism and capitalism. Notably, none of these figures devotes serious attention to the problem of human slavery within the new industrial age.

The Revolutions of 1848, which took place immediately prior to the Crystal Palace Exhibition, might have served as a warning in the midst of the celebration of industrial creativity. Likewise, the passage of one of the most oppressive fugitive slave laws in the United States portended the American Civil War, which was just over the horizon. Most of the slogans and advertisements celebrating the Great Exhibition as an expression of European cosmopolitanism emphasized some form of freedom resulting from the new technology. This sentiment, however, was not apparent to those who had been enslaved and oppressed within the United States.

In what follows, I examine the lives and works of five African Americans: Martin Delany, William Wells Brown, George Moses Horton, Frances Harper, and Amanda Berry Smith. In the words of Orlando Patterson, these authors and reformers suffered a "social death": they suffered under slavery and experienced the oppression and degradation of a segregated society.[12] Yet, each seeks and expresses a new form of freedom. The desired freedom possesses elements of Protestantism and capitalism, for some more than for others, but in none of these persons are these elements normative. Rather, the fragmented elements indicate the context of modern cosmopolitanism and industrialization. Each reformer pursues the creation of a moral community, which under an ideology of democratic freedom would mean a civil society. Since these

African Americans were excluded or enslaved by a democratic free society, such a notion of freedom is problematic. Aware of this, they seek a society that acknowledges its shortcomings, is willing to make amends, and is capable of transforming the tragic into the redemptive. They seek a society of intimacy, at least within a common past, as well as a just social order.

These authors may not have spoken of cosmopolitanism directly in philosophical debates or treatises. However, their imaginative writings critically engage with notions of world citizenship, freedom, and restraint. They express what Charles H. Long refers to as a "culture of contact," creolized and in-between traditions in which they are neither wholly indigenous nor enslaved nor European. This book explores how temperance provided a religious orientation for these reformers to enter the discourses of the Enlightenment and modernity, and to enact and imagine another epistemological stance.[13] As Long has shown, "religion did not disappear simply out of the Enlightenment pronouncements."[14] On the contrary, the interrelation between capitalism and Protestantism that Weber explored was complemented by a new understanding of materialities in a desacralized world. *Temperance and Cosmopolitanism* traces a new form and modality of exchange developing in discourses of temperance that emerged at the same time as new modes of modernity and cosmopolitanism.

From this perspective, my book is about therapeutic freedom and religious recovery: healing from individual addiction and from "intemperance," or what became known as "slavery to the bottle," but also healing for a country in recovery from the legacy of chattel slavery. The institution of chattel slavery and the traffic of human beings and commodities encompass the Atlantic world and connect with transnational perspectives. Temperance acquired its primary meaning as opposition to alcohol in the nineteenth century, but temperance also indicated a new time of freedom, civilization, and bodily reform. African American authors and reformers challenged the nationalist discourses of the temperance movements in critically cosmopolitan and often transnational ways. This book contributes to an ongoing conversation about the legacy of slavery and addiction by probing the voices of these nineteenth-century authors and reformers who reimagined national, cultural, and racial identities as intersecting with meanings of cosmopolitan freedom and temperance.

Both before and after the American Civil War, whites associated alcohol and drugs with blackness and enslavement. The white supremacist fear of African American freedom manifest in stereotypes of drunkenness or the propensity to violent and addictive behavior was exacerbated in the period of Jim Crow segregation after Reconstruction. Many African American men were lynched because of such stereotypes.[15] The association of excess, lust, and unrestrained passion with Africans, however, began long before the Civil War. While that association is a product of the transatlantic slave trade and the creation of a "black Atlantic," the revolutionary and antebellum periods in the United States were formative in conflating inebriety with enslaved Africans. During slavery, theories of "black savagery" and the predisposition to lust and intemperance were commonly associated with African people. For instance, in the early 1800s Thomas Jefferson drew on prerevolutionary theories such as those proposed by the Swedish botanist Carolus Linnaeus, which divided the human species into five classifications, with Homo Europeanus the gentlest and best mannered. In *Notes on the State of Virginia* (1803), Jefferson defended Homo Americanus against Linnaeus and other Europeans who thought its members were degrading in racial constitution as a result of the American climate. According to Jefferson, members of Homo Afer remained subject to the passions, prone to crime (theft in slavery), and culturally and racially inferior in artistic and intellectual capacity because of their skin color.[16] By the 1830s, ethnologists developed theories of polygenesis to defend claims of the different origins of the species, black inferiority and "rascality," white supremacy, and the necessity for black enslavement or criminalization.[17]

The racism that often accompanied temperance and prohibition is somewhat ironic given that temperance and abolition were strongly interlinked—most white and black abolitionists were temperance reformers. While some scholars have considered African American involvement in temperance, the treatment of temperance often suffers from many of the same stereotypes associated with white American temperance reformers. Temperance is considered either as adaptive to Protestant asceticism and its work ethic, or as a corollary to stereotypes about puritanical behavior in Protestant evangelism of the nineteenth century. Some critics argue that early temperance reformers were most concerned with the inculcation of middle-class capitalism or Protestant values and the regulation of work and society.[18] Yet, temperance reformers were not always "anti-intellectual," fundamentalist, Protestant conservatives.[19] Because of the popularity of the temperance movement by the end of the nineteenth century, temperance could encompass more partisan associations.

Temperance and abolitionism were both international movements that to a large extent found their roots in Protestant evangelism and reform. Ian Tyrell has studied the internationalism of the Woman's Christian Temperance Union (WCTU) and comments on its Methodist underpinnings and connections to missionizing. He notes that the internationalism of the movement helped expand its patriotic Americanist notions. Nonetheless, "the social and ideological climate for temperance was more favorable in the United States, and it was from there that reformers elsewhere in the Anglo-Saxon world principally looked, whether to be informed, shocked, or horrified."[20] Oftentimes, evangelical or internationalist language held distinct meanings for African American authors and reformers grounded not only in Protestant millennialism or cosmopolitanism but also in transatlantic slavery and efforts to forge new civil societies from the ruins of excess. Most significantly, many African American reformers concerned themselves with founding temperate, transnational, and cosmopolitan diasporic communities in the creolized situations created by the involuntary traffic of Africans to the American continents.

THE TRAFFIC OF BODIES AND THE METAPHOR OF SLAVERY

Alongside abolitionism and women's rights, temperance was the most prominent reform movement in the nineteenth century—and it was intertwined with both movements as the foundation of either moral or civil behavior. At the Constitutional Convention after the Revolutionary War, the issue of chattel slavery was talked about almost every day.[21] Yet neither the word "slave" nor the word "slavery" was used in the initial document, nor were these words found in the Declaration of Independence, except in excised passages. On the other hand, "slavery" began to be used as a metaphor for a variety of oppressions.[22] In the aftermath of the revolution and the proliferation of many reformers in the Second Great Awakening, for instance, the word "slavery" intensified as a "figurative expression of the impotence of the will—the failure of self-control in the face of extreme temptation."[23]

The symbolic use of slavery appears problematic when juxtaposed with the literal institution of chattel slavery. The latter relegated actual human beings to the status of property and denied them social identity, citizenship, and legal protection. Revolutionaries used the slavery metaphor in relation to King George III, for example, which is instructive because it was often complemented by the metaphor of intoxication. According to Robert Levine, "In the writings of Franklin, Benjamin Rush, and Anthony Benezet it was regularly argued that British desires to maintain authority over colonial Americans were the desires of enslavers intoxicated by power." He continues, "The conjoining of temperance and antislavery in Revolutionary rhetoric helped make temperance reform particularly appealing for Northern free blacks, who formed some of the first temperance groups in the United States in the late eighteenth century."[24] Temperance became an essential value for free African Americans, and by the 1840s, as both Donald Yacovene and Benjamin Quarrels have noted, temperance became "synonymous with antislavery."[25]

Moreover, historians often argue that Christian evangelism was the most significant venue for black abolitionists and reformers to expand temperance.[26] Certainly, temperance had early moorings in religious denominations, manifest in the publication of the reformed Calvinist and evangelist Lyman Beecher's *Six Sermons on Intemperance*, and perhaps culminating in the founding of the generally Protestant WCTU in 1871. In 1846, Beecher made specific connections between slavery, the Middle Passage, and intemperance. He boldly stated that inebriety was the worst form of slavery because the suffering was for an "eternity": "Yes, in this nation there is a middle passage of slavery, and darkness, and chains, and disease, and death. But it is a middle passage, not from Africa to America, but from time to eternity; and not of slaves whom death will release from suffering, but of those whose sufferings at death do but just begin. Could all the sighs of these captives be wafted on one breeze, it would be loud as thunder. Could all their tears be assembled, they would be like the sea."[27] Perhaps ignoring the literal, transatlantic aspects of intemperance and enslavement, Beecher placed inebriety in a universal context of the afterlife.

The United States had become a slave society, and in the nineteenth century metaphors of enslavement permeated temperance. It had indeed become a land of excess—what W. J. Rorabaugh in 1979 called *The Alcoholic Republic*. Drawing on Rorabaugh's statistics, Woodruff notes that during the period of heaviest drinking in 1810 and 1830, "American drank 7.1 gallons of absolute alcohol per person per year."[28] If temperance developed as part of a revolutionary sentiment, alcoholism also increased with the excessive pursuit of individual happiness and a ubiquitous sense of individual freedom. The American tradition of alcoholism, according to Rorabaugh, also developed because of the frontier experience, tavern culture, and the American taste for "strong drink." Notably, few popular sources on temperance reform connect the spirit of American individualism and the pursuit of excess to the simultaneous presence of millions of slaves on democratic republican soil.

To be sure, temperance began to be tied to alcohol use in the eighteenth century, particularly during the revolutionary era. At that time, intoxication was understood to be sinful, but moderation was viewed as more virtuous than abstinence, which could be intemperately excessive. Temperance has been prominent in many religious traditions; however, in the colonial period, not even the New England Puritans were "temperance" activists.[29] Only in the late eighteenth and nineteenth centuries did temperance begin to be equated with an opposition to alcohol in "Europe and North America," as Cook notes.³⁰ The birth of American temperance, on the one hand, initially appeared with the nationalist revolutionary ethos that expressed the desire for widespread civil society: "temperate" behavior suggested a rational, restrained, and public character. On the other hand, temperance movements acquired an evangelical quality in the social context of enthusiastic religious "awakenings."³¹

Whereas temperance in the revolutionary era meant moderation and abstinence from distilled liquor, many evangelical reformers and temperance societies, like the Washingtonians who developed in the 1830s, would promote total abstinence. Revolutionary-era temperance coincided with a spirit of republicanism and the development of a rational and restrained character. In 1784, Benjamin Rush published *An Inquiry into the Effects of Ardent Spirits upon the Human Body and the Mind*. The pamphlet focused mainly on the undesirable physiological effects of distilled spirits and, as Jack Blocker notes, commented only secondarily on the damaging moral or spiritual consequences. Poverty and disease, as well as crime and death, were attributed to alcohol use.³² While Rush was clearly concerned with regulating the developing capitalist order, he suggested the healthy civic body would be white and argued that black skin was a result of leprosy—after he focused on the disease of intemperance.³³

The association of black skin with disease and alcohol with the disease of poverty bear similarities, as does chattel slavery and the metaphors of slavery to the bottle. Both chattel slavery and alcoholism were states of powerlessness and humiliation for a society developing highly individualist and white supremacist ideologies. The traffic of slaves and the beginning of the rum and distilled alcohol trade have often been connected. As William H. James and Stephen L. Johnson point out, in the eighteenth century the patterns of European American drinking—and the increased availability of rum, whisky, and gin—depended on a circular business in which slaves were traded for sugar to distill into rum, the profits from which were used to enslave people in West Africa and bring them back into American slavery.³⁴ The intertwined nature of African bodies as commodities and commodities like sugar and rum (and tobacco) also undergirds the meaning of freedom for numerous African American temperance reformers who understood temperance as coeval with actual political and social freedom.

Such was the case for Frederick Douglass and his promotion of temperance, which Robert Levine discusses at length. However, Douglass often presents freedom as an inner state of consciousness and temperance as an inward battle of the will. Addressing the popular association of chattel slavery and blackness with absolute degradation, David Brion Davis refers directly to Douglass's account of his battle with the "slave-breaker" Edward Covey in his *Narrative*. In this famous passage Douglass described his beatings as extinguishing any human consciousness: "My natural elasticity was crushed, my intellect languished, the disposition to read departed, the cheerful spark that lingered about my eye died; the dark night of slavery closed in upon me, and behold a man transformed into a brute!" Davis interprets this passage as a statement that slavery can "deny a person's capacity for self-transcendence."[35] The master tends to reduce the slave to a position of total otherness leading to "social death." Nevertheless, Douglass's experience of total brutality and nontranscendence has also been problematized as characteristically masculine and individualist in its understanding of freedom as inner consciousness.

Part of the problem with Douglass's description of slavery (and inebriety) can also be found in his characterization of freedom. Although it becomes political, liberty often seems removed from a social or communal identity, apart from the overriding sense of liberation from physical abuse and harm. When Douglass decides to fight back and challenge Covey rather than accept the beatings, he views himself as almost free:

> This battle with Mr. Covey was the turning-point in my career as a slave. It rekindled the few expiring embers of freedom, and revived within me a sense of my own manhood. It recalled the departed self-confidence, and inspired me again with a determination to be free. The gratification afforded by the triumph was a full compensation for whatever else might follow, even death itself. He only can understand the deep satisfaction which I experienced, who has himself repelled by force the bloody arm of slavery.... It was a glorious resurrection, from the tomb of slavery, to the heaven of freedom.... And I now resolved that, however long I might remain a slave in form, the day had passed forever when I could be a slave in fact.[36]

The "fact" that Douglass can no longer be "whipped" makes him feel as though he at least possesses a type of internal and mental freedom. Of course, Douglass was aware that "freedom" needed legal and external manifestation to be real. Even then, however, his sense of freedom remains highly individualistic—he will repeatedly proclaim his desire to "become [his] own master"[37]—and he focused on self-control, restraint, and the achievement of liberal rights, albeit through revolution and resistance.[38]

In the *Narrative* Douglass, like a number of other authors of slave narratives and antislavery texts, described many slaveholders and overseers as "drunkards" (think of Harriet Beecher Stowe's Simon Legree, who kills Uncle Tom in a fit of drunkenness and whose evil is clearly associated with inebriety). According to Douglass, for slaves "it was deemed a disgrace not to get drunk at Christmas; and he was regarded as lazy indeed, who had not provided himself with the necessary means, during the year, to get whisky enough to last him through Christmas." Douglass views holidays within slavery, and the drunkenness that is promised in them, as "keeping down the spirit of insurrection" and as "safety-valves, to carry off the rebellious spirit of enslaved humanity." The holidays are "part and parcel of the gross fraud, wrong, and inhumanity of slavery," and they "disgust their slaves with freedom, by plunging them into the lowest depths of dissipation."[39] As such, the so-called privilege of drunkenness indoctrinates slaves to believe they cannot manage their own freedom.

While Douglass's interpretation of alcohol use became a popular variant among black abolitionists, Kenneth Christmon notes that "by the beginning of the Civil War, slave-holding states prohibited or controlled the consumption of alcoholic beverages by Blacks. The danger of mass drunkenness and potential revolt was heightened following Nat Turner's and Denmark Vesey's revolts. Laws were enacted that placed tighter controls on drinking and even prevented African Americans from owning stills. For example, South Carolina in 1931 passed a law prohibiting any free Black from owning or operating a still."[40] Granting any revolutionary power to alcohol use went beyond the republican and temperate civility promoted by Douglass and most of the reformers I address. However, both Brown and Horton play with the limits of excess in a creolized aesthetics of temperance or restraint. Indeed, unique forms of temperance emerge; heightened asceticism or individual self-control is not, for instance, the goal of the temperance practices and behaviors these writers envisioned. Temperance could, however, simultaneously be mobilized by recently freed African Americans for economic motives and to emulate values of thrift, self-reliance, and moral purity. Temperance informed the founding of diasporic communities and civil societies to heal those who have been affected by the pursuit of excess in the transatlantic slave trade and the individualist pursuit of happiness.

The contradictory discourses and practices of excess and restraint and of slavery and freedom shaped the lives, writings, and civilizing counterdiscourses of this representative group of African American writers in the antebellum period. Other writers—including Frederick Douglass, Walt Whitman, John B. Gough, William and Ellen Craft, Sojourner Truth, Frances

E. Willard, and Ida B. Wells—either offered visions of temperance as a nationalist discourse of democratic purity or created alternatives for imagining new modes of exchange and models for diasporic foundings of "civilization." They imagined temperance in conflicting ways as part of groups as diverse as the Washingtonians (Whitman), the Sons of Temperance (Brown), the Good Templars (Brown), and the WCTU (Harper and Smith).

The use of the slavery metaphor is instructive: most reformers used it to imply understandings of inner and outer captivity. The argument over the inward (bondage of the will, or "slavery to the bottle") and the outward (denial of political freedom in chattel slavery) persisted during the post-Reconstruction period in debates between Ida B. Wells and Frances E. Willard, the most powerful temperance leader in the latter part of the nineteenth century. Wells confronted Willard in 1893 over segregated chapters of the WCTU in the South and Willard's lukewarm condemnation of lynching. For the sake of cleansing the inner self from slavery to alcohol, many white temperance activists were willing to allow a system of quasi-slavery to continue and to permit the public degradation of personhood. These tensions between African American and European American reformers continue in many contexts of temperance, and the authors analyzed in this book devise alternate public meanings of temperance reform in response.

One of the central concerns of this book is how African American reformers imagined entering into U.S. and then world history. African American reformers participated in a public temperance movement, not strictly an inward experience without outward action. They worked to constitute significant creative, often critically cosmopolitan, forms of temperate civil society. Alcoholism was, of course, viewed as harming others and impinging on the normative moral laws of domesticity and family as well as economic prosperity. African American reformers often went beyond this individualist and nationalist sense of internal liberty to define a public, temperate cosmopolitanism that entailed freedom of movement and the creation of creole public spaces.

SLAVE TRADE AND RUM: THE TRAFFIC OF COSMOPOLITAN AND SUBLIME COMMODITIES

While nineteenth-century temperance reformers made the metaphorical conflation of slavery and alcoholism central, the slave trade itself is a testament to the developing field of excess, promoting the addictive commodities of sugar and rum, cultivating a culture of consumerism from mercantilism, and commodifying the bodies of Africans as chattel. In Stephanie Smallwood's characterization of the Middle Passage, she notes that "slaves became, for the purpose of the transatlantic shipment, mere physical units that could be arranged and molded at will—whether folded together spoonlike in rows or flattened side by side in a place."[41] Packing Africans as tightly as possible on a slave ship, "on average some three hundred or more people," increased profit and highlighted the new nature of modern slavery in which human beings were chattel to be shipped and discarded in horrific conditions across the Atlantic.[42] The commodities exchanged for African labor included guns and gunpowder, utensils, textiles, tobacco, sugar, and rum. As the trade developed, rum became a prime commodity in the trade for African people. As Christmon comments, "Owners of slavers carried Africans to South Carolina and brought back to New England naval stores for their shipbuilding, or to the West Indies and brought back molasses. The molasses was made into the highly prized New England rum and shipped in hogsheads to Africa for more human cargo. Thus the American involvement is often referred to as the triangular slave trade. Twenty gallons of rum could purchase a muscular young man. It was profitable to spread a taste for liquor on the coast."[43]

Indeed, in the introduction to Theodore Canot's account of being a slaver in the early 1800s, Malcolm Cowley writes, "To make the venture pay, the slaves were packed as tightly as cases of Scotch whisky."[44] The metaphor is apt, given that rum, along with guns and gunpowder, figures prominently in Canot's account as a way to bribe other Europeans once the slave trade was illegal or to trade with West Africans for slaves. And the rum is almost always described as originating from "New England." While the North is not always considered as deeply embedded in the slave system as the Southern plantation states, Northern states did have slaves, and economic growth was imbricated in the web of the triangular trade. According to Sidney Mintz, two trading triangles developed in the seventeenth and eighteenth centuries. The first triangle was, of course, the one that "linked Britain to Africa and to the New World: finished goods were sold to Africa, African slaves to the Americas, and American tropical commodities (especially sugar) to the mother country and her importing neighbors." But it was the second that went contrary to the "mercantilist ideal": "From New England went rum to Africa, whence slaves to the West Indies, whence molasses back to New England (with which to make rum)." The main problem, as Mintz points out, was that slaves, even when thought to be commodities, were not commodities. They were part of the consumptive web, and their existence as humans required they also use the "products made by Britons—cloth, tools, torture instruments" for the "creation of wealth."[45] The new nature of the commodity as human being paralleled the culture of consumption and the developing taste for sugar, and Mintz's study *Sweetness and Power* makes clear the cosmic and cruel ironies involved in the cultivation of a sweet tooth.

A deep investment in alcohol production was formative in the American republic, and the equally important addiction to sweets was central for both Britain and the United States. The traffic of goods and bodies was complemented by the development of cosmopolitanism and an "enlightened" capacity to view the traffic primarily as producing abstract goods—sometimes dispassionately, and sometimes with passionate sympathy. According to Ian Baucom, cosmopolitanism and the cosmopolitan subject's capacity for a "sublime" rendition of history and suffering correlate with the transatlantic slave trade in the development of the commodity within capitalism. In his words, "Finance culture that preceded, enabled, and secured this circuit of cross-Atlantic commodity exchange; the bank, stock, credit, insurance, and load-derived money forms of value that underwrote this cycle of accumulation, presided over its rise, and . . . have returned to dominate what Braudel calls its moment of 'autumn.'"[46] Baucom's study probes philosophers, poets, and economists from Kant to the romantics to Adam Smith, highlighting various understandings of cosmopolitanism and the sublime. The abstract and speculative modes of exchange inherent in the cosmopolitan subject position (detached, interested, or disinterested) become the "conditions of possibility" for the triangular trade, particularly related to "all the variant forms of 'paper money' derived from the establishment of a modern, credit-issuing system of banking."[47]

Marx and Engels had implied that all humans were commodified and reified according to their labor use- or exchange-value within capitalism. Baucom's argument furthers this insight by considering how the traffic of slaves in the Caribbean and in American ports depended on promissory notes and interest-bearing negotiations for bankers and insurance agents. Slaves were not only commodities but also "a flexible, negotiable, transactable form of money."[48] Captain Luke Collingwood and others involved in the infamous *Zong* massacre in 1781 relied on this to murder 132 slaves by throwing them overboard to claim insurance for ill or damaged "cargo" that they could not support through the journey with inadequate provisions. In fact, the owners had overloaded the ship significantly, had taken too long on their voyage (thus accumulating interest), and, according the legal case, did not have enough water or provisions to

Introduction • 15

transport the commodities. Though abolitionist Granville Sharpe and insurance agents presented the case as murder, the courts would initially rule that the crew was protecting its investment, a decision later overturned by Lord Mansfield. Baucom considers this event, which is notable in the development of abolitionism, to correspond with a mode of capitalism and cosmopolitan "specters" of the sublime that develop in conjunction with the traffic of bodies on credit and interest.

Certain forms of cosmopolitanism and sublimity go hand in hand with modernity and New World slavery, which undergird the construction of the Enlightenment subject and its universalism. But other forms and meanings of cosmopolitanism correspond to a critical and temperate cosmopolitan subjectivity—a form of diasporic subjectivity that, while linked to aspects of creolization and *métissage* discussed by Baucom and Paul Gilroy, has been overlooked and underestimated. A temperate cosmopolitanism was linked to creolization and was one of the main modalities of civil identity for African American reformers who critically engaged the specters of Enlightenment rationality.

I focus on a fugitive and temperate cosmopolitanism bound to the land and reflections on diasporic resettlement. For the fugitive and temperate cosmopolite, for whom the process of leaving "home" was not usually a choice, the search for a meaningful land and place is always creolized rather than being racially pure or abstractly sublime. This in-betweenness is a consequence of being the excess, the interest, and the trafficked commodity.[49] As a fugitive slave, Brown lived in Europe from 1849 to 1854 and wrote *Three Years in Europe* (1852), the first travel narrative published by an African American. Certainly, many other fugitives, including Frederick Douglass and William and Ellen Craft, made their way abroad as well. Brown's cultured and at times traditional cosmopolitan outlook led some to view him as mimicking the manners and values of the European elite. John Ernest has called Brown's musings a "fugitive tourism"—a fugitive cosmopolitanism is not far removed from such a conception but shows a longing for and attachment to place that diverges from Enlightenment cosmopolitan outlooks.

According to David Harvey, Kant's thoughts on cosmopolitanism have influenced contemporary liberal cosmopolitanism, even eliciting remarks that the European Union may be a manifestation of the "Kantian dream of a cosmopolitan republicanism."[50] However, cosmopolitanism had also developed within Christianity and other religious traditions. Understanding cosmopolitanism as simply transcending local customs and ethnic or national identities overlooks the fact that most versions of cosmopolitanism (especially Kant's) entailed the legitimacy of the nation-state and the command of patriotic attachment. Kant and Enlightenment thinkers mainly viewed world citizenship and a peaceful commonwealth as manifest in the right to "host foreigners." The establishment of sociability among citizens and the constitution of civil society for Kant presaged the feasibility of a "federation of nations."[51]

Debates about cosmopolitanism continue today. Martha Nussbaum defends liberal cosmopolitanism as an ethical subjective stance consistent with a type of nonpatriotism and enlightened disposition, and Anthony Appiah forwards a "rooted cosmopolitanism" emphasizing the need to remain rooted in local communities open to ethnic differences, particularly for formerly colonized peoples.[52] As the anthropologist Pnina Werbner points out, "Against 'globalisation,' a term implying the free movement of capital and the global (mainly Western) spread of ideas and practices, cosmopolitanism is a word used by the new cosmopolitans to emphasise empathy, toleration and respect for other cultures and values."[53] The postcolonial theorist Homi Bhabha entered the debate by using the term "vernacular cosmopolitanism" to describe cosmopolitanism from the perspectives of the marginalized in opposition to the elitism and enlightened detachment of the bourgeois class.[54] The term has recently been aligned with the position of the oppressed political subject, such as refugees and people experiencing homelessness, who have developed unique cosmopolitan memories and communities.[55]

This book considers cosmopolitanism from the perspective of the fugitive first, then the enslaved, and then the recently freed, all of whom attempt to establish diasporic communities with temperance as the fundamental mode of embodiment that would undergird civility. This alignment of temperance with cosmopolitanism can be understood by again considering Kant's assumption of rationality as the privileged position from which to achieve specular cosmopolitanism or liberal cosmopolitanism.

The sublime was the aesthetic realm most closely related to cosmopolitan subjectivity for Kant. The experience of the sublime and the response to it unleashed the possibility for disinterested sympathy: "This event consists neither in momentous deeds nor crimes committed by men.... No, nothing of the sort. It is simply the mode of thinking of the spectators which reveals itself in this game of great revolutions, and manifests such a universal yet disinterested sympathy."[56] Kant's emphasis on the spectator position and disinterestedness has been criticized by many. However, Baucom persuasively argues that the cosmopolitan subjectivity—a detached, disinterested position—is not entirely at odds with the interested position of sympathy proposed by many other theorists of the Enlightenment, such as Adam Smith, and even the British romantics, such as William Wordsworth. As Baucom writes, "The subject of the Kantian sublime . . . is, formally at least, a virtual analogue—counterintuitive as this may seem—of the sympathetic subject of Smith's *Theory of Moral Sentiments*." He clarifies that Kant's "historical sublime" requires the subject to experience or witness "trauma," "the terrifying spectacle of historical events, 'deeds,' and 'crimes.'" The Kantian subject's experience of sublimity must then transfer the actuality of events "to the mode of thought of the spectator who becomes aware of them and who, becoming thus aware, comes to recognize in itself the capacity to invest a disinterested sympathy in the idea of humanity at large, and so to emerge ethically enriched by its speculative consumption of the spectacle's abstract historicity."[57]

The Kantian subject achieves the realm of the imagination and the grandiosity of the ego in distancing and restraint. Sublimity is a purely mental process of abstracting from the surrounding historical event, local place, or material world in order to experience a cosmopolitan sympathy for historical suffering or the tragic. The lack of any specificity characterizes the sublime and parallels the cosmopolitan position and its valuation of the human mind and imagination. The experience of the sublime in this individualist paradigm also requires pleasure and pain, as is true of the experience of drugs and alcohol—or the experience of controlling or quitting one's addiction through the use of reason. Richard Klein observed this in *Cigarettes Are Sublime*: trying to quit smoking but never succeeding is, for Klein, a fascination with the sublime. Certainly, addictive behavior entails a familiarity with the dichotomy of pleasure and pain inherent in the experience of sublimity. As Klein writes, "For Kant, the sublime, as distinct from the merely beautiful, affords a negative pleasure because it is accompanied, as its defining condition, by a moment of pain. By pain he strictly means the normal feelings of shock or fear aroused by the presence of whatever impresses us by virtue of its sheer magnitude, giving rise to awe or respect."[58] Beauty, on the other hand, gives rise to a more finite experience of aesthetic satisfaction. The sublime and the experience of suffering that arises from the excesses of alcohol or slavery cannot be controlled through acts of human reason, imagination, or individual egotism. African American temperance reformers such as Brown, who played with the limits of an aesthetic sublime and cosmopolitan modes of restraint, linked their subjectivities to specific materialities, memories, attachments to the land, and diasporic communities in an attempt to externalize freedom and create civil public spaces.

African American reformers rarely romanticize an ecstatic or highly individualistic relation to the irrational passions, as was common for many romantics. For many temperance reformers, however, though the sublime experience might be viewed as consistent with drunkenness, common sense and reason afforded ways to control the appetite through willpower. Frequently, an ascetic response to the experience of uncertainty, excess, imagination, or passion prevails. For instance, the Methodist and Chautauqua founder John Heyl Vincent suspected that "imaginative people" had "weak wills," and he banned certain types of literature, including novels, and staged theater.[59] Reformers often favored other types of edifying literature, songs, and advice manuals. Charles Fowler gives a clear example of the fears some reformers placed on overly imaginative literature: "A single book may make or mar a life. Voltaire learned an infidel poem when he was five, and it molded his life."[60]

Notably, Brown, Horton, Harper, and Smith all composed "edifying" temperance literature, but they focused on different forms and meanings of temperance as consistent with a republican, cosmopolitan, but creolized character. While theater was generally considered suspect by white temperance reformers, a one-man reading of a play without staging—which is what Brown did with his play *The Escape* (1858)—might have been acceptable. Generally, African American reformers did not avoid the passions or the imaginative realm of what might be called the "suffering" of the sublime, but they did depart from both the romantic and the rational-transcendent response, given that they were commonly perceived as the direct object of the sublime as well.

The preoccupation with the sublime (and cosmopolitanism) also manifests itself as a concern with the land and nature, usually the vastness of space over against the limited, local place of communities. For Kant, being a citizen of the world entailed a certain comfort with the speculative and disinterested traveler. Brown seems at times to share this vision in his *Three Years in Europe*, but there are important departures in the creolized text, performances, and strategies of diversion. Brown's travel literature also creates a diasporic revision of cosmopolitanism, which clings to the land, revisits sacred sites speculated on by many British romantics, and re-creates, almost in pantomime, the manners of French and British society from the point of view of a symbol of the excess.

Temperance and Cosmopolitanism considers both the metaphoric and actual spaces of creole cosmopolitan and fugitive temperance from the perspective of those concerned with the founding of spaces for recovery of the displaced diaspora. Viewing temperance through the lenses of literary reformers perhaps encourages a different meaning of temperance than political or philosophical treatises can capture. Because of their ability to address multiple audiences and mobilize heterogeneous discourses, fiction, poetry, autobiography, the travelogue, and the slave narrative evoke the imaginations of what I call a temperate and creole cosmopolitanism in a way that direct political speech often cannot. All these literary-historical visions present creolization in various ways that differ in meaning, style, literary form, and language.

Temperance was central to Martin Delany's and William Wells Brown's diasporic imagination of cosmopolitan space and place. Delany imbibed temperance and often approximated a more typical understanding of it as a corollary to the Protestant work ethic, even as his writing expressed conflicting visions and imaginative attempts to consider a creole cosmopolitanism. Though Delany did not consider himself a literary author, his novel *Blake*, his emigrationist writings, and his reflections on Masonry allow for glimpses of a temperate, creolized, and cosmopolitan space.

Brown experimented with a variety of genres that display strategies of creolization and diversion, and he sought a creolized style that allowed for the enactment and representation of a new temporality and space of freedom. The oral poetry of George Moses Horton was embodied and performative, and his public performances fit generally within a desire for temperate and cosmopolitan space. In my discussion of Harper, I am most concerned with heterogeneous discourses placed in tension, which permits the reader to discern hints of a hemispheric and creolized imagination of temperate freedom.

The book concludes with an analysis of Amanda Smith, whose writing—part spiritual autobiography, part travelogue—becomes an excessive depiction (more than five hundred pages) of the transrational space of her life. It does so through its recursive structure, creolized diversion, and pastiche of speeches and other performances from her life. Smith's autobiography approaches literacy "circumspectly," and the dialogic structure of her conversations with Satan, God, and community challenges much of the masculine slave narrative genre that often focuses on individual improvement, literacy, and uplift. The genre itself reflects her temperance cosmopolitanism, performances, and exchanges with a diverse array of communities.

All the authors in this study traveled and expressed various forms of temperance and cosmopolitanism. The experience of travel opened up both external space and imaginative space. Delany traveled throughout the North and South American continents and to West Africa. Brown explored Canada, Europe, Haiti, and his "Southern home" as possible settlements. Brown also negotiated the meaning of civility and cosmopolitanism by founding black temperance societies, by expressing a continued commitment to temperance and abolition, by engaging in activism in the Underground Railroad, and by reforming communities in Reconstruction. As an outsider to the Kantian ethical code, a displaced commodity, and an abstracted sublime object for the speculative and rational mind, he nevertheless performed a creole and tempered cosmopolitanism.

Though chapter 3 outlines George Moses Horton's particular position as an enslaved person who wrote about his drinking problem and his performative interpretations of temperance and republicanism at the University of North Carolina, I also explore there a critical cosmopolitanism reflected in his longed-for freedom and travels. Critics speculate that Horton may have ended up in Liberia after moving from North Carolina to Philadelphia following the Civil War. While Horton was not a reformer or activist, his poetry and performances show a commitment to reimagining home and the nature of republicanism through positing a new temporality, a new time of freedom.

Harper also traversed the continent and traveled into Canada while working in the Southern states during Reconstruction. Her fiction reflects on the meaning of cosmopolitan space through revisions to a "hemispheric" Haitian and creole history in Louisiana connected to a history of intemperance. While Harper highlights ambiguities in the association of inebriety with African Americans, or "black creoles," in her fiction no color is immune from the slavery of intoxication, and the traffic of liquor is bound to the traffic of slaves.

Harper and Amanda Smith were both active in the WCTU, but each had a different experience of the organization. Smith traveled to India and West Africa with her Holiness and Methodist evangelism. In her autobiography, she experiences a temperance-based understanding of cosmopolitan and creole cultural exchange for diasporic healing with the indigenous people. Smith's continual movement through liminal spaces empowered transnational gospel temperance throughout the world. Harper challenged the domestic spaces and national white Protestant character idealized by the WCTU. All of these authors critically engaged temperance as a central discourse and practice rooted in the desire for excess by Europeans. They also creolized and negotiated doctrines of restraint and cosmopolitanism.

Temperance and Cosmopolitanism views the actual spaces for cosmopolitanism as complemented by imagined ones, and a temperance aesthetics of freedom appears in diverse forms of creolized writings. A creole cosmopolitanism challenges the abstract aesthetic realm of sublimity and individualism that transcends space to achieve rationality and self-control. Paul Gilroy posits what he calls a "slave sublime,"[61] which ranges temporally from the more immediate experience of pain and bitterness to the redemptive eschatologies, such as Ethiopianism and Zionism, in the black and Jewish diasporas. A creole and temperate cosmopolitanism presents an in-between position more concerned with founding community and healing in recovery from slavery.

Brown commonly approached the sublime and the position of spectator indirectly through vignettes following juxtapositions, in trivial accounts, and by "circling back" to similar problems and historical events with "fanciful" diversions, perhaps what Baucom following Edouard Glissant calls "errancy."[62] The interest in the seemingly trivial and Brown's penchant for ironic performance characterized much of his work.

I opened with Brown's satirical and performative gesture at the Crystal Palace, along with that of other fugitive slaves, at the cosmopolitan display of commodities—products of woodworking, glass, iron, and art. His presence as a fugitive "commodity" provides an ironical relation to the liberal cosmopolitan understanding of matter and exchange, and the abstract mode of the sublime inherent in capitalist modernity. Brown's performance critically addresses European cosmopolitanism and sublimity: the nature of the commodity, excess, and violence is excluded by the abstract presentation of the whiteness and purity of the "Greek Slave" and the cosmopolitan spectacle. The mannerisms and the cultivation of self that Brown continually performs are not simple "mimicry" of European manners and civility. Nor are they quite the "sly civility" that Homi Bhabha made well known in his discussion of the hybrid and in-between subjectivity of the colonized in British India.[63] Rather, civility, manners, cultivation, and, above all, temperance are part of a reorientation process, evidenced in Brown's notion of freedom for the diaspora, which touches the major exchanges at the heart of European civilization and cosmopolitanism. African American reformers had to rethink their approach and how to temper the excess and surplus that were their bodies. Norbert Elias described "the civilizing process" of cultivation and manners that disguised the sensual body and its functions, just as the sublime and cosmopolitanism often disguised the actual bodies and local places and geographies displaced by the slave trade and imperialism.[64] This book traces the emergence of a fugitive and temperate cosmopolitanism in African American reform as an alternate discourse to imagine the creolized process of founding community and place through transatlantic slavery.

CHAPTER 1

William Wells Brown and Martin Delany
Civil and Geographic Spaces of Temperate Cosmopolitanism

A temperate and cosmopolitan sense of space and place is challenging to imagine for enslaved Africans who were involuntarily uprooted and transported as chattel goods and commodities to an intemperate land. Yet, such a temperate cosmopolitanism developed through African American movement and escape that was rooted in a simultaneous search for settlements, civil societies, and "homes." Most white Europeans voluntarily immigrated to the Americas and to what would become over centuries mythologized as their "promised land" in the United States. If they sometimes imagined themselves as "cosmopolitan," they were mainly cosmopolitan of choice—not necessity. While the "land of the free" would retain slavery for a century after its Declaration of Independence and Revolutionary War, both oppressor and oppressed created novel forms of community and conceptions of space and place in the nineteenth century.

This chapter focuses on the imaginative meanings of civil space and geographic place for two African American authors, abolitionists, and temperance reformers: William Wells Brown and Martin Delany. Both imagined temperance as a founding discourse for antislavery and freedom, and as a necessary disposition for the formation of civil space. However, the two diverge slightly in their understandings of a temperate disposition. Delany's form of cosmopolitanism depends on a hierarchical and purified freedom rooted in discourses of temperance, moral uplift, masculine heroism, and African elevation, even though some of his writings are open to a creolized sensibility. In contrast, though Brown shares the basic commitment to elevation and uplift, he imaginatively suggests a temperate character involved in creolized cosmopolitan performances that could facilitate new forms of civil and cultural exchange. Both agree that an educated and temperate populace, whether based on cultivated culture or pragmatic business acumen, was needed to establish a creole and critical cosmopolitanism.

Brown's imagined and actual civil spaces challenged discourses of American nationalism, individualism, and progress because they were enmeshed in diasporic understandings of temperance and geographically rooted meanings of exchange. For Brown, cosmopolitanism was not simply an abstract or imaginary concept but arose from his escape from slavery and travels to Canada, Europe, and Haiti. He promoted Haitian emigration and reflected on which other geographic spaces could complement and facilitate temperate civility. Delany became a more forceful emigrationist following his co-editorship of the *North Star* (1847–49), and he reflected on possible settlements in Canada, Haiti, South and Central America, the West Indies, and the Niger Valley in West Africa. This chapter culminates with Brown's hemispheric rationale for a temperate and creole cosmopolitanism needed for black diasporic settlements away from the North American continent. African American temperance reform and Freemasonry inform decisions about the location for the diaspora. Delany's and Brown's criticisms of the Canadian "promised land" or "refuge" indicate that, for them, Canada did not satisfactorily fulfill ideals of home or temperate cosmopolitan exchange. Delany's involvement with temperance and with another prominent civil society, the Masonic movement, also demonstrates how he was involved in experimental forms of cosmopolitanism, transnationalism, and geographic reorientations.

Delany, like Brown, was committed to a broader meaning of temperance intertwined with antislavery and freedom, and he was active in temperance societies in the earlier phase of his career. I am primarily concerned with Delany's and Brown's pre–Civil War development as black leaders who broke with the moral suasionist agenda of white abolition to pursue political and public goals of national and cosmopolitan freedom, a freedom that led them both to promote emigration. In Brown's literary and historical works, temperance is a consistent point of reference. For Delany, while the allusions to temperance are not as pervasive, temperance remains an undercurrent, consistent with self-control and a form of heroic self-determination.

Glenn Hendler considers Delany's commitment to temperance and his attention to two modalities of reform: the construction of a rationalist public, civil space similar to an Enlightenment Habermasian model and an inward disposition of civility. Delany was a temperance reformer for most of his life, beginning as "recording secretary of Pittsburgh's Temperance Society of the People of Color in the late 1830s. Indeed, he was involved in virtually every institution of the public sphere accessible to a black man in the middle decades of the nineteenth century, including the press, the scientific community, Freemasonry, the U.S. military, state politics, and the novel."[1] Delany, however, never conceived of himself as a literary author in the way that Brown would: he saw his public life as primarily pragmatic and useful, something that only indirectly characterizes literary authors. Similarly, his involvement in temperance was useful for public success.

Robert Levine has addressed Delany's and Frederick Douglass's commitments to temperance and moral uplift in their letters and speeches in the *North Star*. He notes that black temperance moves away from conformity to larger white goals of moral suasion and improvement toward political action and legal freedom. Levine notes, "Martin Delany had himself, during the 1830s and early 1840s, embraced temperance reform; and though Delany would eventually break with Douglass on a number of issues, he continued to share Douglass's belief in the worth of temperance to the free blacks. In one of his 'Western tour' letters to Douglass, printed in a March 1848 issue of the *North Star*, Delany proclaimed, 'The Temperance cause is beginning to 'look up,' I having, by invitation, addressed the Pittsburgh Society of Washingtonians.'"[2]

The political orientation of Delany's temperance commitment would continue to inform his work into his emigration phase and his Niger Valley expedition in 1859, during which he negotiated a treaty with the Aleke of Abeokuta for the settlement of African Americans on the land of the Egba people. In his "Report of the Niger Valley Exploring Party" (1861), Delany provides his recommendations for improving health and founding "civilization" in the region, and he highlights the need for "temperate" habits, with abstention from "malt or spirituous drink." He specifically charges the "Christian lands" as those who "produce and send bad spirits to destroy those who go to Africa." Only in rare exceptions would alcohol's medicinal use be of value.[3] While Delany promotes temperance as a moral necessity, he believed it would also support the development and profitability of cotton producers in Protestant West Africa that could create a "metropolis" and counter the hegemony of slave producers. Whether this future civilization would be cosmopolitan in a critical sense and avoid reproducing the speculative aspects of European Enlightenment cosmopolitanism is dubious. Nevertheless, Delany possesses a complex reputation as a black nationalist and pan-Africanist. More recently, Ifeoma Nwankwo foregrounds Delany's *Blake* in her discussion of "black cosmopolitanism," which she argues is a "cosmopolitanism from below" that draws on but challenges Enlightenment cosmopolitanism.[4] Delany's challenge can be located within discourses of temperance and Masonry, but his cosmopolitanism is generally more oppositional and pragmatic than is Brown's enactment of *créolité*.

Delany composed many speeches, essays, and pamphlets, but his novel *Blake; or, The Huts of America* (serially published from 1859 to 1862) was ostensibly written to raise money for his Niger Valley emigration program.[5] In it, the morality of temperance shapes the heroic, pure, self-controlled, and pragmatic nature of the main character. *Blake* seems to have been primarily written while Delany was living in Chatham, Ontario, from 1856 to 1859. While temperance references are sparse, their presence suggests Delany's assumption that bodily purity and self-control inform heroic masculinity and the temperate character necessary to forge an Africanist nation. While in the work of other authors, such as Brown and Douglass, enslaved and newly freed people are not immune to excessive alcohol consumption, in Delany's text drunkenness among slaves, Henry Blake, or the diaspora is nonexistent. For instance, a slaveholder, Ralph, asks, "'Rachel, don't you nor Jerry ever take any spirits?' 'No, Mau Rafe, not any,' replied the old woman. 'Maybe your friend there will take a little.' 'I don't drink, sir,' said Henry."[6]

Blake's discourse of internal purity pervades his racial identity (or vice versa). As the narrator remarks in the first chapter, "Henry was a black—a pure Negro—handsome, manly and intelligent in size comparing well with his master, but neither so fleshy nor heavy built in person. A man of good literary attainments—unknown to Colonel Franks, though he was aware he could read and write—having been educated in the West Indies, and decoyed away when young."[7] A "pure" racial identity and an elite education complement Henry's freeborn identity. Significantly, Delany, too, was freeborn, and a distancing from slavish inheritance or dependency informs his politics. Gilroy gives Delany's work a prominent place in his understanding of the "black Atlantic" and the "counterculture of modernity" by emphasizing Delany's black nationalism and the way his work prefigures contemporary concerns in "Afrocentrism."[8] Gilroy highlights Delany's "pure" African ancestry, which Delany claimed was "royal."[9] Delany was born free in Charles Town, Virginia (now West Virginia), and he also "claimed to be a descendant of West African chieftains."[10] He has received much critical attention since Gilroy and others situated him as central to discussions of transnationalism. However, as Robert Levine points out, prior to the black pride movements of the 1960s and 1970s, Delany's reputation suffered because preference was given to the more integrationist and racially neutral approaches of abolitionists like Brown and Douglass, who were understood to be civil rights activists.

Delany, like many abolitionists, including Brown and Douglass, portrayed inebriety chiefly through the image of the master consumed with power, and he also drew attention to the tavern keeper and the inebriety of poor uneducated whites. In *Blake*, the protagonist Henry and his companions are escaping to Canada when a group of lower-class whites briefly capture them. Delany writes, "On the way to Canada through Indiana" they were approached by a "dumb blacksmith and his wife." The conversation ensues: "'Take little something?' asked he; stepping back to a corner, taking out a caddy in the wall, a rather corpulent green bottle, turning it up to his mouth, drenching himself almost to strangulation. 'We don't drink, sir,' replied the fugitives. 'Temperance, I reckon?' enquired the smith. 'Rather so,' replied Henry."[11] Delany describes the lower-class whites as "inmates of the tavern [who] reveled with intoxication," "victims of excessive indulgence in the beverage of ardent spirits." After being captured, the fugitives are able to break free, and Henry forces the sentinel, "already partially intoxicated," to drink as much alcohol "as possible, which soon rendered him entirely insensible."[12]

Two problems in Delany's works affect the depiction of a temperate cosmopolitanism: the often-conflicted sense of racial and masculine purity and black nationalism, and the specific form of educational hierarchy that influences the structure of space and place. Henry Blake's purity and the lack of education associated with inebriety are suggestive of these problems. To be clear, they are not distinctly Delany's problems, as Brown also shares a certain elitism, though of a different sort. Nonetheless, as Glenn Hendler asserts in outlining Delany's public sense of civility, "Delany's elitism in undeniable, but those aspects of his political and rhetorical strategy that cut across territorial and racial boundaries complicate his designation as a black nationalist."[13] Elitism was present in Delany's earlier writings on black Masonry, which were also complicated in their depiction of so-called black nationalism because they simultaneously bring to light the cosmopolitan origins to Masonry. Delany's black Masonry facilitates a counternarrative to Enlightenment cosmopolitanism by recovering Africanist origins without necessarily challenging the general structure of the capitalist nation-state.

Arguably, it is contradictory to characterize racial nationalism as cosmopolitanism, but the nation-state and civil societies undergird and make possible modern forms of cosmopolitanism, which adhere to Kant's ideal of states being open to hosting foreigners. Enlightenment cosmopolitan philosophers were not addressing the situations of stateless persons, runaways, or refugees, whereas recent postcolonial theories of cosmopolitanism focus on refugees and stateless status to define cosmopolitanism as a liminal position. For Brown, Delany, and many abolitionists, questions of diasporic settlement, which were at times nationalist, necessarily complemented "refugee" status. But the civil and material spaces they recommended for the newly freed suggest their desire either for open and cosmopolitan exchanges at the very heart of what constitutes the "nation" or for more exclusive notions of a self-contained group. Portrayals of the creolized populations in New Orleans and Havana in the second half of Delany's *Blake* suggest a diverse yet hierarchical ordering of the diaspora to seize the means of production in a revolution that would, nevertheless, ambiguously embrace elite forms of "black capitalism." Temperance was crucial to the development of the character necessary to form a countercultural movement, and diasporic settlements could nurture a disposition that would foster cosmopolitan exchange. Temperance could facilitate creolization but could also fuel discourses of purity and asceticism. Likewise, it could become a means for achieving capitalist wealth, as Delany sometimes suggested.

The tension between Delany's black nationalism and the positions of more moderate, integrationist black abolitionists obfuscates their intersections and often neglects the differences between creolization and assimilation. Likewise, temperance is often wrongly viewed as assimilated to a white Anglo-Saxon Protestant ideology of asceticism rather than a radical political concern, when in fact it also led to oppositional movements of black nationalism. Significantly, although temperance was fundamental to the founding and organization of most African American civil societies and diasporic communities, considerations of revolutionary "counterculture" or diasporic identity and alliance do not usually address temperance as essential. Freemasonry was one of the first Enlightenment cosmopolitan spaces. While Delany's use of temperance discourse often appears moralistic, his involvement in Freemasonry presents an oppositional and countercultural form of cosmopolitanism that opens itself to creolized exchanges.

FREEMASONRY, EXCLUSIVITY, AND THE "SECRET" OF REVOLUTIONARY FREEDOM

Freemasons, both white and black, have the reputation of being more countercultural and revolutionary than do temperance reformers. Although the temperance movement shared many revolutionary aspects as a quasi-secretive civil society, it was associated primarily with the Protestant work ethic, prohibition, and the politics of the Woman's Christian Temperance Union. Yet, as David Brion Davis comments, many black reformers, particularly those in the tradition of black nationalism, including David Walker, Maria Stewart, and Martin Delany, "were not kowtowing to whites when they set the highest priority on black uplift and moral improvement. When they called for education, industry, temperance, self-confidence, ambition, regular work habits, and Protestant religion, they were seeking black empowerment."[14] Temperance and civility were fundamental to Masonry, but temperance as a civil society organized for moral improvement does not commonly possess Masonry's aura of radicalism; in fact, temperance usually connotes assimilation and adaptation to the moral norms of white American Protestantism.

Although the Freemasons are shrouded with a conspiratorial and revolutionary mythos, their association with the founding of the American republic and American revolutionaries suggests that their "secret" values were consistent with the Anglo-Saxon Protestant basis of American democracy pervasive at the time—an open secret of sorts in which the performance of rituals *was* the secret. Catharine Albanese explains that, in the prerevolutionary context, "it seems almost that the secret had disappeared from the secret society. The dark, mysterious, and theosophized universe of Hermeticism had dissolved in the clarified presence of Enlightenment-style deism. . . . One turned confidently toward a just deity who functioned as a kind of upper-end counting-house manager, rewarding virtue and punishing vice after death and encouraging benevolence and good works before that."[15] In the United States, Benjamin Franklin formed his Junto club and other civil societies while sharing the rationalistic social vision of Masonry, and George Washington is known to have given the Masonic sign on occasion. According to Albanese, perhaps half of those who signed the Declaration of Independence had some connection to Masonry. In fact, she notes, "at least two Freemasonic authors have attributed the notion of union among the colonists to the brotherhood."[16] The metaphysical values of Masonry were consistent with liberty, equality, and fraternity; Enlightenment rationalism; and the founding principles of the United States. Margaret Jacob connects Masonry in the eighteenth century with the rise of modernity and republican social ideals as well as a cosmopolitan sensibility inherent in its reception and hosting of foreign "brothers."[17]

In his discussion of the countercultural role of black Masonic movements and Delany's role in Freemasonry, Corey Walker elaborates on this American revolutionary connection. Although Masonry contains the outlines of a counterculture and its sacred spaces hold a "ritual of race," Walker frames African

American Masonry within reformist norms of American democracy: "African American Freemasonry enacts a political culture that coexists within the operative logics of American democracy while simultaneously challenging the norms and understandings of American democracy in the postemancipation world."[18] While Masonry has a mystical aura, "free" masonry was commonly a civil society organized by "free" blacks, even if the society ideally opened its doors to fugitives and those who were recently enslaved. Delany's 1853 lecture on Masonry argues that Moses was a slave and fugitive, thus proving that the white Masonic requirements of free birth for Masonic membership were unjust.[19] Delany explains, "Policy alone will not permit of the order to confer Masonic privileges on one while yet in captivity; but the fact of his former condition as such, or that of his parents, can have no bearing whatever on him."[20] Moreover, he argues that ancient Freemasonry had only considered "voluntary slavery" or slavery resulting from a crime as legitimate reasons for barring access to membership.[21] Free selfhood and sovereignty, literacy and education, and race pride were highly valued. White American Masons did not accept African American Prince Hall Masonry, but "even in its Prince Hall version, black Freemasonry replayed white practices, for not all blacks were candidates for lodge membership." Some fugitive slaves, for instance, could not meet the educational requirements. Masonry was "an exclusionary society, and exclusivism was essential to their union, for lodge members were keepers of privileged knowledge."[22]

Though elitist on certain educational requirements, African American Freemasonry is a critical expression of the European transatlantic and American revolutionary contexts in a couple of ways. First, according to legend, Prince Hall, founder of black Freemasonry in the United States, became a Mason to partake in the Enlightenment ideals of fraternity, equality, and liberty. He and fourteen other free blacks petitioned the grand lodge in Massachusetts for admittance but were rejected. Subsequently, they petitioned to "foreigners" in 1775, and the Grand Lodge of England admitted them. Though Prince Hall's origin had been assumed to be an American and a Bostonian free black, Walker identifies research showing he came from Barbados, a point "which underscores the centrality of the Caribbean to the later cultural production of Freemasonry."[23] The Haitian and Caribbean Masonry networks Walker documents are part of a broader black diasporic alliance portrayed in Delany's *Blake*.

Second, Delany's 1853 lecture presents Ethiopianism as the origin of black Freemasonry and revises the Enlightenment meaning of cosmopolitanism as countercultural. Delany, like many nineteenth-century African American reformers, argues that civilization originated in Ethiopia and Egypt. He challenges the racial exclusivity of white European and American Masons by appealing to the biblical figures of King Solomon and Moses. Solomon gathered "men of all nations and races" to build the temple, and afterward "commenced the universality of the Order, arising from the going forth of the builders into all parts of the world."[24] By recognizing the building of the temple as a cosmogony, Delany re-centers in Ethiopia the dispersal of the cosmopolis throughout the world. Challenging the "racial ethnographic science" of his era, which Levine notes was a primary concern for Delany in this period, Delany concludes that "to Africa is the world indebted for its knowledge of the mysteries of Ancient Freemasonry. Had Moses and the Israelites never lived in Africa, the mysteries of the wise men of the East never would have been handed down to us."[25] The knowledge of Euclid, Pythagoras, and the word "Eureka" can be found in Africa.[26] While Delany's order of Masonry includes men of "every country, clime, color, and condition (when morally worthy)," it maintains the mysterious knowledge of a master builder contained in the revelatory word "Eureka," with which, Delany comments, he has "revealed the Masonic *secret*, and must *stop!*"[27]

Secrecy, essential to exclusivity, was fundamental to both African and European Masonry—in the latter case, partly because many members of the bourgeois public who valued the formation of civil societies in Europe during the Enlightenment believed the right to privacy and private association to be intrinsic to the founding of free nation-states. The "dichotomy" between public and private "remains central to much of modern social experience," and the public was more than the coffeehouse or print culture of the novel that many theorists of the Enlightenment have characterized as transparent rational space: "The paradox at the heart of early modernity lay in its creation of a new public sphere that simultaneously championed the private, the interior, and the exclusive. The same public that read novels silently in the comfort of home also found 'secret' lodges fashionable, even alluring."[28] The protection of secrecy and secret societies was essential for the foundations of the Enlightenment and revolutionary bourgeois public space. Jacob notes that the value of secrecy, particularly with societies like the Masons, may be dangerous because "unwittingly, by taking up the habits of secrecy, eighteenth-century advocates of the cosmopolitan gave hostages to the future enemies of democracy, many of whom would in turn use secrecy to their own advantage."[29] Jacob is alluding to militant organizations of the present, but many African American organizations, who, of necessity, had to remain secretive, used secrecy in positive ways for revolutionary and just ends.

In planning paths to freedom, any organized community, fraternity, or civil society of African-descended people needed secrecy for the simple reason of safety in a context of white supremacy. As Walker notes, "The possibility of death—either by blacks involved in the planning of the rebellion or by whites if the conspiracy was discovered . . . bound them together in this 'free-mason society.'" Walker finds Masonry in Gabriel Prosser's Rebellion in Richmond, Virginia, in 1800, and he makes persuasive links to the Haitian Revolution and French coconspirators from Haiti or New Orleans who provide a context for Prosser's "appropriation" of the symbols of Freemasonry.[30] Freemasonry in Gabriel's Rebellion intertwines with Delany's involvement in black Masonry. The implied rituals Delany's novel alludes to depended on Freemasonry. Blake "develops a secret network" in his liberationist plans. The "huts" could be understood as Freemason lodges "that dot the Atlantic world" and facilitate, according to Walker, Blake's "revolutionary 'Freemasonry' and secretly communicate the plans for a hemispheric insurrection." Given that the huts appear "throughout the Americas, Delany hints of the diasporic destinies that connect the Americas, the Caribbean, and Africa as well as the global dimensions of Freemasonry."[31] However, the "secret" in *Blake* is also repeatedly connected with the knowledge of how "capital" is circulated. Blake's Masonic secret becomes the open secret of capitalist wealth necessary for freedom and for achieving hegemony to counter the white slaveholding capitalist order. When Henry first reveals the "secrets of his organization" to some of the slaves after "prayer," a slave named Charles exclaims, "'Capital, capital!' . . . 'What fools we was that we didn't know it long ago.'"[32] The secret of the movement Henry is organizing is to amass as much capital as possible from the slave owners—to be sure, a necessary first step that touches on the heart of exchange and wealth involved in the transatlantic trade. Africans who were commodities reclaim their own right as the source of value in shaping the modern world, but socialist meanings seem far from the revolutionary plans.[33]

Delany's attention to capital in *Blake* is also couched in images of American patriotism. For instance, Blake's secret organization depends on wealth in every moment of "passing" and crossing borders—money becomes the passport to freedom and Americanism. As the narrator comments on Henry's escape from slavery with other men, "Having by this time become so conversant with the patriotism and fidelity of these men to their country, Charles handing the Indianan a five-dollar piece, who on seeing the outstretched wings of the eagle, desired no further evidence of their right to pass, conveying them into the state, contrary to the statutes of the Commonwealth."[34] While Delany ironically presents the fact that national identity and national currency are equivalent, the correlation between economic wealth and political power continues throughout the novel and permeates—indeed, reifies—most levels of the pan-African revolutionary organization.

Perhaps this reification of wealth also suggests one of the reasons for the failure of any revolution in the novel. The final four chapters of Delany's novel are not extant, and the serialized form presents a fragmentary and often conflicted engagement with questions of interracial alliance, possible transnational links, and the possibility for black freedom in the midst of terror. The novel's bleak ending, with assaults of both the revolutionary poet Placido and Ambrosina Cordora, the daughter of a wealthy Cuban woman who is part of Blake's revolutionary group, also reflects Delany's challenge in imagining a geographic space for black empowerment. As Katy Chiles notes in her discussion of *Blake*'s serial form, the novel contains fragmented and often anachronistic allusions to Delany's enmeshment in political discourses about the American nation and with African American abolitionist debates over emigrationist politics and the status of the "nation within a nation."[35] Among these debates was whether Haiti was a preferred destination for emigration. Delany initially supported Haitian emigration but turned to support African emigration around 1858, mainly because whites led the Haytian Emigrationist Bureau. Cuba, the location for the proposed revolution in *Blake*, is doomed to failure because, as Chiles notes, Delany thought the geographic space itself was not large enough and the area was dominated by European interests. In Delany's words, "To these general unfavorable contingencies Africa can never be subject, being a vast continent, peopled by one of the great enduring, fixed, reproducing, absorbing races of the earth, which must continue throughout all coming time—as it has time past—only ceasing when the world shall pass away."[36] Thus, for Delany, West Africa presented a more realistic territory for expanding African interests that could potentially counter slavery and white European domination.

Although Delany's conception of racial affiliation was more fluid than some scholars have recognized, his famous 1854 seven-hour speech and pamphlet *Political Destiny of the Colored Race on the American Continent* highlights that Delany did not seriously consider "the question of civil rights for a minority." Indeed, Delany's "was a plan for political hegemony" for blacks (or rather, what he calls 'colored people,' which ultimately seems to include nonwhites if we take seriously his statistical analysis of the population of the Americas). Still, he "did not simply reverse the hegemonic 'logic of power.'"[37] Ultimately, Delany's conception of African racial identity seemed more open when it came to matters of uniting a minority population—of pure-blooded Africans—in the United States. However, Delany repeatedly criticized "mulattos" and creoles in his work, perhaps justifiably since creoles often occupied a planter class in the racial hierarchies of Cuba and New Orleans. In *Blake*, creoles are commonly the worst slaveholders, and "mulattos" dangerously mimicked white racism in organizations like "the 'Brown Society[,]' an organized association of mulattos, created by the influence of the whites, for the purpose of preventing pure-blooded Negroes from entering the social circle, or holding intercourse with them."[38] This criticism begins early in the novel, but when Blake arrives in Cuba he makes alliances across pure racial boundaries and allows for fluid affiliations for the sake of the revolution. However, the mixed characters involved are primarily from the upper classes.

Nwankwo, following Gilroy, argues that race is a matter more of political commitment for Delany than of "common cultural condition" or phenotype.[39] She also provides several examples from *Blake* of "intraracial bonding" for the purposes of transnational revolution, particularly in the representation of Placido, the racially mixed Cuban poet. Nonetheless, the Great Gathering of those involved in Blake's revolutionary society at Madam Cordora's in Havana includes those from elite classes: "Among the leading persons [were] Madame Cordora and Ambrosina, the wife and daughter of a deceased wealthy mulatto merchant; Madame Cordelia Barbosa, a wealthy young quadroon widow; Madame Evelina Sebastian, a refined wealthy mestizo lady; Carolus Blacus, a wealthy tobacco dealer; Madame and Señorita Seraphina, his wife and daughter, both accomplished black ladies; Andro Camina and Madame Tripoli and Tripolitan, his lady and daughter, a refined family of wealthy blacks, retired on a great fortune; and Justin Pompa, a distinguished black artist of rare accomplishments."[40] The diversity does not significantly challenge the cultural and economic elitism and is held in tension with other more pronounced black nationalist assertions.

For example, Henry's religious position also seems more consistent with an Enlightenment Christianity and cosmopolitanism than with a syncretic or creolized orientation that would allow various traditions to comingle. Blake is guided by divine Providence, with allusions to Moses in the "wilderness" throughout. Indeed, his initial plans converge with "Divine Providence," and, toward the end of the novel, his final speech concludes "Then let us determine to be ready, permitting nothing outside of an interposition of Divine Providence to interfere with our progress."[41] As Jerome McGann comments on this final scene and the role of religion in the novel, "Religion dominates the political action in *Blake*. It maps the struggle between what is perhaps the most basic repetition/comparison in the work: between a false religion that justifies and promotes racist oppression and a religion of promise."[42] Even while Henry accepts and incorporates other religious orientations into his community, his religious disposition draws on a heroic messianism consistent with a Protestant and individualist "self-reliance."[43] Moreover, consistent with Delany's Masonic "secret" of redemption and freedom, Henry appeals to a cosmopolitan and Christian Ethiopianism to unite with his Catholic hosts: "Ethiopia shall yet stretch forth her hands unto God; Princes shall come out of Egypt."[44]

Earlier in the novel, Blake assumes the role of "High Conqueror" to manipulate the lower-class Africans who believe in conjure, and he comments to his peers about having done so: "Now you see, boys . . . how much conjuration and such foolishness and stupidity is worth to the slaves in the South. All that it does, is to put money into the pockets of the pretended conjurer."[45] And yet, there are moments in *Blake* that acknowledge the creolized ceremonies and performances in Cuba. In chapter 72, "King's Day," Delany's voice intercedes to present a brief moment, a day of cultural and religious integrity, that depends on a creolized tradition. Forgetting his character Blake, the author-narrator Delany interjects that he is "indebted for the following description of the grand Negro festival to a popular American literary periodical, given by an eyewitness to the exhibition." In the passage, he goes on to describe "native Africans" dressed in "finery" with the freedom to "assemble according to their tribes." King's Day is the "only day the black can call his own; the law gives it to him, and no master has the right to refuse his slave permission to go out for the whole day." The specific details of "ranks" and "African paraphernalia" include "the hideous mask with horns" and "magical powers" that cause whites to fear the day. After a thoughtful description of songs and performers, Delany remarks, "The whites of Havana are rejoiced when the day is over."[46] Despite this moment of acknowledging diverse religions and classes, the tendency is generally to move toward a Christian Protestant elitism that depends on wealth.

Jeffory Clymer suggests that *Blake* shows "that Cuba's wealthy people of color can learn to forego their class privilege and instead join forces with the island's slave population in an effort to overthrow Spanish rule and form a pan-African republic."⁴⁷ Yet this tension remains unresolved. While the class hierarchy seems to favor the diverse and racially intermixed characters, suggesting a more politically than racially charged black nationalism, Delany continued to emphasize racially purified meanings of blackness and a hierarchical ordering that seems an inversion of Protestant and European cosmopolitanism. In *Blake*, creeds and practices are absorbed into a "unified" enlightened vision that points to the inward moralistic purity of the heart: "'Our ceremonies, then,' continued Blake, 'are borrowed from no denomination, creed, nor church: no existing organization, secret, secular, nor religious; but originated by ourselves, adopted to our own condition, circumstances, and wants, founded upon the eternal word of God our Creator, as impressed upon the tablet of each of our hearts.'"⁴⁸ Blake's overarching goal for a unified Africa for Africans is to "assimilate themselves to civilized customs . . . producing the greatest staples of wealth to the world."⁴⁹

In *Principia of Ethnology* (1879), Delany's final work before his death in 1885 and one often used to support his position as black nationalist, he ambiguously reverses the logic of white superiority by making a counterargument for the superiority of pureblooded Africans over and against the racially mixed. In Delany's words, "The white and black, the pure European and pure African races, the most distinct and unlike each other in general external physical characteristics, are of equal vitality and equally enduring." He continues: "The sterling races, when crossed, can reproduce themselves into their original purity, as before stated. The offspring of any two of the sterling races becomes a mixed race. That mixed race is an abnormal race. Either of the two sterling races which produced the abnormal race may become the resolvent race."⁵⁰ Delany argues that the "mixed" or half race produces a "quadroon" of one sort or other and so on, until the offspring becomes either black or white or red once more. Levine notes that Delany's "ethnological tract, written at a time in which blackness was almost universally regarded by white scientists and social scientists as an essential mark of inferiority, sought to reverse the conventional wisdom and restore a spiritual and national (Africanist) pride to beleaguered African Americans."⁵¹ Delany had explained, in less biologically essentialist terms, some of his rationale for promoting race pride and, seemingly, the superiority "of pure and unmixed African blood," in *The Condition, Elevation, Emigration, and Destiny of the Colored People of the United States* (1852). He argues that "elevation" of all people of color depends on "the elevation of the pure descendants of Africa; because to deny his equality, is to deny in a like proportion, the equality of all those mixed with the African organization; and to establish his inferiority, will be to degrade every person related to him by consanguinity; therefore, to establish the equality of the African with the European race, establishes the equality of every person intermediate between the two races. This established beyond contradiction, the general equality of men."[32] His argument is compatible with both a "black nationalism" and a creolization process that appeals to co-presence and mutuality in the experience of an in-between or intermixed position in civil and political society.

Despite the contradictions and tensions in working through the meaning of black identity and civil ordering, Delany's fundamental commitment to temperance and Masonry reveals the different political modalities of temperance and demystifies stereotypes about black involvement in temperance as limited to assimilationist practices. Like Masonry, temperance provided escaped slaves and emigrating free blacks a cosmopolitan and transnational structure: networks of meetings and affiliations throughout Europe, the United States, Canada, and in most settlements of the diaspora, including in Haiti, the West Indies, Liberia, and other parts of Africa. Brown would eventually find himself attracted to the more cosmopolitan structure of the Independent Order of Good Templars but struggled with the exclusionary practices of civil societies. Delany's temperance commitment intersects with the diasporic and pan-African concerns in Brown's fugitive cosmopolitanism.

Delany's pragmatic expression of a temperate cosmopolitanism remains in tension with the creole stylistics of Brown, and yet the two are similar in their emigrationist impulses and their elitism. Nevertheless, their elitism differs: Delany promotes a pragmatic work ethic and business education as foundational for success while working within the discourses of race science to empower those of "pure" African descent. Brown, in contrast, emphasizes the cultural and literary aspects of an educational and cosmopolitan elite. In many ways this dichotomy presages the well-known debate at the turn of the twentieth century between the Protestant work ethic orientation of Booker T. Washington and the cultural elitism of W. E. B. Du Bois. In *The Condition, Elevation, Emigration, and Destiny of the Colored People of the United States*, Delany argues that African Americans had moved too quickly to acquire cultural and literary educations: "We jumped too far; taking a leap from the deepest abyss to the highest summit; rising from the ridiculous to the sublime; without medium or intermission." Foreshadowing Washington's disgust at witnessing a "young man ... sitting down in a one-room cabin, with grease on his clothing, filth all around him, and weeds in the yard and garden, engaged in studying French grammar," Delany asks, "What did John Jacob Astor, Stephen Girard, or do the millionaires and the greater part of the merchant princes, and mariners, know about Latin and Greek, and the Classics? Precious few of them know anything."[53] Du Bois had wondered in *The Souls of Black Folk* "what Socrates and St. Francis of Assisi would say to this."[54] While Delany consistently rejected "menial" positions, his recommended education for former slaves begins with learning "useful" trades to build themselves up and into a merchant and business class.

Delany's and Brown's diverging perspectives toward elite black heroes appears in their depictions of the African American poet James Whitfield, who worked as a hairdresser. In *The Condition, Elevation, Emigration, and Destiny of the Colored People of the United States*, Delany acknowledges Whitfield "of Buffalo, New York, though in an humble position (for which we think he is somewhat reprehensible), is one of the purest poets in America. He has written much for different newspapers; and, by industry and application—being already a good English scholar—did he but place himself in a favorable situation in life, would not be second to John Greenleaf Whittier, nor the late Edgar A. Poe."[55] Delany's praise is qualified by implying that Whitfield is responsible for not "plac[ing] himself" in a more profitable position. Brown also celebrated Whitfield in several texts, and in his travel narrative he remarks, "I have often read with pleasure the sweet poetry of our own Whitfield of Buffalo, which has appeared from time to time in the columns of the *North Star*. I have always felt ashamed of the fact that he should be compelled to wield the razor instead of the pen for a living. Meaner poets than James M. Whitfield are now living by their compositions; and were he a white man he would occupy a different position."[56] Brown does not impute the responsibility for his "menial" position to Whitfield but rather suggests that cultural positions of leadership are political necessities for African Americans that need to complement an economic rise to power.

While their opposition has traditionally been framed as black nationalism versus integrationism, Brown and Delany diverge mainly in their forms of elitism, with Delany maintaining an economic orientation and Brown envisioning a temperate cosmopolitanism rooted in cultural performance and intellectual exchange. Delany continued to promote African emigration until the American Civil War, even though he was consistently wary of the American Colonization Society in Liberia despite having to gain their support for his own Niger Valley expedition. His proposed treaty with the Aleke in Nigeria was reneged in 1859. Delany and Brown also share a common interest in emigration, though by the 1860s when Brown was supporting Haitian emigration, Delany had already rejected its viability. This tension likely influenced Brown's parody of Delany in his report "The Colored People of Canada," written for *Pine and Palm* in 1861 while an agent for James Redpath's Haitian emigrationist program. He writes, "Considered in respect to hatred to the Anglo-Saxon, a stentorian voice, a violence of gestures, Dr. Delany may be regarded as the ablest man in Chatham[, Ontario], if not in America."[57] Brown, ever the ironist, also remarked that Delany's plans when he arrived in Lagos were to "take off the head of the old king." He suggests that Delany's achievements were matched by his arrogance. Notably, Delany replied, chastising Brown for his somewhat hypocritical association with Redpath's Haitian emigration bureau and commenting that he had "always treated Mr. Brown as a gentleman, and heretofore regarded him as a friend, and would now notice his uncouth (and certainly unwarranted) attack, only to correct this shameless misrepresentation."[58] Brown's irony, sarcasm, and playful literary stylistics were often less transparently sincere and uplifting than were Delany's pragmatic, scientific, and rationalist modes of self and community reform.

A TEMPERATE COSMOPOLITAN FREEDOM: WHY NOT CANADA?

Brown was a well-known abolitionist, but he was also a man of letters who authored the first African American novel, *Clotel; or, The President's Daughter* (1853), travel narratives, plays, and various historical and autobiographical works. Clearly, Brown took some creative liberties with his historical representations, but his commitment to freedom and temperance was unquestionable. He early became one of the most prominent African American temperance reformers. After his escape from Missouri slavery in 1834, he founded some of the first temperance societies in Buffalo in 1836, and he continued lecturing on temperance in Europe and across North America throughout his life.[59] Brown spent 1849 to 1854 in Europe, primarily in London and Edinburgh. (He went initially as a delegate for the International Paris Peace Congress.) *Three Years in Europe; or, Places I Have Seen and People I Have Met*, the first travel narrative by an African American, was published in 1852 in London and later revised in an 1854 edition titled *The American Fugitive in Europe: Sketches of Places and People Abroad*. Prior to leaving for Europe, Brown was a steamboat operator and lived in Buffalo for nine years, and he transported fugitive slaves through either Detroit or Buffalo during the 1830s and 1840s. Buffalo's proximity to the Canadian border seemed strategic, given the potential need for his own flight, but he never moved to Canada.[60]

Though a cosmopolitan traveler abroad, his cosmopolitanism develops from the perspective of a fugitive slave and cannot be conflated with a European individualist detachment associated with Enlightenment cosmopolitanism, that of Immanuel Kant in particular. Brown's creolized and parodic visions of culture affected his notions of freedom, temperance, and civility—and, as witnessed in his caricature of Delany, he sometimes bordered on incivility.

In 1854, Ellen Richardson purchased Brown's freedom from Enoch Price, and he would no longer be a "fugitive," making it relatively safe for him to return to the American continent. Seven years later, he toured Southern Ontario in a somewhat contradictory effort to promote Haitian immigration, given that some positive aspects of black communities in Ontario appear in the report. However, the negative aspects of racism in Canada overshadow those moments. Allegedly, Brown also had visited Haiti, Cuba, and the West Indies in 1840.[61] During the Civil War, Brown, like many reformers, seemed to abandon his support for emigration and turned to Reconstruction. He was consistently involved in temperance and fully committed to temperance movements and civil societies as necessities in the postwar era.

When he moved to Buffalo in 1836, according to William Farrison, "Brown discovered many who, like himself, had freed themselves from chattel slavery; but among them he also found many who were being victimized by servitude to intoxicating drinks. In order to abolish this kind of slavery, Brown organized a temperance society—one of the first to be organized in western New York—and served as its president for three terms."[62] This society gained about three hundred members, but Brown stepped down from its presidency as he became more involved with abolitionism.[63] After the "legal" end of chattel slavery in the United States, Brown resumed a more activist role in temperance, though he never abandoned his temperance associations while an abolitionist.

Brown participated in the Order of the Sons of Temperance and the Independent Order of Good Templars, "two national secret orders replete with regalia, rituals, and passwords, and with international affiliations."[64] The Washingtonians were also one of the first white masculine temperance groups formed, and their manner of association did not clearly follow any principle of "secrecy": they often delivered very public performances based on emotional appeal. As I will discuss in the next chapter, Brown was critical of John Gough and the public performances of Washingtonian reform, which highlighted sentimentality and sympathy for the drunkard. The Washingtonians often backslid from their pledges, and in 1842 the Sons of Temperance originated to address this problem. The Sons "adopted a policy of secrecy to remove the liability of public exposure from both the organization and its individual members."⁶⁵ Brown became involved with the Sons in the 1860s and in 1866 served as chief representative of the John Brown Division in Massachusetts, but he continually struggled with their racist and segregationist policies.⁶⁶ He would eventually commit to the Good Templars in 1875, though racial tensions continued in that group as well.⁶⁷ The Independent Order of Good Templars (IOGT) also seems to bear more in common with Freemasonry in its "quasi-masonic ritual brotherhood" and cosmopolitan "transoceanic membership."⁶⁸

In the United States, temperance was most prominent in the Northern states during the antebellum period, though white temperance unions existed in parts of the South. Temperance was also affiliated with Methodist churches and the AME Church in the South, without necessarily requiring religious faith and testament.⁶⁹ Most African Americans who joined the IOGT were moderate drinkers or teetotalers and did not classify themselves as "alcoholics seeking to save themselves from a drinking problem."⁷⁰ According to Fahey, African Americans found the "universalism" and relative cosmopolitanism of the IOGT attractive in comparison to other temperance organizations or civil societies.⁷¹

African American leaders in the antebellum period recognized the problems that alcohol posed for the poor, often prone "to turn to drink as an anodyne, an escape," and therefore they linked "abstinence" with "abolition."⁷² Temperance movements strove for universalist and international goals of individual sovereignty, restraint, and enlightened freedom—the hallmarks of civil society and public space promoted in Enlightenment modernity. Nonetheless, while the movements were international, they often expressed themselves in nationalistic form. White American temperance movements promoted many of the middle-class, domestic, and individualistic values associated with the Protestant work ethic and its inner-worldly asceticism. Likewise, often their organizations became racist even as they expressed their freedom as overcoming "slavery to the bottle": freedom was understood as controlling the willpower in an attempt to gain an individual and internal purity. The desire for restraint and bodily purity as a correlative of temperance could coexist with ethnic chauvinisms for black nationalists just as an ideology of masculine bonding, identity formation, and self-control tended to be dominant in many temperance organizations.⁷³ To be sure, African American men had a strong need for fraternal bonding and for redefining masculinity in light of slavery's emasculating violence and representations of black masculinity. Women were allowed in many meetings, particularly those of the IOGT.[74] However, even branches of women's organizations like the WCTU often adhered to racist and typically gendered norms of middle-class Protestant domesticity.

The newly freed faced considerable problems such as poverty, and the potential existed for alcohol abuse as "anodyne," but temperance organizations also facilitated a much-needed opportunity for fostering social connections. Potential alcohol abuse among the recently freed or escaped was a primary reason Brown became involved in temperance after his escape from Missouri slavery in 1834. He had also witnessed the effects of alcoholism as belligerency in the master class. In his *Narrative* (1847), Brown describes how in the last six years of his life in slavery, he was hired out to "at least ten different" employers in St. Louis. One employer was the tavern keeper, Major Freeland. Brown characterizes Freeland as "'a horse-racer, cock-fighter, gambler, and withal an inveterate drunkard,' with whom 'when he was present, it was cut and slash— knock down and drag out.'" Freeland's "tyrannical" and "diabolical" treatment of Brown appears to have played an important role in his rejection of alcohol and participation in the temperance movement.[75] The excesses and inebriety of the master class (either slaveholders, whites who hire out, or overseers) often served to demonize slaveholding in abolitionist literature.

Brown's biography, nonetheless, suggests that he did enjoy drinking as a young boy. William Farmer writes in his introduction to *Three Years in Europe*:

> Although William did not get the religion of his master, he acquired a family passion which appears to have been strongly intermixed with the devotional exercises of the household of Dr. Young—a love of sweet julep. In the evening, the slaves were required to attend family worship. Before commencing the service, it was the custom to hand a pitcher of the favorite beverage to every member of the family, not excepting the nephew, a child of between four and five years old. William was in the habit of watching his opportunity during the prayer and helping himself from the pitcher, but one day letting it fall, his propensity for this intoxicating drink was discovered, and he was severely punished for its indulgence.[76]

Brown's narrative does not in fact depict this incident as dramatically as Farmer implies. Brown wrote that he enjoyed the julep and was "about as happy as any of them" drinking. But he says he "accidentally let the pitcher fall upon the floor." As a result, he was "severely chastised."[77] He says nothing about having a "propensity for this intoxicating drink" nor of being punished specifically for "indulgence"; rather, the fact that he broke the pitcher seems to be the cause. Farmer's rendition makes it appear as if Brown attributed the punishment to his inebriety, thereby implying that such actions were prohibited for slaves. Yet, Brown indicates that drinking among slaves was not uncommon, though not always permitted.

Brown's writings, however, less frequently depict slaves as inebriated and generally present the slaveholder and overseers as inebriates, as Robert Levine points out, "drunk with power."[78] In a version of the "tragic mulatta" story in Brown's well-known novel *Clotel; or, The President's Daughter* (1853), Horatio Green is a "defeated" politician, perhaps modeled on Jefferson, and had taken Clotel as his concubine. Green attempts to find solace "in that insidious enemy of man, the intoxicating cup" and, in a dishonorable act, agrees with his white wife's plan to sell Clotel "to the far South."[79] Brown's defense of "amalgamation" as a whitening process (assimilation linked with temperance) is linked, Levine argues, to the metaphor of "blacking" and its momentary conflation with drunkenness in *Clotel*. "Blacking" refers to the blackening or polishing of shoes and boots, usually performed by servants or slaves. In a humorous scene in *Clotel* a Connecticut minister defends the Maine Law (passed in 1851 to legislate prohibition) to a Southerner who is providing caricatures of "teetotalers." The minister says that before he was a teetotaler he used to keep liquor on his premises because his "servant" (who was "addicted to strong drink") claimed that he needed the whiskey to mix with the blacking. The minister spied on his servant and discovered him drinking "the whisky, blacking, and all."[80]

Brown's temperance discourse, according to Levine, concludes by promoting "amalgamation" and "deracialized union" to found Brown's notion of a free civilization.[81] Conversely, temperance for Brown might be viewed instead as creolized, cosmopolitan, and diasporic—at least until he promotes integration and the intermingling of the races during the Civil War and Reconstruction (and even then, creolization is different from whitening). Brown's commitment to temperance was also linked to his commitment to diasporic settlements and cosmopolitanism. Levine's integrationist reading highlights the issue of class raised in Brown's metaphor of "blacking." In this rendering, Brown associates drunkenness with those who abuse their power, but he also at times associates alcoholism with the poor or laboring classes (not necessarily the enslaved). For instance, in a letter from Europe, Brown had remarked about some of the British laboring class that "very much of their degradation is brought upon by themselves." He continues: "The amount of drunkenness is frightful.... It is enough to horrify any one to go amongst these people, who seem abandoned to the varied evils that neglect, ignorance, and vice have produced.... Many of those appear so worn in countenance, form, feature, and expression, that one is almost led to doubt whether they are of the same species with the well-organized and the noble of the race." From this quote, Levine argues that Brown "places the burden for the 'elevation' of the working poor on the poor themselves."[82] Still, Brown was also empowering the poor rather than viewing them with liberal sympathy or as an object of pity. For Brown, inebriety leads to "ignorance and vice," making the laboring classes another "species" in this passage, though not quite "slaves."

In Brown's work, intoxication was more commonly a metaphor not for blackness but rather for a poverty of cultural and cosmopolitan development; temperance, on the contrary, was associated with "peace." Brown notes in *Three Years in Europe*, "The name of Elihu Burritt, for many reasons, should be placed at the head of the Peace Movement. No man was ever more devoted to one idea than he is to that of peace. If he is an advocate of Temperance, it is because it will promote peace. If he opposes Slavery, it is upon the grounds of peace."[83] Moreover, Brown praises the white British laboring classes who are demonstrating at the Crystal Palace as part of the temperance (and peace) cause:

> Their number while going to the Exhibition, was variously estimated at from 15,000 to 20,000, and was said to have been the largest gathering of Teetotalers ever assembled in London. They consisted chiefly of the working classes, their wives and children—clean, well-dressed and apparently happy: their looks indicating in every way those orderly habits which, beyond question, distinguish the devotees of that cause above the common labourers of this country. On arriving at the Exhibition, they soon distributed themselves among the departments, to revel in its various wonders, eating their own lunch, and drinking from the Crystal Fountain.[84]

Certainly, both Brown and Delany tended to view the poor and laboring classes, both black and white, as at greater risk for intemperance than the upper classes. However, all classes were portrayed as potentially succumbing to intemperance.

For both authors, Canada shared similar values and class tensions, and proved unsatisfactory as a permanent settlement for former slaves—except possibly in areas of Ontario like Toronto and more heavily populated black settlements like Chatham, where Delany lived and practiced medicine for several years. When Delany moved to Chatham in 1856, he had aligned with some of the goals of Canadian emigrationists, such as Mary Ann Shadd Cary. In *The Condition, Elevation, Emigration, and Destiny of the Colored People of the United States* (1852), Delany discussed the limitations of emigration to Canada due to the predominantly white population and the values they shared with white Americans, as well as his belief that the United States would eventually annex Canada. In his words, "The Canadas are no place of safety for the colored people of the United States; otherwise we should have no objection to them. But to the fugitive—our enslaved brethren flying from Southern despotism—we say, until we have a more preferable place—go on to Canada. Freedom, always; liberty any place and ever—before slavery. Continue to fly to the Canadas, and swell the number of the twenty-five thousand already there."[85] Increasing the number of blacks in Canada remained important to Delany several years later when he wrote "The Political Aspect of the Colored People" (1855), in which he acknowledged the successes of black Canadians.[86]

In *Blake*, a poor escaped slave named Andy did not realize that his mythological "Canada" would be as racist and exclusionary, and as segregated in its institutions, as parts of the American South: "He little knew the facts, and as little expected to find such a state of things in the long-talked of and much-loved Canada by the slaves. . . . It had never entered the mind of poor Andy, that in going to Canada in search of freedom, he was then in a country where privileges were denied him which are common to the slave in every Southern state—the right of going into the gallery of a public building."[87]

Brown always veered away from any semipermanent habitation of Canada, though he occasionally romanticized the image of Canada in his first slave narrative and in *Clotel*. He also worked to transport fugitives for the Underground Railroad. Canada would do, in other words, until better and more cosmopolitan spaces for settlement were secured. Brown and Delany both viewed Canada as part of a hemispheric "America." In his 1861 report "The Colored People of Canada," Brown depicted an uncivil, uncosmopolitan space, heavily populated by white European immigrants who shared much in common with the white European immigrants in the United States, such as racist and intemperate dispositions—habits that complemented each other and to which the poor and laboring classes were easily susceptible.

Southern Ontario, part of Canada West from 1841 to 1867, was among the more prominent destinations for fugitive slaves traveling by way of the Underground Railroad in the decades preceding the American Civil War.[88] Canada, for escaped slaves, may have appeared an imagined promised land, a "new Canaan," but while it was an escape from enslavement, it was not necessarily a space of freedom that could meet the political, cultural, and material needs of new communities. Not coincidentally, the early American Puritans and Protestant sects often saw themselves as escaping the Old World to the "promised land" just as the ancient Israelites had escaped from Egyptian captivity. Captives in chattel slavery and abolitionist literature often mobilized such rhetoric to promote an escape from a traumatic past, but the location of a promised land was far from certain. Canada was, as many noted, "convenient" because of its proximity to the United States and the relative ease of crossing the border. However, the attachment to Canada was far from unanimous, and many black abolitionists found that its racism and large white population made forming strong black communities and a cosmopolitan civil society more challenging. As Brown would note in his 1861 report, "Canada has so long been eulogized as the only spot in North America where the Southern bondsman could stand a freeman, and the poetical connection of its soil with the fugitive, the 'North Star,' and liberty, had created such an enthusiastic love in my heart for the people here, that I was not prepared to meet the prejudice against colored persons which manifests itself wherever a member of that injured race makes his appearance."[89]

Nevertheless, from at least as early as the 1820s, fugitive slaves arrived in the Niagara region and St. Catharines from Buffalo; others crossed to Ontario through the Detroit-Windsor border for refuge, escape, or an opportunity to create settlements and permanent homes. For fugitive slaves in Canada West, temperance became a fundamental badge of character.

From the beginnings of abolitionism, temperance was a required practice and disposition. This may be because it is easier to become economically successful while sober, a fact that Benjamin Franklin knew so well, or perhaps these were some of the white Protestant values inculcated by African American reformers. Both are partly true, but the actual problems created by alcohol use need not be downplayed to recognize the significance of ideological and discursive practices. As Mary Ann Shadd Cary's plea for a temperance boarding house in Chatham, Ontario, shows, "The planned black settlements in the province either required or recommended temperance. In communities throughout Canada West, local blacks formed societies, like the African Temperance Society of St. Catharines, to promote abstinence from intoxicating beverages."[90] The practice of temperance appears throughout Benjamin Drew's collection *The Refugee*, and some settlements, like the Elgin community formed by William King in Buxton, were dry communities. In Buxton "the temperance principle is strictly acted on through the whole settlement,—no intoxicating drinks being either manufactured or sold."[91] The Refugee Home Society in Windsor, sponsored by Henry and Mary Bibb and James T. Holly, followed suit: "The claims of temperance are kept fully in view. A by-law provides that 'No house shall be used for manufacturing or vending intoxicating liquors on any lot received from the Society.'"[92]

Henry Bibb wrote a well-known editorial in 1851 in his newspaper *Voice of the Fugitive* attributing "Color-Phobia in Canada" to slavery and inebriety. Racism was a "contagious disease" in the United States that was "striving to get a foothold in Canada." Color-phobia, according to Bibb, is particularly contagious

> among the lowest class of white people.... Its origin sprang from old Capt. Slavery, who has enlisted thousands in his services to carry on the work of prejudice, malice, and hatred, death, and devastation among the human family.... The rum shop is substitute for the school house and his soldiers are mostly men [of] intemperate habits; always ready to go at the bidding of their leader to break up an anti-slavery meeting, to engage in the work of kidnapping, man stealing, breaking up the bands of human affections by selling children from parents and husbands from their wives.[93]

Most reformers agreed, and Samuel Ringgold Ward said in an 1851 letter to Henry Bibb that "Rum and Negro-hate, the two great evils of our adopted land, shall receive undying fight from me during my life."[94] Arriving in a "free land" did not mean the space was healthy, temperate, or cosmopolitan, and a legal definition of freedom was not enough to sustain a sense of community or identity. Brown's thoughts on Canada suggest the need for a temperate cosmopolitan space nurtured by civil society. Such a space should include cultural memories beginning with the experience of the transatlantic trade, following various "leaps" to freedom and cosmopolitan travels, and still honoring the immediacy of local, material history, lived experience, and traditions.

Brown's farcical 1858 play *The Escape; or, A Leap for Freedom* hints at the meaning of Canada as a future promise for escaped or freed slaves. As in other slave narratives to Canada, such as Henry Bibb's, little is said about the land and people in Canada once the destination is reached. The favored house slave and protagonist Cato, who is also a would-be doctor and dentist among slaves, dreams of pulling teeth in Canada: "As soon as I get to Canada, I'll set up a doctor shop, an' won't I be poplar? Den I rec'on I will. I'll pull teef fer all de people in Canada." Escaping also requires changing one's identity; therefore,

Cato desires a name change to "Alexander Washington Napoleon Pompey Caesar."[95] As John Ernest points out, "When Cato first escapes, he is barely able to believe his good fortune; he asks himself, 'I wonder if dis is me?'"[96] This question about the performance of identities and disguises unveils Brown's continual attention to the construction of race and to which ritual or "race" could provide a temperate and cosmopolitan home.

A space of freedom would provide not only the social, political, and economic conditions but also the cultural conditions, including religious possibilities, for an authentic identity entailing a relationship to the land and community. Escaped slaves who immigrated to Canada often did not have those links to a larger community and, in many cases, returned after the Civil War to the United States, where they had such links. Of necessity, African American migrants from chattel slavery had become cosmopolites as part of a diaspora stolen from their homelands and displaced through enslavement. In such a situation they formed relationships to create new African American identities. Although cosmopolitanism is a popular concept in much recent critical theory, Simon Gikandi points out that Enlightenment visions of being "citizens of the world" appeared at the same time as the Middle Passage and the triangular trade complicated the claims of enslaved persons to European cultural sophistication and cosmopolitanism.[97] This sense of homelessness and lack of cultural ties, though attractive as a free-floating geography of the mind to many men of the Enlightenment and of good "taste," presented more ambiguity in the experience of those who were the commodities and displaced bodies that made such a geography possible.

While the "flight" to Southern Ontario was a hopeful escape, Cato's question, "I wonder if dis is me?" remained part of efforts to envision a location of freedom. Ironically, Thomas Jefferson, as Hannah Arendt notes, referred to Cato when reflecting on the necessity of and problems in constituting elementary republics and "wards."[98] For Cato (and Jefferson), a republic could succeed on the basis of the civil organs and spaces that encourage participation in government. For the Enlightenment thinker Jean-Jacques Rousseau, Cato was "a symbol of political liberty" who possessed the republican virtue that Diogenes the Cynic nostalgically viewed as no longer available.[99] Diogenes was the first to proclaim he was "a citizen of the world" in reply to a question about his origins. If Brown, though cosmopolitan in his numerous travels, emphasized republican virtue as central to his ideal political community, he also had Cato question the possibility of that identity in Canada. Cato substitutes a problematic classical and indeterminate multiplicity by merging

European and American emperors in his new Canadian name and identity: Alexander Washington Napoleon Pompey Caesar.[100] That republican freedom had become a matter of classical and biblical European rhetoric rather than lived experience is implied when Cato at the end "got religion" and decides to add "Rev." to his name.[101]

Enslaved Africans made many spaces within republican American slavery "home," but the sense of home would always be a fragmented memory of sacred space and cultural dislocation. Canada, as another colonial space, offered the "freedom of British soil" or "Victoria's shore" in Brown's imaginative work, but the culture was not indigenous.[102] For many of the enslaved, it was the remnant of Africa that provided a cultural and spatial link to their past. As Gikandi notes, "For slaves, culture itself had to start as a ruin, a fragment that represented both connection and disconnection from Africa."[103] Whether through music, dance, shouts, or the drum and other ritual objects, cultural and symbolic forms during the decades preceding the Civil War usually entailed some relation to past events and to material space.[104] In the earliest generations for slaves, those cultural ties to West Africa, despite the tragedy of the Middle Passage, still appeared in Africanisms and syncretic traditions. By the mid-nineteenth century, this continuity was not as forceful and the geography of resettlement for the diasporic imagination was much more diverse, though back-to-Africa movements appeared and reappeared throughout the nineteenth and twentieth centuries. Many critics refer to the French historiographer Pierre Nora's concept of *lieux de mémoire* (sites of memory) to clarify the process of remembering home, not simply as nostalgia but as part of the tragic reconstruction of personal and collective identity.[105]

The Underground Railroad shares in this mnemonic reconstruction. Though the Underground Railroad was an early, effective, and symbolic means of escape for African Americans, the part Brown explored around Buffalo, New York, and St. Catharines, Ontario, does not loom large as a *lieux de mémoire* for black freedom. Nevertheless, Brown, a fugitive slave who was also a conductor for the Underground Railroad, critically assesses the possibility of a centering meaning of black freedom for descendants of the transatlantic slave trade in his varied writings on Canada.

In the slave narrative that prefaces *Clotel*, written by Brown in the third person, he echoes the abolitionist belief in Canada's promise as the "new Canaan." He recounts how he persuaded his mother to attempt an escape with him to Canada, though she "did not wish to leave her children in slavery." They had "nothing but the North Star to guide them."[106] While this first attempt failed, the North Star shines on as she urges him to continue his quest for liberty despite her enslavement. Brown's escape north is disappointing: "What crushed the poor slave's heart in his flight most was, not the want of food or clothing, but the thought that every white man was his deadly enemy. Even in the free states the prejudice against color is so strong that there appears to exist a deadly antagonism between the white and coloured races."[107] Nonetheless, upstate New York was as far north as he would settle on the American continent. In the first version of his slave narrative, his desire is to venture north to Canada—the reader anticipates his crossing into the "promised land." Yet, just within reach of the border, he arrives in Cleveland. In his words, "I had no money, and the lake being frozen, I saw that I must remain until the opening of the navigations, or go to Canada by way of Buffalo. But believing myself to be somewhat out of danger, I secured an engagement at the Mansion House, as a table waiter, in payment for my board." He stays there "until spring" and then finds "good employment on board a lake steamboat."[108] At this point Brown became involved with the Underground Railroad and abolitionism, combining his skills as a steamboat pilot with his antislavery interests while remaining in Buffalo and organizing temperance societies.

Brown was evidently proud of the number of slaves he transported across the border when he claimed in his slave narrative, "During the season of 1842, this fugitive slave conveyed no less than *sixty-nine* runaway slaves across Lake Erie, and placed them on the soil of Canada."[109] His use of the word "soil" complements his idealization of Canada, regardless of his own in-between identity traversing national borders. Stephen Lucasi calls this a "traveling subjectivity" and notes that Brown's slave narrative is unique because it transgresses the typical journeys and arrivals and "reflects a broadening of those conventions through its hybridization of the slave narrative and travel narrative."[110] A "traveling subjectivity" and a mobile subject position capture much of Brown's life and the potential energy of many reformers who escaped from slavery, though the "soil" recurs in Brown's work in a register reminiscent of the imaginative aesthetic and sacred spaces of pilgrimage. Brown's constant travels—his escape from slavery, his movement from Buffalo to Canada, to Europe, and then to his beloved Massachusetts, as well as his contemplated (though this is speculation) immigration to Haiti before his final return "home"—imitates the structure of a pilgrimage, complete with reflections and ambiguous tragic liminalities. Some have characterized Brown as a "fugitive tourist" and "trickster," but the ambivalence toward space in his narratives might also be understood as a search for the intimacy of home that resonates with a *lieux de mémoire*.

This is informed by romantic concepts of the folk, the meaning of tradition, and the nature of civil society in a cosmopolitan republican democracy.

While free "soil" holds the promise that African Americans be recognized as equals, Canada does not appear in Brown's writings as a potential "home" or as the site of a revolutionary rebirth for a cosmopolitan subjectivity. In his 1861 report Hamilton and Toronto do garner more praise from him than do the more rural farming areas. Part of the reason for this seems to be that the rural areas were typically more segregated than were the urban and cosmopolitan regions. Also, as immigrants to the American continent, poor white laborers who may have had a sense of tradition and history in the segregation of "British soil" directed the formation of black settlements. The metropolitan areas fared a little better because of cultural activity and smaller populations integrating over time. Brown remarks on Toronto, "The number of colored people in Toronto is about 1400. Every Southern state . . . [has been] amalgamated into one conglomerated mass; and these are scattered in every part of the city."[111] Notably, the city is much more integrated and cosmopolitan in the common sense of the word than the rural regions and areas with more fugitive slaves. Brown praises the educational institutions as "the finest" of any city "in America" and notes the presence of physicians and businessmen, as well as "benevolent associations" and "temperance" organizations.[112]

Brown also comments on the issue of "passing" as white European, a dominant theme in his literature. He writes that, in Toronto, African descendants who are light-skinned often "pass for foreigners, and under that guise, almost any mulatto may push himself through the crowd, if he can rattle off a little French, German, or Spanish. With some of our class, this is an inducement to study the languages."[113] George Green, a main protagonist of *Clotel*, passes while in Europe, though not while in southwest Ontario. Evidently, while he speaks of "passing" in a somewhat neutral tone, as is characteristic of his writing, Brown did not desire to "pass," though he was light-skinned enough to do so.

By the late 1840s, the number of fugitives in St. Catharines, Ontario, had increased, the region was more segregated than Toronto, and it lacked many educational opportunities.[114] The town makes a brief appearance in a scene found both toward the end of *Clotel* and in letter 23 of *Three Years in Europe*, which bears the imprints of the story of Brown's friends William and Ellen Craft, who escaped through Halifax, Nova Scotia, on their way to Liverpool. George Green, the light-skinned son of a statesman and the lover of Mary Green, Clotel's daughter, borrows Mary's clothes and, following the example of the Crafts, cross-dresses to escape "toward Canada" from a death sentence for participation in a revolt in Richmond, Virginia. Echoing romantic abolitionist discourses of the Underground Railroad, George follows "the North Star" across the Ohio River where he, like Brown in his autobiographical accounts, meets a Quaker who assists him. The narrator alludes to an abolitionist poem, "The Fugitive Slave's Apostrophe to the North Star," as his guide through the "night."[115] In *Clotel*, Brown mixes historical and literary documents to shape the revised narrative of American origins. And while Canada appears as the mythological North Star, the brevity of the account suggests ambiguities in Brown's literary perception of the potential new Canaan.

Although George Green escapes from prison and slavery to Canadian soil, this is a temporary asylum. In a brief paragraph, the narrator mentions George's quaint "abode in the little town of St. Catharines" while employed "on the farm of Colonel Street," where he "attended a night-school, and laboured for his employer during the day." His is a dignified reprieve, though "the climate was cold," because "he was in a land where he was free, and this young slave prized [this freedom] more than all the gold that could be given." George also teaches others "what he could"—and we are told that "there are many" other fugitives.[116] The actual numbers in St. Catharines and major settlements such as Chatham, Dawn, and Elgin have been debated. Benjamin Drew, in his famous recounting of the number of blacks in Canada West, most of whom were thought to be fugitive slaves, notes that there were about eight hundred in the total population of six thousand in St. Catharines.[117] In 1861, Brown follows Drew's statistics when he writes, "In the village and its environs, there are not far from eight hundred colored people, representing every Southern State in the late American Union, scattered around, and within five miles, are a large number of farmers, many of whom have become wealthy since escaping into Canada." Brown visits the market where he receives some news about the population from vendors. He provides a positive assessment of St. Catharines at this time: "The houses in the settlement are all owned by their occupants, and from inquiry I learned that the people generally were free from debt. Out of the eight hundred in St Catharines, about seven hundred of them are fugitive slaves."[118] If Brown is promoting Haitian immigration in this 1861 tour, the fact that he notes the property of former slaves in St. Catharines is a significant acknowledgment of progress in the region. Nonetheless, the momentary remarks about progress in the region are countered by his general conclusions: "The more I see of Canada, the more I am convinced of the deep-rooted hatred to the negro."[119]

Clotel was written during Brown's travels abroad to Europe, prior to his Canada West tour in 1861, but after his alleged trip to Haiti in 1840. Notably, it offers a neutral, maybe even positive, description of St. Catharines, though the region seems to be only a place for laboring, not a space for civil society or cultured (and cultural) exchanges. Notwithstanding a significant possibility for community indicated by his instructing the "many" others, George does not remain for long. St. Catharines is more an "asylum" and temporary stop than a genuine settlement. Indeed, in an 1849 welcome speech in Britain published in the *North Star*, Brown gives thanks to God that "there was an asylum still left for the slave and that the Canadas, at the present moment, were the land of refuge for more than 20,000 escaped bondmen (cheers). Nor could he convey to that meeting the feelings which came over him when he landed at Liverpool and felt that he was really free. Then he could indeed adopt the language of the poet, and say—'Old England! old England! thrice blessed and free!'"[120] George Green follows the same route to England and then France after spending time laboring in Southern Ontario.

Canada West is cold, after all, but no colder than Buffalo. Yet, Brown had opened *Clotel* with his slave narrative, including a letter promoting West Indian emigration published in the *London Times* on July, 4, 1851.[121] Notably, that letter makes clear that Brown did not romanticize Europe, as has sometimes been insinuated, and he clearly warns African Americans against coming to England because of the lack of employment.[122] But Brown's representation of the climate also supported the idea of Canada as a wilderness made for labor rather than a space conducive to cultural refinement. Brown, echoing the negative sentiments of slaveholders who depicted Canada as a desolate and cold wilderness, writes, "Although a residence in Canada is infinitely preferable to slavery in America, yet the climate of that country is uncongenial to the constitutions of the Negroes, and their lack of education is an almost insuperable barrier to their social progress." Though Brown "attempted to remedy" the situation "by the establishment of Manual Labour Schools in Canada for fugitive slaves,"[123] that effort was not supported well enough; even such schools likely would not have met Brown's educational ideals. Regardless, George Green in *Clotel* attempts to "obtain education for himself" and teach other fugitive slaves "what he could."[124] While George spends "nearly six months' labour at St. Catharines," as soon as he receives news that Mary had been sold to the New Orleans market and he loses "all hope of getting the girl"—he "resolved to quit the American continent forever" and departs for Liverpool.

Why such a drastic and final decision? One reason is the lack of educational opportunity: "With little or no education, he found many difficulties in the way of getting a respectable living." George works as a "porter" in

Manchester and manages to pursue "private lessons at night" over the course of three years. These are not lessons in manual labor because he becomes a "clerk" and eventually a "partner in the firm" and is set "on the road to wealth" while passing as white, being "somewhat ashamed of his African descent."[125] George vacations in northern France and, while in Dunkirk, chances to encounter Mary, his long-lost love, who was purchased by a Frenchman because she reminded him of his sister; they marry, but he dies, and she subsequently lives with her father-in-law. Of course, the reunion in France is presumably to highlight the fact that European governments have ended slavery at this time, as the narrator remarks, "We can but blush for our country's shame when we recall to mind the fact, that while George and Mary Green, and numbers of other fugitives from American slavery, can receive protection from any of the governments of Europe, they cannot return to their native land without becoming slaves."[126]

Canada, while having a European government, was too close to the United States, and it shares a similar colonial history and white European immigrants. According to Brown's 1861 report, Canada is not an ideal place for former slaves to establish their freedom and independence, mainly because of "the prejudice," which had two underlying causes. First, there was self-imposed segregation experienced in "forming separate churches, taking back seats in public meetings, and performing menial offices of labor, and thereby giving the whites an opportunity to regard them with a degree of inferiority."[127] Brown may appear to blame the victims, and the criticism seems somewhat ironic given that he desired to establish a manual labor school. However, Brown also shares this view with others, such as Mary Shadd Cary, who was critical of the mismanagement of the Dawn Settlement in Dresden, Ontario, founded in the 1830s by the Anti-Slavery Society through charitable help from Oberlin College in Ohio and other sponsors, including the "Quaker philanthropist" James Cannings Fuller.[128] The settlement became associated with Josiah Henson, the presumed biographical source for Uncle Tom. Brown also directly criticized the segregated settlement, the use of white philanthropy rather than mutual help (or self-help), and other examples of voluntary segregation that were not culturally empowering.[129] And while Brown promoted black independence and segregated civil and cultural life in some contexts, such as in his promotion of Haiti and in the final reflections of *My Southern Home*, he realized that in situations in which African Canadians were a minority population, integration (or, to use his word, "amalgamation")—presumably without "passing" or denying one's heritage—would be more empowering.[130]

The second reason for prejudice, one that perhaps became more pronounced after Brown's five years in Europe, was that, in his words,

> [t]he main body of the population of Canada appears to be made up of the lower class of the people of England, Scotland, and Ireland. As I walk the streets here, I look in vain for that intelligent portion of the middle classes that I used to meet in London, Edinburgh, and Dublin. This lower stratum, coming from the old world, and feeling keenly their inferiority in education and refinement, and being vulgar and rude themselves, try, like the editor of the London Free Press, to draw attention from their own uncouthness, by directing the public eye to the other degraded class.[131]

Brown acknowledges that this is not the case everywhere in Canada. The tensions are not a simplistic elitism but echo complaints of African Americans later in the nineteenth and early twentieth centuries when race riots broke out as a result of resentment from competing immigrant workers who believed whiteness provided some level of superiority and entitlement. Brown recognized that class tensions increased racial resentment and that a fair laboring situation for the former slaves could be achieved more effectively in majority-black areas, such as Haiti. In a different context, such as Canada, the focus had to be on integration and the establishment of educational and civil organizations that could facilitate cosmopolitan, cross-cultural exchange.

While Brown criticized uneducated whites in "The Colored People of Canada," he had also done so in his writings on the northern United States. For instance, in *The Black Man, His Antecedents, His Genius, and His Achievements* (1863) he answers with a bit of irony the objection that whites will not receive blacks on equal terms: "I have some white neighbors around me in Cambridge; they are not very intellectual; they don't associate with my family; but whenever they shall improve themselves, and bring themselves up by their own intellectual and moral worth, I shall not object to their coming into my society—all things being equal."[132] Still, New England seems preferable to London, Ontario: a couple of years earlier he remarked, "The equality meted out to colored persons in the hotels of New England, are unknown in Canada. Nowhere here, are our people treated with any kind of respect in the hotels; they are usually put off into inferior rooms by themselves, fed at separate tables from the whites, and not permitted to enter the common sitting rooms of the inn. Most of the towns have excluded the colored children from the common schools." One might conclude that most of the northern regions of the northern American continent displayed cultural and intellectual limitations as a result of prejudice. Notably, while white immigrants emit the disease of racism, with copious amounts of "bad beer and poor whisky," Brown notes, "I have not yet seen any colored inhabitants intoxicated."[133]

Brown's interest in founding temperance organizations and spaces for cultural exchange, and his focus on the land itself, was not quite consistent with upper-class or European elitist cosmopolitanism or its types of privileged societies. The "soil" was significant for Brown in imagining a more rooted version of civil society and a tradition of freedom for the African diaspora and descendants of American chattel slavery. While Brown often presents cosmopolitan situations and lived on the territorial and racial periphery in his own life, he did not see "passing" as "white" in a Eurocentric culture as consistent with his ongoing exploration of settlements for African colonization. Southern Ontario fell short as a location for developing Africanist civil societies that could integrate without whitening because of a series of limitations: a predominantly white population, a lack of long-term indigenous connections that would solidify cultural memory, and the segregation of black organizations. Canada remained an important location for black temperance organizations, specifically the Sons of Temperance, and other civil societies with which Brown was involved. In 1866, following the U.S. Civil War, the National Division of the Sons of Temperance, which included branches in Ontario, desegregated. Brown would soon become chief officer of the John Brown Division of the Sons of Temperance in Massachusetts.[134] Nevertheless, he committed himself more exclusively to the internationalism of the Good Templars in the 1870s.

The northern "American experience," whether in Canada or the United States, with its constant influx of immigrants, could not offer African-descended people the same connection to the soil or the stable ethnic communities they could find elsewhere. Cato's question "I wonder if dis is me?" likely plagued many immigrants, including lower-class European immigrants whose less secure identities often legitimated defensively racist anxieties and violence. Brown's and Delany's responses to Canada can lead to a critical understanding of the cosmopolitan ideals explored in their experience of movement and their attempts to found civil societies both locally and internationally.[135] Prior to the Civil War, Delany directed his sights toward West Africa. Brown looked to Haiti over against Canada as a possibility while placing his primary hopes in the acceptance of African Americans within the United States, where they had taken root over centuries of slavery—and which they ambiguously called "home."

CHAPTER 2

Brown's Temperate Cosmopolitan "Home"
Creole Civilization and Temperate Manners

General discussions of cosmopolitanism often consider the ability to forge alliances across ethnic, national, gendered, or cultural geographies. In Kant's speculative model of civility, those alliances depend on an empathetic ability to view the other as oneself. But a speculative, detached empathy does not clearly indicate what networks of civil society, ideals, and forms of behavior may encourage the practice of peace. William Wells Brown develops a continued investment in temperance and a rooted cosmopolitanism in his travel writings, his writings that concern Haiti, and his reflections on the American South after the Civil War in his final autobiography, *My Southern Home* (1880). In these works, Brown demonstrates a temperate aesthetics of "creolization" and explores, as well as performs, the imaginative possibility of founding a creole civilization to complement a temperate cosmopolitanism.

Ifeoma Kiddoe Nwankwo considers cosmopolitanism to be "the definition of oneself through the world beyond one's origins" intrinsic to "modernity" and the Enlightenment. She claims that imperialism and orientalism were "forms of European cosmopolitanism, and more specifically of the ways Europeans constructed their definitions of self and community in relation to and through their relationship to the broader world."[1] Using the example of the Haitian Revolution she explains how a network of black identifications was created at the same time as the white development of European modernity and cosmopolitanism. Through a literary analysis of the Cuban poets Placido and Juan Francisco Marzano, Martin Delany, Frederick Douglass, and the West Indian slave narrative author Mary Prince, Nwankwo persuasively argues that alliances of the African diaspora in the nineteenth century formed a cosmopolitanism "from below," which gained particular strength in light of the Haitian Revolution.

Addressing Nwankwo's near omission of William Wells Brown, Martha Schoolman argues that Brown's travel narrative of his time in Europe shows an "engagement with the imperial relations between Europe and the Caribbean and a growing effort to see Europe from a Caribbean point of view."[2] Brown considers these issues in his criticism of the lack of labor opportunities for fugitive slaves in Europe and his brief recommendation of emigration to the West Indies. Schoolman and Charles Baraw also oppose Elisa Tamarkin's representation of Brown as the elitist tourist or admirer of high culture by showing Brown's critical consciousness of "Europe's violent past."[3] In his discussion of John Ernest's phrase "fugitive tourist," Baraw notes Brown's attention to "signs of historical disturbance, whether in the ironic form of Milton's service as Cromwell's secretary or in the more sensational recollection of scenes of political violence."[4] Schoolman situates Brown's imaginations and peregrinations as a response to "modernity's epochal reply to Enlightenment universalism: the Haitian Revolution."[5] Although she mentions Haiti, Brown's interests in Haiti are of his imagination rather than real political or historical practice. Schoolman presents Brown's cosmopolitanism as divorced from pragmatic black abolitionism and linked too closely to European thought: "Brown's Haitian turn remains a European production, presented as if in near isolation from the broader intellectual ferment of black abolitionism. As such, it lacks explicit ties to a subaltern cosmopolitanism of the sort theorized by Mignolo and Nwankwo. Soon, it would become plausible to claim that Haiti was in effect Brown's own Tintern Abbey."[6] The comment seems reductive. Brown admired the "sacred spaces" and cultural tradition of British poets as well as the history of the land and its attendant civil orderings and drew on aspects of European cosmopolitan thought in his burgeoning admiration for Haiti. An international and cosmopolitan context necessarily affected meanings of civil and political space for African American abolitionists and emigrationists.

As such, Haiti became a sacred site for many African American abolitionists involved in a transnational dialogue with European reformers. Brown's cosmopolitanism, while tied to an imaginative analysis of Haiti, was never simply imaginary. His admiration of sacred space and his aesthetics of creolization allow him to depart from reductively equating cosmopolitanism with an individualistic, speculative perspective. Brown's lifelong involvement in temperance organizations inheres in *The Rising Son* and *My Southern Home*, and his consistent recommendations for reconstructed civil manners, restraint, and customs in communities recovering from chattel slavery directly opposes the equation of cosmopolitanism with a state of mind divorced from material processes. The creolization he recommends and performs in his aesthetic processes are in direct dialogue with the "broader . . . ferment of black abolitionism," including dialogue with European nations in an international and cosmopolitan context.

Schoolman's focus on a critical cosmopolitanism also draws on what Benedict Anderson calls its "privileged modes of impersonality, objectivity, and critical distance."[7] Yet, Brown's work presents theoretical counters to discourses of distance and "restraint" because his cosmopolitanism is fundamentally rooted in a temperance practice and a creolized disposition toward the founding of modern "civilization." For Schoolman, "Brown's approach, which he develops over the course of *Three Years in Europe*, is . . . to develop a critical-cosmopolitan alternative by inverting the preferred temporalities of elite cosmopolitanism in order to discover political possibility in Europe's violent past rather than its reformist present."[8] However, rather than considering the "violent past" and "reformist present" as separate, Brown depicts both the present and past as violent yet intertwined; a space apart and a temporality in between or alongside European temporalities repeatedly appears. His musings on the land and tradition in Europe show indigenous cultures and structures of civil society opening themselves to cosmopolitan possibilities.

Temperance aesthetics are modified in Brown's works, given his tendency to creolize. Temperance emerges from the Latin root *tempus*, meaning temporality. In the classical period temperance also meant the "mean" or midpoint between extremes, and during the neoclassical period such a mean was employed as part of an aesthetic.[9] Alexander Pope's neoclassical poetics entail balance and harmony, universal ethics, and aphorisms, which Brown notes in *Three Years in Europe* and expands on in *The American Fugitive in Europe* (1854).[10] Though Brown was not, like Pope, enamored with heroic couplets or neoclassical aesthetics in their traditional form, he admired Pope as an "independent writer," a "translator of Homer," and a poet who "suppress[ed] vice."[11] Whereas the midpoint for Pope might have been between the ancients of Western culture and the modern, Brown's cultural positioning placed the midpoint between past and present within a simultaneous history of diverse voices, often derived from African civilizations and folk cultures, which he juxtaposes with the modern European age. In *Three Years in Europe* he praises writers from Shakespeare to Pope and the British romantics to Robert Burns, though he also mentions African American poets such as James Whitfield of Buffalo. Burns, unlike Pope, is criticized for his inebriety. If we view Brown's discussions of European culture as too concerned with the fact that it is European, we miss his attention to temperance and structure, which he also applies to other cultures and situations.

While Brown's literature was not outwardly "religious," much temperance reform was rooted in Methodism and the Methodist *Book of Discipline* (1784). In its earliest forms, John Wesley recommended temperance; later reformers created a discipline of temperance.[12] Travel literature was another way of promoting temperance. Although Charles Fowler's works were published in the 1870s (and therefore later than Brown's travel narrative in Europe), Fowler notes that "standard" travel literature, advice manuals, biographies, and "a little standard fiction" were suitable.[13] Debates over what qualified as edifying literature were common from the beginning of temperance reform; though theater "staging" and "luxuriating scenery" were suspect, some temperance reformers considered it acceptable to read a play publicly, as Brown did with his one-man play *The Escape*.[14] Along with temperance and cosmopolitanism, other restraining discourses, as well as his shifting and seemingly ubiquitous personal narrative voice, may have influenced Brown's choice of genre. His narrative voice is usually inaccessible, hidden, and restrained. Considering some of the contexts and practices of temperance reform as consistent with a critical cosmopolitan discourse allows for a fuller understanding of the ways in which those who were enslaved reconceived of alliances both within the black diaspora and also across cultures and races. Travel literature served as one of the main genres for Brown to reflect on the possibilities of a temperate civilization, a theme that also permeated the creolized genres of his other works.

COSMOPOLITAN CIVILIZATION: THE PROMISE OF HAITI AS A TEMPERATE CRÉOLITÉ

After a discussion of temperance and *Clotel*, Robert Levine concludes, "Temperance would remain central to Brown's antebellum and postbellum writings, both as a metaphor for unrestrained patriarchal power and as a program for black elevation."[15] In addition, Brown's *My Southern Home* "extends temperance beyond the literal act of drinking to encompass various aspects of corporeal self-control [to show that] 'all intoxicants' are desires for vengeance, inordinate wealth, power, and sexual gratification."[16] Brown's involvement with temperance as a bodily discourse of emotional and affect control characterizes a desire to found a "civilization" situated between the "new" democracy and "past" aristocracy, both forms that support slavery. He interrogates the ambiguities in empire and modern nation-states, exploring a revolutionary and cosmopolitan civil space that prefigures current positive imaginings of a hemispheric transnationalism at home and expressing novel forms of "civilized" manners, speech, and cultural exchange abroad in Europe.[17] This is not meant to imply that empires are aristocratic and nation-states democratic. Indeed, the ambiguities Brown faces in promoting temperance internationally result from the need to found transnational structures of freedom for enslaved Africans in the United States. He could not support American exceptionalism, nor could he uncritically endorse the detached universalism or cosmopolitanism of empire. Brown's use of temperance as a corporeal regimen complemented his experience of a creole identity involved in continuous passages inherent in the diasporic situation of emerging from New World chattel slavery.

Brown's notion of a democratic civilization differed from that expressed at the founding of the United States and from that supported in mythic accounts of New England origins transposing into an ideology of free labor—though it can at times appear that he offers a "mythic account of [national] origins" in *Clotel*.[18] American "democratic" foundations supported individualistic orientations and an abstract "law of nature" that implied various racial hierarchies. Brown promoted democratic values throughout his abolitionist career, but his eliding of the foundation of "home" through movement, escape, travel, and pilgrimage clarifies a meaning of civilization, custom, manners, and restraint contrary to American values of individual self-control and work ethic that encouraged viewing the land as a commodity subject to the resources of the human will. Even though popular American temperance reformers emphasized bodily reform of diet, alcohol, and the dynamics of domestic relationships, they rarely extended their ideas about temperance to the land as a material and "cultured" sacred space not simply created for consumption.[19]

Indeed, while it could be argued that many abolitionists and temperance reformers promoted social elevation and somewhat simplistic laissez-faire freedom associated with the Protestant work ethic, to do so overlooks more nuanced uses of temperance to enact communal meanings of sobriety, civil exchanges, freedom, and spatiality. Space is thus not only the constructed civil space for associations but also a larger receptacle for transcultural exchange to establish communal identity and value. For Brown, in his travels and final return "home," the land itself becomes a resource and limit to the self—a restraint—that allows him to garner meanings of culture and exchange as he instills the customs of a well-tempered public character.

The descriptions of the countryside and land in *Three Years of Europe* have drawn some attention, mainly for their unreliability. As Baraw and Schoolman indicate, Brown juxtaposes progress with violence and criticizes class disparities. Many moments in the text, if isolated, indicate an uncritical relationship to the pastoral surroundings, the periphery, and the metropolitan center. However, such moments are quickly problematized by the surrounding context. As Brown comments, in leaving Boulogne en route to Paris for the 1849 International Peace Congress, for which he was a representative, "It was a beautiful country through which we passed from Boulogne to Amiens. Straggling cottages which bespeak neatness and comfort abound on every side. The eye wanders over the diversified views with unabated pleasure, and rests in calm repose upon its superlative beauty. Indeed, the eye cannot but be gratified at viewing the entire country from the coast to the metropolis. Sparkling hamlets spring up as the steam horse speeds his way, at almost every point—showing the progress of civilization, and the refinement of the nineteenth century."[20] Here, Brown seems to romanticize the peasant classes, as he does elsewhere: they show a charming "neatness and comfort." He emphasizes a spectatorial detachment with the "eye wander[ing]" in "unabated pleasure" and "repose," though one might pause on the phrase "diversified views." The periphery of the countryside seems, in general, to reflect the power of the "metropolis" and the "progress of civilization." Nevertheless, the next paragraph indicates Brown's awareness of the violence of previous revolutions inherent in the metropolitan center: "Where, a few months before was to be seen the flash from the cannon and the musket, and the hearing of the cries and groans behind the barricades, was now the stillness of death—nothing save here and there a gens d'arme was to be seen going his rounds in silence."[21]

Brown critically reflects on the emerging "civilizations" in Europe, which fascinate him, one assumes, because the focus on civilization, the beauty, and the geographic relationship of the countryside to the center reflect the ordering of imperial and world history. The word "civilization" does not grow out of American democracy and its revolutionary founding, but rather emerges from modern European imperialism and its structures of civil society. The word is particularly Eurocentric and was not in frequent use until the eighteenth century, first in France and then in England. The historian of religions Charles H. Long observes that "the meaning of this term cannot be understood apart from the geographies and cultures of the New World that are both 'other' and empirical."[22]

European modern "civilization" also goes hand in hand with theories of cosmopolitanism between nation-states. And for Brown, the achievement of "civilization" depends on recognizing the "genius" and contribution to world history of those who were enslaved or colonized. This is not simply integrationist and does not mimic Eurocentric values because, of course, such values would be altered when viewed from diverse peripheral perspectives. However, it would be misleading to present a cosmopolitanism "from below" that did not deeply acknowledge the dialogical tension and centrifugal interaction with the centers of Europe, the Americas, and the "world." At the end of *Three Years in Europe*, Brown comments that the education at Cambridge of the "sons of Africa," including Alexander Crummell, "has made such rapid strides towards civilization." This tribute to civilization leads him to recall, in an oft-cited passage also repeated in *The Black Man*, "a Toussaint, once laboured in the Sugar field with his spelling-book in his pocket, amid the combined efforts of a nation to keep him in ignorance. His name is now recorded among the list of statesmen of the past. A Soulouque was once a slave, and knew not how to read. He now sits upon the throne of an Empire."[23] While it is tempting to isolate the passage with reflection on the "sons of Africa," Brown immediately notes that even the lower ranks of society like "Franklin" were, with the promise of democratic civilization, able to become "American statesmen."[24] In other words, Brown indicates that both whites and blacks have a shared history of enslavement—a strategy of historiography that he repeats and develops in *The Black Man*, *The Negro*, and *The Rising Son*.

Marnie Hughes-Warrington argues that Brown attended to the shared heritage of blacks and whites in slavery: "Brown's remedy for such invisibleness was to argue that white and black alike shared a heritage in slavery, and out of a comparison of their activities in bondage, to suggest that blacks had the potential to create an empire of the mind far more powerful than the political empire of the United Kingdom or the economic empire of the United States. His work is thus neither a straightforward affirmation of Enlightenment narratives nor a 'counter' work, such as is favored by theorists of 'radical black subjectivity' such as Henry Louis Gates or bell books."[25] While Hughes-Warrington does not use the word "cosmopolitan," Brown's in-between position and desire to speak of the development of a diversified "civilization" is rooted in a creolized and temperate cosmopolitanism. The metaphorical "empire of the mind," however, is also complemented by Brown's activist work creating the foundational organs of democratic society and cross-fertilizing broad alliances across national, racial, and cultural boundaries.

While he was himself an empirical other—recognized negatively as an enslaved person—Brown consistently wrote of such figures as the "tragic mulatta" and the predicament of one-drop racism in the United States, with positive views of the eventual "amalgamation" of the "races."[26] In *My Southern*

Home amalgamation becomes a fluid cosmopolitan exchange rather than a whitening process. Discussions of Brown's work commonly allude to the self-consciously constructed aspects of his identity, such as his lack of a fixed identity; his biracial, nearly outwardly "white" appearance that made it possible to almost "pass"; and the multiple roles he played in his life and writing.[27] These roles begin with his name. As a child on the plantation, his name was changed from William to Sanford because another white child was named William.[28] He was eventually renamed William Wells Brown, a name "bestowed upon" him by the Quaker, Wells Brown, who helped him escape.[29] From that fluid and uncertain position, he assumed various vocational and activist roles: steamboat operator, barber, banker, husband and father, gentleman among the ladies, radical abolitionist and republican revolutionary, anglophile, temperance activist, consummate man of letters, historian, playwright, novelist, and, in the 1870s, medical doctor of uncertain qualifications.

This intermixture of roles and identities also disrupted the familiar binary of "primitive/civilized." Brown conceived of the inherently Eurocentric concept of civilization in creolized ways—living an intermixture that opposed a neat opposition of terms. Indeed, what some have understood as Brown's liminal, "trickster" identity could be viewed as a restrained cosmopolitan orientation characterizing the structure out of which Brown saw a modern civilization emerging.[30] This notion of civilization came to fruition not only through Brown's European travels (1849–54) but also through his reflections on African civilizations. These civilizations are signified in the creolized possibility of Haiti for African descendants, through Egypt and intermixtures with Islam, and in Brown's later pilgrimage for "home." In Brown's travels, temperance remained the locus for a new, creolized civilization, expressing a sociogenetic and psychogenetic restraint forged in light of transatlantic slavery and an imagined revolutionary founding, as well as countering the excesses inherent in modern "civilized" exchanges.

The creolized civilizational mode can be seen as an expression of the "passivity of power," a strategy in which the lack of dominating power is turned to creative ends. The most obvious example appears as diversion rather than direct or impassioned polemics. According to Edouard Glissant, "Diversion is the ultimate resort of a population whose domination by an Other is concealed: it then must search elsewhere for the principle of domination, which is not evident in the country itself: because the system of domination (which is not only exploitation, which is not only misery, which is not only underdevelopment, but actually the complete eradication of an economic entity) is not directly tangible. Diversion is the parallactic displacement of this strategy."[31] Such might be Brown's in-between position, the position of one who agrees in principle with many principles of democracy and civilization but who has been raised with a rhetoric of "concealment," so familiar in the founding of a republic that retains chattel slavery. Diversion resembles what John Ernest has clarified as Brown's use of the "incidental" and anecdotal. In *The American Fugitive in Europe*, for example, Brown tells, and retells, a seemingly inconsequential anecdote about the British landlady who left him wet sheets that he threw out the window. Ernest notes that some incidents—Brown outwitting members of the Klan who are planning to lynch him, for instance—are not light asides. In the Klan incident, "Dr. Brown had with him a syringe and a supply of 'a solution of the acetate of morphia,' which he injected into the ailing man while pretending to perform a kind of conjuring ritual."[32] This "incident" occurs in the introduction to Brown's *The Rising Son; or, The Antecedents of the Advancement of the Colored Race* (1874), presumably written by Alonzo D. Moore, but then, ironically, the book leaves conjuring and wit and seriously outlines the history of African civilizations and heroes. The use of diversion is more like pastiche than irony, without an intervening narrative point of view or judgment. The narrative distance leads John Ernest to ask, "Where in the world is William Wells Brown?"[33]

Brown's narrative strategies may sometimes appear close to what Baucom, following Glissant, calls "errancy," or an "interested cosmopolitanism" that refuses detachment and transcendence, refuses sympathy or the indulgence of transcendent sublimity.[34] The readers may be frustrated by Brown's texts, wondering what his position is. This diversionary narrative position is consistent with a modified creolization, though dialogue is not always offered in creole language or the "dialects" of those enslaved. At the same time, however, we do find many examples of directly creolized dialogue in Brown's fictional works, such as *Clotel* and *The Escape*, and even in his nonfiction, such as *My Southern Home*.

Although Brown refuses sympathy and does not come to a point of narrative judgment, he does display a subjectivity of restraint. This restraint may bear similarities to the Kantian cosmopolitan subject of rationality, but in Brown's case the temperance and restraint leads not to transcendence but to parallel points of view. Brown's somewhat disruptive topic shifts are similar to what Glissant describes as a parallelism: "Ask a Martinican peasant or native, I suppose, the way: the directions he will provide have nothing to do with the precise and objective nature of the location that is at stake. He will play with it. You will also find that he will not attempt to impose on you any set notion of time. He will offer a version parallel to your own." This strategy makes room for multiple histories and temporalities, as Glissant notes, "The struggle against a single History for the cross-fertilization of histories means repossessing both a true sense of one's time and identity: proposing in an unprecedented way a revaluation of power."[35] Such repossession speaks to Brown's quest for a temperate culture for formerly enslaved people that allows for simultaneous histories from a restrained and balanced point of view.

While practicing wit and irony, diversion, camouflage and subterfuge, Brown also demonstrates restrained and "civilized" manners at both "psychogenetic" and "sociogenetic" levels. These are Norbert Elias's terms from his study *The Civilizing Process*, in which he outlines the development of modern civilization from the medieval period forward in the "West." To be sure, as Long argues, the concept of civilization not only was an "internal development in Western Europe" but was also intimately tied to the "discovery of the New World" and "primitive" others against whom Western society could pose its superiority.[36] What Elias discusses as psychogenetic aspects of affect control and restraint correspond to sociogenetic manners, customs, traditions, and, ultimately, economic value in modes of exchange. White American temperance societies commonly emphasized reforming the inner and psychogenetic aspects through greater stress on controlling the will rather than understanding "affect control." For Brown, temperance was tied to intermingling and polyvalent conceptions of civilization, the folk, culture, and value, understood in terms of exchange and consumption. Modern civilization, as Elias points out, "plays down the national differences between peoples; it emphasizes what is common to all human beings or—in the view of its bearers—should be."[37] Brown desired to found a local yet transnational identity that would acknowledge the former slaves' relationship to the land while establishing a broader sense of modern civilization.

Clearly, Brown hoped for the development of a black republic and "national character" that could be further creolized in broader association with European nations. Arriving in a "free land," like Canada or European soil, was not enough to nourish or sustain a sense of community or identity. A restrained relation to the land was needed to manifest an in-between point of historical memory. The diasporic imagination proposed many options for constructing a temperate and cosmopolitan republic, among them Haiti and the West Indies. Brown was open to Louisiana, particularly New Orleans, because of its link to South American, Central America, and Haiti. Following the Haitian Revolution, Haiti became an imaginative (and real) space for a diasporic black consciousness, one Brown memorialized in his 1863 history *The Black Man, His Antecedents, His Genius, and His Achievements*.³⁸ As Elizabeth Ruth Bethel comments, "Hayti held a central position in that identity and historical consciousness at mid-century. Toussaint L'Ouverture and Crispus Attucks were claimed equally as Afro-American heroes; and the Haytian and American Revolutions were declared equally crucial political events in the shaping of Afro-American political and cultural identity." Haiti had become the first republic formed by those of African descent, and in *The Black Man*, Brown paid homage to figures such as Toussaint L'Ouverture, Jean-Jacques Dessalines, and Henri Christophe. Bethel continues, "The origins of those *lieux du mémoire* relocated [from Africa] in the milieu of the Haytian Revolution and the successive waves of Afro-American migration which began in the 1820s and continued into the 1860s."³⁹

Although Redpath's Haitian emigrationist bureau, for which Brown was an agent, did not succeed, "several hundred black Canadians settled in Haiti during the fall and winter of 1861–1862" to escape prejudice in Canada, though many would return because of the harsh conditions.⁴⁰ About three thousand African Americans immigrated to Haiti following President Geffrard's 1859 incentive plan for African descendants in the United States and Canada, and bishop James Theodore Holly, also part of the emigrationist bureau, would immigrate with his family to Haiti permanently.⁴¹ The emigrationist scheme that seemed promising following the Fugitive Slave Law in 1851 and the Dred Scott decision in 1857 faced challenges once the Civil War began, including difficulty in securing steamers for transportation.⁴² With the impending American Civil War, Douglass and other abolitionists now opposed the idea of leaving the United States. Freedom seemed like a possibility in the United States, which, for all its history of blood and terror, had been their "homeland" for the past couple hundred years. According to Brown in *The Rising Son*, the political and economic situation in Haiti was not as encouraging as emigrationists initially hoped. President Geffrard faced widespread opposition, both to the Haitian emigrationist schemes and his other policies, and had to flee the country in 1867 for Jamaica. As Brown notes, for black Americans and Canadians it would have been "better for them and Hayti had they remained at home." In his words, "The liberal offer of the Haytian president to Americans and other blacks to come to the Island, and his general progressive efforts to elevate his people, were not appreciated by the Haytians, and the spirit of revolution which had so long governed the Island, soon began to manifest itself."⁴³ Although such circumstances diminished his enthusiasm for Haiti, there is little indication that Brown limited his options for building diasporic African communities to the island nation.

Brown repeatedly expressed concern about the lack of restraint shown by political leaders, even if he understood the historical pressures and the contexts of violence they faced. While he criticized statesmen in Europe, he also engaged critically with Haitian leaders in *The Rising Son*. As an escaped slave from Kentucky, Brown seems to draw on Southern imaginations of agrarian republicanism and tradition. In his reflections on African heroes of the Atlantic world, such as Toussaint L'Ouverture, and in his repeated focus on restraining passions, Brown may also have been responding to proslavery uses of Aristotelian legitimations of the "natural slavery" of "barbarians."

Of course, differences exist between ancient and modern forms of "slavery," but Brown knew that Southerners used classical examples of slavery to obfuscate the legal complexities of modern chattel slavery. For instance, the names of Brown's characters, such as Cato who renames himself "Alexander Washington Napoleon Pompey Caesar," are ironic gestures to those slaveholders who used to give their slaves Roman names, also ironically, much as they would to their pets.[44] Proslavery racialist thinking often considered Africans as "natural slaves," even though race was not the qualifying factor in ancient slavery. In theorizing the difference between natural slaves and civil slaves, Anthony Pagden notes, Aristotle had pointed to the dual aspects of the "intellect (*nous*) and the subordination of the passions (*orexis*), for the intellect is the logical and the passions are the alogical parts of man's bipartite soul (*psyche*)." According to ancient thought, and to many who continued to draw on Aristotle to justify enslavement, "The passions are, by definition, unable to govern themselves; but the intellect of the fully grown male will, unless of course his mind has been impaired, be able to master this part of the whole character and direct it toward the good. It is, indeed, man's ability to use reason in this way, together with his capacity for speech, which distinguishes him from all other animals." Pagden explains that though the "natural slave is clearly a man," his "intellect has, for some reason, failed to achieve proper mastery over his passion."[45] Differentiating further, Aristotle claimed that while the natural slave might exercise understanding, he was "incapable of practical wisdom," unable to make judgments.[46] Restraint of the passions and the proper, dignified, and balanced "capacity for speech" echo Brown's temperance concerns.

Examples of the restraint of passions abound throughout Brown's works. When Brown praises Toussaint L'Ouverture's character, he emphasizes, "Toussaint was entirely master of his own appetites and passions," a man of "great sobriety."⁴⁷ Levine points out that Brown's temperance orientation also leads him to propose less violent revolutionary activity: "Commenting on the French revolutions of the 1790s and 1840s in *The American Fugitive in Europe*, for example, Brown attacks Marat . . . and praises Lamartine as a more temperate leader who, 'by the power of his eloquence, succeeded in keeping the people quiet' and under control." Brown commends "Toussaint L'Ouverture and Madison Washington as models of self-restraint," praising Toussaint's "humanity."⁴⁸ On the one hand, these comments could support a reserved and mildly conservative view of political and social change, as well as the virtues of self-control and an ascetic work ethic. On the other hand, they appear to be part of Brown's argument about the use of restrained "humanity" to counter common stereotypes of Africans, as well as to support his temperance aesthetics that characterize the balanced statesman. We encounter Toussaint again in *The Rising Son*: "Toussaint himself lived with an austere sobriety, which bordered on abstemiousness. Clad in a common dress, with a red Madras handkerchief" around his head, proclaiming "liberty!" And Brown repeats, "Toussaint was entirely master of his own appetites and passions," with the "art of governing" indicated by his "polished eloquence."⁴⁹

Brown revised misplaced Southern discourses of ancient thought by arguing that culture, tradition, and cosmopolitan relations, along with temperance, will accomplish restraint. In doing so, he countered common white Northern notions of temperance that located restraint in individual willpower, situating restraint instead in tradition, manners, or custom. Excessive passions and intemperance were indicative of the slave trade, not of the development of African civilizations. Discussing slave traders in *The Rising Son*, Brown repeats Remond's equation of drink with the traffic: "Fired with ardent spirits and armed with old muskets, these people would travel from district to district, leaving behind them smoldering ruins, heart-stricken friends, and bearing with them victims whose market value was to influence the avaricious passions of the inhabitants of the new world."⁵⁰ The "passions" seem part of a generalized disorder connoting an inferior disposition. Brown's depiction of African cultures' general sobriety stands in contrast to the descriptions of those who are driven by passions.

Brown did not locate the restraint of passions in a Protestant asceticism, an American domestic space, or even a civic fraternity. On the contrary, temperance was a key virtue in the founding of ancient civilizations and the "amalgamation" and intermingling of Islam with the "pagan" religions of Africa. Perhaps surprisingly, Brown praises Islam for providing restraint to the passions. He writes in *The Rising Son*, "Mungo Park, in his travels seventy years ago, everywhere remarked the contrast between the pagan and Mohammedan tribes of interior Africa. One very important improvement noticed by him was abstinence from intoxicating drinks."[51] According to Brown, "Throughout Central Africa there has been established a vast total abstinence society; and such is the influence of this society that where there are Moslem inhabitants, even in pagan towns, it is a very rare thing to see a person intoxicated." Traders from Europe and America, however, bring "ardent spirits" to the "coast at Caboon."[52] Brown plays on a statement Mungo Park made in his *Travels in the Interior of Districts of Africa*: "'The beverage of the pagan Negroes,' he says, 'is beer and mead, of which they often drink to excess; the Mohammedan converts drink nothing but water.'"[53]

Perhaps extrapolating from Park's comments on Islam, Brown sees Islam as one step toward Christianity, and finally to "progress in civilization," the title of one of Brown's chapters. All the trappings of civilization seem present in Africa: the "Veys" have a "written language"; the "Abyssinians" "have fine schools and colleges" and "agriculture, that great civilizer of man, is carried on here to an extent unknown in other parts of the country." Liberia "will yet be developed" with "steamship" and "locomotive," and "the Corn Exchange, London and Wall Street, New York," will move it out of the "moral wilderness."[54] Nonetheless, even if the book at times reads like a celebration of freedom as American and European commerce, Brown's locus of "civilization" is in Ethiopia: "So it is that we trace the light of Ethiopian civilization first into Egypt, thence into Greece, and Rome, whence, gathering new splendor on its way, it hath been diffusing itself all the world over."[55] These African syncretic and creolized origins of temperance speak to Brown's continuous attempt to reform transatlantic history and culture through reinterpretations of ancient traditions and character.

Brown located restraint at the foundation of transculturation and custom and expressed direct concern for the restrained traditions of his "Southern home." Such eloquence and restraint was, much to Brown's chagrin, not always present in temperance reform movements or in the egotistical sublime of some British romantic authors who, though he may have admired them, were often intemperate.

TEMPERANCE UNIVERSALISM AND THE LAND: ARISTOCRATIC CREOLIZATIONS OF "DEMOCRATIC" CIVILIZATION

Unlike Frederick Douglass, who often highlights his "manhood" and self-control in autobiographical descriptions of his transition from slave to freeman, such as when he overpowers overseer Edward Covey, Brown does not fit neatly within the individualistic or representative man paradigms.[56] William L. Andrews notes that compared to Douglass's oratorical flourishes, "Brown's decidedly understated, restrained, almost deadpan manner of recounting his life seems artless."[57] Some of his work does, nonetheless, find its home among the domestic and sentimental literature of the time. To be sure, he also celebrated the possibility of "manhood" on British soil: "No sooner was I on British soil, than I was recognized as a man, and an equal. The very dogs in the streets appeared conscious of my manhood."[58] Yet this boasting, made somewhat tongue in cheek, is a consequence of the denial of manhood to African American men who were enslaved and could not adopt the patriarchal gender roles that shaped European American society.[59] As Andrews comments, "Brown seems to have almost deliberately refused to identify himself according to Douglass's myth of the heroic resister" and thus comes across as "nonheroic" or "antiheroic" in his *Narrative* and elsewhere.[60] Neither the ambiguous identity of the trickster nor the status of temperance reformer is as "lofty" as the folk "culture hero." To pay homage to the antiheroic in the midst of enumerating black heroes in *The Black Man*, Brown diverts to account for "A Man Without a Name."[61]

In the early 1850s, following the passage of the Fugitive Slave Law, Brown experiences situational irony as an escaped slave in Europe, a vantage point from which the United States appeared uncivilized and barbaric. His early celebrations of "civilization," or at least "civility," in Europe did not indicate a burgeoning Yankee pietism, though he champions the democratic virtues of his fellow abolitionists. Brown was a fugitive American tourist and cosmopolitan, and he looked to the promises of European civilization (including those articulated by earlier "Americans" and revolutionaries) for his sense of identity in Europe. In addition, he studies the modes of "civilized" behavior, the "mores" and customs, just as de Tocqueville and Gustave de Beaumont studied the American situation for the development of democratic culture and civil society. Similarly, Brown's final autobiographical work, *My Southern Home*, often feels like reading a sociological study: he discusses religion, conjuring, and dietary and shopping habits. Tocqueville, despite recent debates over his support of European imperialism, provides a productive link to Brown's thoughts on democracy and Southern "customs." In addition, Beaumont, Tocqueville's traveling companion, expresses similar hopes for a creolized amalgamation and attends to the effects of manners and customs of temperance, along with other dietary reforms, on interracial unions and cosmopolitan exchanges.

Beaumont's 1835 novel *Marie* was the first to imagine a positive sexual relation with "an American woman of Creole background."[62] Brown revised the negative connotations of the tragic mulatta and miscegenation as a result of rape and slavery, particularly in *Clotel*. He promoted an "aestheticized ideal" of cosmopolitan exchanges and "amalgamated" manners. Manners and the practice of restraint were the psychogenetic and sociogenetic foundations of such spaces. For some French writers, such as Brissot and Beaumont, "once miscegenation was purged of its association with colonial exploitation, it could become the most visible symbol of the new republic's enlightened, equitable trade policy toward the U.S.: a bilateral commerce, based on an aestheticized ideal of courtly manners, yielding to both parties an equal benefit and pleasure."[63] Moreover, as with Brown's interest in temperance, opposition to alcohol, and restraint in speech and civil manners, for Beaumont in *Marie*, "the table in turn becomes the abolitionist's political medium for imagining the civility and legitimacy of mixed-race sexual unions, and for initiating otherwise occluded gender relations and forbidden forms of intimacy into the discussion of national affairs."[64]

A creolized civility undergirds the construction of civil space in Brown's work; *Clotel* is a version of the tragic mulatta motif involving President Jefferson's imagined granddaughter tragically sold into slavery. In the first edition, freedom can only be imagined as a creolized union abroad in France because the United States could not make social, cultural, or political space for those with African blood. Notably, as he remarked to Frederick Douglass in an 1851 letter, Brown's daughters attended "one of the best Seminaries in France, instead of being in an American school, where the finger of scorn would be pointed at them, by those whose superiority rests entirely upon their having whiter skin."[65] His daughters were educated abroad and then taught white European children, an opportunity they would not have had in the United States or in Canada. In the 1860 revision of *Clotel*, Brown's two lovers are reunited just outside Geneva, while in the 1867 version "Clotelle" returns to the continent, becomes an "Angel of Mercy," and works to support black communities throughout the South.[66] She returns to New Orleans and eventually purchases "Poplar Farm," Brown's autobiographical "home" when he was a child enslaved near St. Louis. Poplar Farm also figures prominently as a reconceptualized home in *My Southern Home*. French civilization continued to fascinate Brown; both Brown and Frances Harper created an imaginative space in the transamerican hemispheric context of Haiti. And for both authors, the influence of slavery, the possibility of a black republic in Haiti, and *créolité* on the American land itself led them to pursue temperance reform work in the South during Reconstruction.

Although he lived in Boston, Brown was organizing for temperance and education in Kentucky in 1868 when briefly captured by the Ku Klux Klan—though he escaped by means of his wit and the drugs he gives them—and he continued temperance work for the Sons of Temperance and the Independent Order of Good Templars throughout Reconstruction and after.[67] According to Fahey, in the 1870s Brown "organized lodges in Virginia, West Virginia, and Tennessee" for the Good Templars.[68] Brown never made the "South" his "home" again—he lived in Boston in his later years, and his life was, as Schoolman points out, "proleptically cosmopolitan."[69] However, to a certain extent, he considered the "South" his birthplace and "home," and he continued to devote much of his reformist energy toward temperance and education there until his death. For several months in 1879 and 1880, following Reconstruction and before the publication of *My Southern Home*, Brown toured "the new South," "partly in the interest of temperance, partly to satisfy his curiosity."[70] In his final memoir Brown recommends immigration north for African Americans in the South, yet his recommendation was clearly a last resort.[71] Brown remarks, "If he cannot be protected in his rights" or if Jim Crow and white supremacy create "conditions whereby he could do little but starve," then "he should leave."[72]

Brown strongly criticized the racism he confronted in London, Ontario, and his continual critique of lower-class whites and white supremacy coincides with his allusions to the problematic development of democracy in the United States. Yet in *My Southern Home*, Brown indicates a deep connection to the soil of the Southern states—or to his Poplar Farm, at least—and the need for the formerly enslaved to build civil societies and gain economic self-sufficiency in the "homes" they had labored for and with which their lives were intertwined. In *Clotel* Brown surely sympathizes with Georgiana, a white female reformer in the South, who argues against sending her former slaves to Liberia in support of colonization: "Why should they go to Africa, any more than the Free States or to Canada. . . . Is not this their native land? What right have we, more than the negro, to the soil here, or to style ourselves native Americans? Indeed it is as much their home as ours, and I have sometimes thought it was more theirs. The negro has cleared up the lands, built towns, and enriched the soil with his blood and tears."[73] She continues to remark on their revolutionary heroes, such as Crispus Attucks, and their rightful claim to republican freedom. Brown echoes Georgiana almost thirty years later in *My Southern Home* when he writes, "By common rights, the South is the negro's home.

Born and 'raised' there, he cleared up the lands, built the cities, fed and clothed the whites, nursed their children, earned the money to educate their sons and daughters; by the negro's labor churches were built and clergymen paid." Thus, while Brown prefers emigration to starvation and death, he clearly desires that African Americans' relation to the place of their birth will be recognized as intrinsic to the development of their culture. By being rooted in a relation to the land, their "cultivated character," their stories of birth and survival, and their musical and artistic talent will flourish, he hopes.[74]

Brown begins investigating the habitus of cultures in Europe and continues this study in his final work. In *Three Years in Europe*, most of his comments on positive civil behavior and manners are reserved for Europeans: "There is a lack of good manners among Americans that is scarcely known or understood in Europe," "few nations are more courteous than the French," and so on.[75] Seemingly Eurocentric comments of this sort abound throughout the book, but the desire for civility, restraint, and temperance continue in his representations of a dignified black (creole) national civilization. In fact, Brown is critical of the prevalence of civility and custom in European society because it can lead to social pressure for intemperance. In *The American Fugitive in Europe*, Brown notes that he often felt "awkward" at the dinner table in Britain because "it takes more nerve than most men possess to cause one to decline taking a glass of wine with a lady." English "society" apparently believed wine necessary for good "health." Fortunately, a woman in the company devised a plan to fill one of the decanters with "raspberry vinegar," for which Brown was relieved from being an "object of pity": "No one of the party, except the lady knew of the fraud; and I was able, during the remainder of the time, to drink with any of the company."[76] This willing identity as a fraudulent wine drinker seems surprising for a prominent temperance reformer, from whom one might expect a lecture on abstinence, but it also shows the primary place of manners in Brown's vision of cultural exchange. Even in temperance reform, it seems, "restraint" must be present for civility to transpire. Brown also notes that gender intermingling has a positive effect on the conversation, for after dinner when the women and men separated, "topics of conversation were materially changed, but not for the better. The presence of women is always a restraint in the right direction."[77]

While reflecting on the nature of civilization and civility, Brown observes various problems with public speech evident in an inability to restrain the passions. In *Three Years in Europe* (1852) and its American version, *The American Fugitive in Europe* (1854), Brown regularly remarks on the lack of restraint in speech as a gauge for a troubled or untrustworthy character. At the Paris Peace

Congress, he observes about Henry Vincent, "His speech was one continuous flow of rapid, fervid eloquence, that seemed to fire every heart; and although I disliked his style, I was prepossessed in his favor."[78] He saves an expanded criticism of British Hartley Coleridge for the American edition of his travel narrative. Hartley "early became the slave of intemperate habits, from which no aspirations of his own heart, no struggle with the enslaving appetite, and no efforts of sympathizing and sorrowful friends, could ever deliver him."[79] Brown comments that, for so many of the figures of "brighter fame," such as "Burns, Byron, Campbell, and others . . . they looked 'upon the wine when it was red,' and gave life and fame, and their precious gifts, and God's blessing, for its false and ruinous joys."[80]

Brown suggests that signs of an intemperate disposition might also be present in excessive speech: "It is equally dangerous, we think, to be known as a good talker. The gift of rapid, brilliant, mirth-moving speech, is a perilous possession. The dullards, for whose amusement this gift is so often invoked, know well that to ply its possessor with wine is the readiest way to bring out its power. But in the end the wine destroys the intellect, and the man of wit degenerates into a buffoon, and dies a drunkard."[81] Indeed, temperance evinced an open, refined, and cosmopolitan character that stood in contrast to the sentimentalized, affected performances of reformers who appeared to Brown as mere confidence men.

Though Brown expressed disdain for lowbrow Americans' lack of restraint, he could not easily be classified as highbrow or elitist. His most forceful criticism of unrestrained speech and confidence-man techniques was reserved for American temperance reformer John B. Gough, the most famous Washingtonian. Brown's criticism appears in the British rather than the American edition, which suggests he may not have wanted to make this criticism as directly to an American audience. Brown writes, "This gentleman was at one time an actor on the stage, and subsequently became an inebriate of the most degraded kind." Calling him an "orator" with "dramatic powers of address," Brown then undercuts his faint praise: "While speaking, he acts the drunkard, and does it in a style which could not be equalled on the boards of the Lyceum or Adelphi." Acknowledging that Gough has surpassed all in attracting members to the "temperance pledge," Brown comments that Gough regularly breaks his pledge. He then questions the people who follow Gough, remarking that Gough has "water upon the brain" and "that Mr. Gough's cranium contained a greater quantity than that of any other living man." Gough's unrestrained passion in speech, "weep[ing] when he pleases," fails to impress

Brown, who declares that "no one can sit for an hour and hear John. B. Gough, without coming to the conclusion that he is nothing more than a theatrical mountebank."[82]

Brown criticizes Gough's exploitation of emotion and sympathy to move an audience to tears with him and thereby convert them to the pledge. This specific use of "sympathy," as Glenn Hendler shows, was essential to the Washingtonian effort to convert "crowds of ethnic and working-class drinkers into the movement, thereby alienating many of the ministers and middle-class men who made up the core of earlier temperance drives."[83] The Washingtonians, however, "constructed whiteness and masculinity as part of a structure of feeling constitutive both of the public sphere in which they took place and of the embodied subjects who populated that sphere."[84] They formed an affective and nationalist public that challenged the presumed feminine structure of sentimentality in the nineteenth century but nevertheless centered on restoring the white American middle-class family and self. Hendler also argues that the "structure of feeling" was in slight tension with, and formed a "counterpublic" to, the dominant bourgeois public and its rational-critical debate.

However, the exploitation of sympathy and the passions is something to which Brown seems adverse. The sublime for Kant entailed a "disinterested sympathy," while for other romantics it has been called an "egotistical sublime" because of their visionary and personal identification with suffering. Though I do not think Brown "blames the victims" (or the poor), he is restrained in his depictions of suffering and veers away from direct expressions of sympathy or personal emotion. For instance, even though *Clotel* is arguably a sentimental novel, its repeated use of "pastiche," such as the interpolation of Lydia Marie Child's story of the "tragic mulatta," distance the audience from the emotional center of the narrator. Likewise, *Clotel* comprises documents, newspaper sources, previous stories Brown has written or delivered in speeches, sermons, and slave songs. Because of Brown's penchant for cultural borrowing, self-borrowing, and self-distancing—his personal slave narratives are rewritten in the third person, for instance—John Ernest considers Brown's role to be that of "cultural editor."[85] *My Southern Home* demonstrates the way that Brown borrowed from his own work, duplicating, "often verbatim, . . . what he had said in the several editions of his *Narrative*, the four versions of *Clotel*, *The Escape*, his *Memoir of William Wells Brown*, and also *The Negro in the American Rebellion*."[86] In distancing himself from romanticism, which emphasized the original work of one's authorial genius, Brown's temperance aesthetics are again creolized through "errancy," or the "fanciful."[87] Baucom writes that Glissant's tendency to invert a scene of tragedy to one of hope where time is not transcended but "accumulates" is also characterized by an aversion to sympathy: "profound antipathy to romantic liberalism's worldly attitude of sympathetic guilt."[88]

Brown criticized the excessive publicity, egotism, backsliding, and affective theatricality and speech evinced by Gough, and in 1866 he would become involved with the more secretive Sons of Temperance when they began to, halfheartedly, admit African Americans. In 1875 he left for the Good Templars. Though secretive and thus somewhat safe from public exposure of their alcoholism, the Sons did not admit blacks to their fraternal society during the years of slavery and their later attempts to integrate were minimal.[89] Most African Americans—including Brown—were well aware of the racism in white American temperance associations because of the violent attacks that many black societies experienced after the 1840s.[90] Indeed, in a letter to Frederick Douglass recounted in *Three Years in Europe*, Brown comments on the warm reception he and William and Ellen Craft had received at a soiree with the Edinburgh Temperance Society: "This should cause the pro-slavery whites, and especially negro-hating Sons of Temperance, who refuse the coloured man a place in their midst, to feel ashamed of their unchristian conduct."[91]

Brown's early criticism, and later disillusionment, of the uncouth and racist Sons of Temperance indicates a "universalism" that should be distinguished from the American emphasis on reforming the self through restraint or purging emotions through acts of individual willpower or sympathetic suffering. Fahey notes that an "evolving universalist ideology" was the main characteristic separating the Independent Order of Good Templars (IOGT) from their contemporaries.[92] The IOGT was formed in response to dissatisfaction with other movements, and they opened their organization to women, though they shared much of the masculinist ideology and rhetoric associated with drink and reform.[93] From this perspective, men were the drinkers who needed to regain self-control, or manhood, to function in the circle of domesticity. Brown, however, did not always share the same masculinist paradigm. Nonetheless, the Templars' universalism led them to spread their moral reform in Canada, the West Indies, and the British Isles, including Scotland and Ireland. Brown would travel again to Great Britain in July 1877 as a delegate for the Good Templars to attend a convention in Glasgow.[94] Both before and after the Civil War, Brown experienced more equality and inclusion in Britain than he did with whites in the United States. While in Edinburgh in 1851 he was critical of the "negro-hating Sons of Temperance," and in the 1870s he was again in a similar position with the IOGT because the racial equality consistent with the universalism and internationalism at the foundation of the order still "had to be advocated by foreigners."[95]

In 1851, Brown's recounting of the soiree for the Edinburgh Total Abstinence Society focuses on a speech from the organization's president published in the *Christian News*.[96] The president wasted no time in criticizing the "Yankees" and "the immaculate laws of immaculate Yankeedom," but the speech opposed slavery under the aegis of temperance. While honing in on the "aristocratic platform" of "educated Edinburgh" and "educated Scotland," the president exclaimed, "Down with the aristocracy of the skin!" Notably, the dignified and honorable "aristocratic Platform" was associated with temperance reform "in the name of universal Scotland."[97] Although earlier temperance societies like the Washingtonians seemed to model their structure on the founding acts constituting the republic and in the name of revolutionary heroes, such linkages between an authentic local civil character and a national identity as put forth "in the name of universal Scotland" would hardly come to mind. Brown seems to have found the broadly conceived "universalism" of the IOGT more promising but still problematic, based as it might have been on the more abstract understandings of Protestant moralism derived from the Enlightenment. Generally, however, reformers in the United States did not appeal to a local identity or to the land, in part because too many local American situations involved slavery or the conquest of aboriginal populations. The concreteness of "universal Scotland," the tradition bestowed by the monarchy, or the land became, in the U.S. context, the more abstract and individualist rhetoric of "life, liberty, and the pursuit of happiness." Brown's search in his travels for a temperate cosmopolitan space directly addresses this problematic hiatus in the constitution of American civic societies and national identity that would prevent its achievement.

My Southern Home was written at a bleak time in American history, following the "failure" of Reconstruction and the rise of Jim Crow, black codes, and the reign of terror in the South. Even in this context, Brown, sometime proponent of American democracy and equality, reveals the value of "aristocratic" dignity. Toward the end of the text, he writes that social equality in Southern Reconstruction could not be achieved for a number of reasons—particularly because, in his words, the South had nurtured "a shoddy aristocracy, or an uneducated class, more afraid of the negro's ability and industry than of his color rubbing off against them." In contrast, "the true nobleman fears not that his reputation will be compromised by any association he may choose to form."[98] This passage is ambiguous, but it is clear that Brown appeals to a higher form of aristocratic culture rather than to overly simplistic meanings of racial uplift and civil society. In *Three Years in Europe*, written thirty years earlier, Brown had also shown his appreciation of the monarchy, the land, the traditions, and the cultures that stemmed from nobility. Nevertheless, perhaps ironically, he felt somewhat too restrained in the European context. During the Peace Congress of 1849, which he attended in Paris as a delegate, he noted that speeches on certain topics were shut down by the congress organizers, and he exclaimed, "Oh! How I wished for a Massachusetts atmosphere, a New England Convention platform, with Wendell Phillips as the speaker, before that assembled multitude from all parts of the world."[99] Whereas Tamarkin draws attention to the regard Brown and other black abolitionists had for "English English" models of culture, civilization, and, often, the aristocracy, I think Brown's attachment to European models demonstrates an effort to reform a temperate cosmopolitanism that promotes social democracy but maintains ties to tradition and the local experience of the land.[100] Clearly, by 1880 Brown's ambiguity toward European democratic values and aristocratic civilization and culture had not resolved itself, but the place of custom, cultivation, and culture overrode any direct appeal to individual will or passion.

Other African Americans in Brown's late temperance cohort seemed to share the ambiguity toward Protestant-derived democracy, even if the origins of American temperance seemed more prominently connected to the Protestant goals of American gender roles, middle-class self-reliance, family, and work ethic. For example, S. C. Goosley was sent by the AME Church to South Carolina but "was unable to get the white Templars there to allow blacks to join the IOGT." Goosley had commented, probably in 1876, "These sanctified whites . . . would refuse to enter heaven if they thought a 'nigger' could get there."[101] Notably, Brown echoes these sentiments in 1880. Indeed, Brown turns to Catholicism in *My Southern Home* to praise a Bishop Kean who had been preaching at a cathedral in Richmond. The bishop wins Brown's approval for addressing the people as "my dearly beloved" while the Protestant minister at an African Baptist Church, though "noted for his eloquence . . . could not rise higher in his appeals to the blacks than to say 'men and women' to them."[102] Brown asked an "intelligent colored man" what he thought of the minister's words, and the man replied, "Before he can make an impression on us, he must go to the Catholic Church and learn the spirit of brotherly love." Brown commends the bishop's appeal to the passage "God is no respecter of persons" and concludes: "The blacks have been so badly treated in the past that kind words and social recognition will do much to win them in the future, for success will not depend so much upon their matter as upon their manner; not so much upon their faith as upon the more potent direct influence of their practice. In this the Catholics of the South have the inside track, for the prejudice of the Protestants seems in a fair way to let the negro go anywhere except to heaven if they have to go the same way."[103] The emphasis on the "manner" rather than the "matter" recurs two pages later in *My Southern Home* when Brown comments on a female vendor in Norfolk, Virginia, who is singing to help sell her strawberries. She is apparently successful with her strategy and her song:

> *I live for miles out of town,*
> *I am gwine to glory.*
> *My strawberries are sweet an' soun',*
> *I am gwine to glory.*
> *My chile is sick, an' hushan' dead,*
> *I am gwine to glory.*
> *Now's de time to get 'em cheap,*
> *I am gwine to glory.*

But preceding the excerpt of the song, Brown contends that "the interest" in the song "centered more upon the manner than the matter."[104] Following the song, he wryly comments, "Upon the whole, the colored man of Virginia is a very favorable physical specimen of his race; and he has peculiarly fine, urbane manners."[105] Brown suggests that private beliefs or pragmatic goals are less important than the overall form or manner of civilization—the style, ceremonies, and symbols that will shape new forms of intermingled, miscegenated, and amalgamated communities, conferred by law and land.

The crux of the matter was also that American individualism and its form of democracy were not inherently opposed to slavery, nor were aristocracies inherently supportive of slavery. The more Brown reflected on the nature of democratic "civilization" in the United States, the more he saw the need to salvage a relationship to the land that echoed the ambiguously aristocratic sensibilities of thinkers like Tocqueville. As Margaret Kohn shows in her discussion of Tocqueville and Beaumont on race and slavery, Tocqueville also saw Protestantism as central to democracy, and he also implied that the tradition of liberal individualism was not inherently antislavery. She offers a quote from Tocqueville's notes for *Democracy in America*, in which he comments, "In general negroes are received in the Catholic churches. Catholicism is, in general, the religion that unlike Protestantism never [illegible] inequality. Protestantism established in the religious order the government of the middle classes and one knows the haughtiness of the middle classes towards the people." Moreover, political leaders in a democracy depend on popular success: "As long as the American democracy remains at the head of affairs, no one will undertake so difficult a task [as emancipation of slaves]."[106] This certainly seemed to be Brown's conclusion when faced with the failed attempts by Protestant sects to achieve social equality for former slaves during Reconstruction. Protestants and politicians, among all the rest, seemed more concerned with the "matter" than their manners.

Brown's focus on "restraint" or "manners" and his constructions of civilization and civility often depart from Enlightenment abstractions about European civilization and its disinterested goals while sharing their desire for custom and tradition. The issue of custom helps us understand Brown's reserved mannerism and championing of restraint. According to Anthony Pagden, Montesquieu "had remarked . . . [that] most of Europe (he was a little uncertain about Spain) is ruled by 'custom' (*les moeurs*); Asia, and the still darker regions of Africa and America, by despots. The rule of law, restraint through custom rather than will, was responsible for the fashioning of societies that provided a space for individual human action, while at the same time ensuring that such action was rarely capable of reducing society to a state of simple anarchy."[107] This ideal image of Europe was problematically positioned against despotism, including that in parts of Africa, and the United States would position itself against Britain in a similar appeal to the rule of law. Yet, the lack of societies or "custom" to restrain and the lack of spaces for human action meant that the rule of law became more centered on the individual will in the United States than it did in Europe.

To be sure, Brown promotes an enlarged, "amalgamated," and critical cosmopolitan consciousness. In *My Southern Home*, he writes, "The colored people of the South should at once form associations, combine and make them strong, and live up to them by all hazards. All civilized races have risen by means of combination and co-operation."[108] At the same time, Brown is consistent about the need for local and rural communities in which the cultivation of the land will be supported and nurtured by the cultivation of the arts and the development of indigenous customs, an argument resonating more with Southern agrarians than with Northerners.

This longing was also evident in *Three Years in Europe*. After visiting Tocqueville's for a soiree as a delegate to the International Peace Congress, he recommended founding reformed civil societies that would refract the past and give birth to a new sense of temporal and democratic freedom in the United States, echoing Tocqueville's criticism that "the American" was rootless, without monuments or ancestors. For entirely different but related reasons, the American slave for Brown was also a stranger in a strange land—not included in the ceremonies to consecrate the land, to confer new identities, or to share sacred stories, contrary to the British peasant. In Europe, Brown draws attention to this homogeneity and inertia among the enslaved: "The past is to him as yesterday, and the future scarcely more than to-morrow. Ancestral monuments, he has none; written documents fraught with cogitations of other times, he has none; and any instrumentality calculated to awaken and expound the intellectual activity and comprehension of a present or approaching generation, he has none. His condition is that of the leopard of his own native Africa."[109]

While Brown everywhere speaks of "civilization," this civilization evokes a sacred relation to the land and encourages communitas, a term Victor Turner uses to describe the openness and intermingling of a variety of cultures and traditions. Both Tocqueville and Brown seem to require this sacred sense of memory and ancestry for communal foundations—calling to mind cultural symbols, myth, art, and the "human bond" of the former slaves in a land that can never quite be "home."[110] Searching for this mode of communitas, Brown ends *My Southern Home* by appealing not simply to self-reliance on the part of the former slave but also to the necessity of nurturing an "inward culture": "We should give our principal encouragement to literature, bringing before our associations the importance of original essays, selected readings, and the cultivations of the musical talent."[111] He continues, "The last great struggle for our rights; the battle for our own civilization, is entirely with ourselves, and the problem is to be solved by us."[112] Without a doubt, Brown's mode of culture and "civilization" harks back to his contemplations of ceremonies, poetry, and tradition recorded while in Europe, but his most considered account of music is in *My Southern Home*. The dance at Congo Square is the backdrop for Brown's model of developing civilization, even if it mimics European patterns. It seemed natural to Brown that all culture would be founded on "total abstinence from all intoxications" and that custom would restrain the passions from the growing danger of consumerism and cynicism.[113] While Brown often disparages the "superstitions" of both slave culture and white culture in the South, this does not stop him from using folklore to shape his own character. The coexistence of these modes of being—elite civilization and folk culture—suggests the situational reversals and irony attributed to the trickster.

My Southern Home situates his ironic "home" "ten miles north of the city of St. Louis, in the State of Missouri, forty years ago, on a pleasant plain."

The land's magnificence and dignity are thwarted by "the killing effects of the tobacco plant upon the lands of 'Poplar Farm'" and by the "want of taste so commonly witnessed in the sunny South."[114] Brown leads us through customs, "superstitions," and problematic but still promising traditions emerging from chattel slavery that point to a world beyond the servile and submissive. He aims to come to terms with the land as home, consecrated and settled by the slaves, and to acknowledge the possibility of founding sacred spaces and building the cultural institutions and associations of renewed democracy and cosmopolitan exchange to be achieved by the former slaves.

Brown ends his autobiography with an appeal to a seemingly black national character, noting, "No race ever did or ever will prosper or make respectable history which has no confidence in its own nationality," and "those who do not appreciate their own people will not be appreciated by other people." He gives the example of the "Jews," who though "scattered throughout the world, are still Jews" because they have a "religion."[115] In the same vein, Brown envied their identification with a homeland that was coeval with the founding of an identity. Thus, he praises the former slaves in Richmond for building a new church and establishing societies. Developing an "inward culture" and an "imagination" through "spare hours [spent] in study and form[ing] associations for moral, social, and literary influence" will foster a local yet transcultural community, with intermixtures of folk culture.[116] He continues, "God will reward us. . . . The best way to have a public character is to have a private one."[117]

A fundamental tragedy, of course, intrudes on his ability to conceive of the South as conferring an identity or home. As a result, emigration may be a necessity. Brown wants to claim the relation to Southern soil as sacred but is pulled into irony and tragedy. After noting that whites could only accept blacks if they continued in servility, he issues the simple command: "Black men, emigrate."[118] Claiming the land and the particular cultural consciousness associated with it is crucial to moving on to an open and cosmopolitan public character capable of a rooted yet transnational exchange.

Brown attempts to sound hopeful about the construction of a regional character, ending *My Southern Home* with an appeal to racial and cultural dignity: "Black men, don't be ashamed to show your colors, and to own them."[119] Nevertheless, the book ends on a tragically ironic note. The efforts to redeem space have turned inward to the realm of consciousness, given the "reign of terror" in the South. Yet Brown strove toward a "rooted cosmopolitanism," an amalgamated, critical, and temperate cosmopolitan culture that depended on the land and recognized its sacredness. Americans had, in general, ignored this meaning of the land and had situated freedom in the realm of privacy and individual consciousness, thereby refracting the conquest and domestication of space. The Fugitive Slave Law was a striking example of this tragedy.[120] After its passage, freedom of the land, even in the North, carried no efficacy because slave owners could violate the "free land" and enslave a person. Rootless forms of democracy and racism had overshadowed the promise of "universal emancipation," a promise Brown narrated in his original panoramic views, displayed in London in 1850. He quotes Curran: "I speak in the spirit of British law, which makes liberty commensurate with, and inseparable from, the British soil—which proclaims, ever to the stranger and sojourner, the moment he sets foot upon British earth that the ground he treads is holy, and consecrated by the genius of Universal Emancipation."[121]

Without the consecration of freedom in the soil, the monuments, and the sacred space and in-between time of civilization, American freedom represented an individualized parody of the possibility for cosmopolitan exchange posed by a revolutionary identity. This is clearer in Brown's final work, which expresses his temperance activism and confronts the limits of a sacred "manner" in modern democracy. Temperance, for Brown, was consistent with a restrained relation to the passions, the world, other cultures, and the land—a land that was not designed to be consumed in intemperate acts of slavery but to be undergone with restraint. Temperance became an indigenous and disciplined program for a new politics in light of transatlantic contact and cosmopolitan exchange, not limited by race or creed but nevertheless holding regard for local customs and manners.

CHAPTER 3

George Moses Horton's Freedom

A Temperate Republicanism and a Critical Cosmopolitanism

Whereas William Wells Brown and Martin Delany are well-known abolitionists, reformers, and authors, George Moses Horton is less prominent in the African American canon. He nevertheless has received recognition, along with Phillis Wheatley, as one of the earliest published African American poets. As William Andrews points out, Horton "not only gave the state its first noteworthy poetic voice. He also became the first poet, and indeed the first belletristic writer, from North Carolina to attract more than a local reading audience."[1] Horton and other North Carolinian African Americans in the nineteenth century, including David Walker, Moses Grundy, Lunsford Lane, Harriet Jacobs, and Anna Julia Cooper, made important literary contributions. Andrews attributes this in part to the context of slavery in the state: North Carolina generally had smaller-scale farming rather than plantation slavery; only one in four white North Carolinians had slaves; many enslaved people in North Carolina lived in cities; and the state had a larger number of slaves who hired out their time, all of which contributed to diverse understandings of freedom and slavery.[2] Horton, unlike Brown or Douglass, never escaped from slavery, though he planned to buy his freedom with the proceeds from his first book: "Horton's early poetry testified to his deep yearning for freedom, but he was not desperate enough to attempt a risky escape to the North."[3] Horton's unique situation leads to enactments of temperance, freedom, and critical cosmopolitanism that differ from his contemporaries.

Horton remained enslaved for sixty-eight years. As a result, his cosmopolitanism is partly imaginative and ambiguous, and he could not be called an abolitionist or even a temperance activist, though he expressed similar sentiments. Still, he was a cosmopolite who left his farm to hire out his time at, of all places, the University of North Carolina, where he sold his poetry. Though tied to the land of his "home," he traveled to Philadelphia and perhaps, as is widely speculated, Liberia, but he also showed an early openness and curiosity about other cultures and traditions at the university, which served as a cosmopolitan microcosm. Indeed, hiring out his time and performing cultural exchanges in public enabled him to disrupt his troubled sense of "home." While deeply critical of his "home" as a slave, he remained "rooted," close to the materiality of animals and sensuousness of the land that surrounded him and attached to the region and to the University of North Carolina. His camaraderie with the students, though often racist and problematic, nevertheless allowed him to develop a sense of performative and cosmopolitan space. He was a poet and orator both inside and outside the culture of the University of North Carolina, and he kept in view the constant prospect of movement and relocation.

    His poetry, oratory, and life context suggest he imagined freedom and temperance in a different manner than that promoted by popular ideologies of abolition and temperance. Much of his poetry possesses thematic and situational complexity that rests uneasily within the abolitionist and temperance canon in which the slave narrative and the rhetoric of progress and purity dominate. Many of Horton's writings show a desire for public distinction that approximates Brown's notions of restraint and creolized performance of a temperance aesthetic, one derived from a republican revolutionary discourse of cosmopolitanism and sublimity. However, Horton's poems display a struggle with the meanings of racial "genius" and sublimity, and some poems empower the romantic sense of egotism and individual creative prowess. Other poems, particularly those published in 1845 in *The Poetical Works*, and his public oratory to the students at the University of North Carolina promote a temperance aesthetics that plays around the edges of the sublime in search of a public space in which poetic "genius" and a performative personality could shine.

HORTON'S BACKGROUND, DRINKING, AND PASSIONATE "GENIUS"

Horton was born in Northampton County, North Carolina, in 1797. The Horton family consisted of George's mother, his seven sisters, and one brother. Their first master, William Horton, owned a small and unprofitable tobacco plantation. When George was a few years old, the Hortons moved to Chatham County to farm wheat, where he was a self-described "cow-boy" for about a decade.[4] He claims to have composed many of his first poems "at the handle of the plough and retained them in [his] head" while young "gentlemen" transcribed his poems when he was "unable to write."[5] Horton expressed a dislike for manual labor and a love for the rhythms of poetry and music. His knowledge of rhyme and meter was enhanced by Wesley's hymns, performed in camp meetings and in church, and by the New Testament.[6] He gained his initial fame by reciting orations and acrostic love poems that he sold to male college students to give to their "belles." Indeed, he enjoyed writing acrostics and continued composing them throughout his life—many are included in his third book, *Naked Genius* (1865). Because of his early success selling poetry, he was able in the early 1830s to convince his master, James Horton, to let him hire out his time and earn profits from his poetry and odd jobs around the university.[7]

Horton eventually learned to write, but he continued with his oratory, and his distinction as an orator and poet early brought him to the attention of Caroline Lee Hentz, who visited the University of North Carolina where her husband was a professor.[8] Hentz was a well-known author whose most popular novel, *The Planter's Northern Bride* (1854), was a critical response to Harriet Beecher Stowe's *Uncle Tom's Cabin*. One of her earlier novels, *Lovell's Folly* (1833), presents a conversation about abolition between a Northerner and a Southerner with a story about a character based on George Moses Horton, whose poetic gifts are "a curiosity, a freakish talented exception."[9] In the novel, as in Horton's life, those who supported his poetry also supported colonization and urged him to immigrate to Liberia.[10] Though she was an apologist for slavery, Hentz believed in Horton's talent and assisted him in his writing—and he acknowledged his debt to her in poems and in his preface to *The Poetical Works*. Hentz likely transcribed many of his poems, and she sent two of them to the *Lancaster Gazette* in 1828. From there, Horton's poems drew increasing attention, including that of David Walker and other abolitionists after *Freedom's Journal* published a poem, "On the Poetic Muse," along with a letter in support of Horton's bid for manumission.

For a moment it seemed that enough money would be raised to purchase Horton's freedom, but this optimism was misplaced.[11] His first book, *The Hope of Liberty*, appeared in 1829, and poems from this book would appear later in abolitionist papers like the *Liberator*. Particularly after David Walker's publication of *The Appeal to the Colored Citizens of the World* in 1829 and Nat Turner's insurrection in 1831, antiliteracy laws were enforced in many areas of North Carolina and the atmosphere became more "restricted."[12] Horton continued throughout his life to appeal to others to help buy his freedom, though those efforts were muted: he wrote a letter to William Lloyd Garrison, for example, but he entrusted it to David Swain, president of the University of North Carolina, Chapel Hill, who never sent it.[13] Horton published *The*

Poetical Works in 1845 while still enslaved, and in 1865 captain William H. S. Banks helped Horton publish a book of poems devoted to the Civil War, titled *Naked Genius*.[14]

Still, to be acknowledged at all by the white Southern literary circles of the time was an anomaly.[15] Although his works are not all widely available for distribution, Joan Sherman has done much to bring them to light in her collection. A few poems have been anthologized, and the University of North Carolina at Chapel Hill has published many of his works online. His presence in literary studies has been recognized by the creation of the George Moses Horton Society for the Study of African American Poetry in 1996. In February 2007, the University of North Carolina at Chapel Hill acknowledged the contribution he made "to the intellectual life of the university" by naming a residence hall after him.[16] And more recently, an anthology has been published to include poets and poems that were not canonized or as widely distributed as the works of Phillis Wheatley and Paul Laurence Dunbar. Many of these poems, including Horton's, are taken from the "early black-owned press ... from 1827 to 1899," documenting developments in such publications as *Freedom's Journal* and the *Weekly Anglo-African*.[17]

While these efforts to recover Horton's life and work are salutary, they remain complicated by his well-known love of the bottle and his backsliding from sobriety. Current critics, notwithstanding Sherman, shy away from addressing his alcoholism even though Horton wrote about his struggles with intemperance in the biography that begins *The Poetical Works* (1845). Earlier criticism considered Horton's inebriety both an impediment to his longed-for freedom from chattel slavery and the logical outcome of his continued captivity. For example, Horton's intemperance is understood in John Hope Franklin's *From Slavery to Freedom* as a stumbling block on the long road to liberty. Franklin, like many, surmises that after writing *The Hope of Liberty* (1829), his "interest in poetry diminished as he took to drink; perhaps he realized that for him there was no hope of liberty."[18] In a completely different vein, Richard Walser's 1966 book claimed he was "a man of pride [who used] drinking—whether heavily indulged in or not—[as] a scapegoat to support his self-conscious [literary] imperfections."[19] Walser even alleges that Horton must have drunk away the money earned by the publication of *The Hope of Liberty*, which was supposed to buy Horton's freedom in order to send him to Liberia: "The curve of fortune aroused the old monster Drink which had been, if not asleep, at least dozing. His small savings, put by from *The Hope of Liberty*, were diverted from the manumission cache, the fund for the down payment on that ticket to Liberia.

Now they were drained into liquor."[20] Overlooking the rarity of manumissions, Walser portrays Horton as a "contented" slave and incapable of—or not really desiring—the absolute sobriety necessary for liberty.

Even if Horton spent some of his money on drink, he would not have earned a large surplus from his publications: Sherman notes that *The Hope of Liberty* "earned scarcely any profit." When he began to hire out his time at the university, he was making "a substantial profit" but not enough to pay for his freedom, and he had trouble convincing James to sell him.[21] Sherman notes Walser's bias in depicting Horton as "an unenergetic loafer who drank, fished," and so on, and she faults Walser for "all but destroy[ing] the man's complex identity and poetic reputation" by "hurl[ing] epithets" like "sycophant, poseur, buffoon, troubadour in motley," and the like.[22] Still, Sherman perhaps overcompensates by placing too much stress on Horton's longed-for liberty and his eventual sobriety. Indeed, "liberty" as a "law of nature" overtakes Sherman's explanation of the "single theme" in Horton's work.[23]

Much of the available information about Horton, particularly his reputation as a drunkard, adds to the ambiguity of his life. The facts, which are also reflected in his poetry, often shadow his life in the same manner as the shroud of mystery that accompanied his death. Horton was an alcoholic, he was enslaved, and he desired to excel and express his "genius" in the literary world, which is particularly shown in his interactions with the white students at the university. Certainly he hoped for "liberty," but liberty for him was connected to his peculiar situation as a poet-slave. His sense of freedom consistently implied the need for a circle of his peers to recognize his literary effort, echoing romantic aspirations for genius and cosmopolitan creative-intellectual exchange. Horton's oratories and poems situate this exchange in classical republican ideals that would have been prominent in their modified form in North Carolina.[24] Horton's life and work is sometimes oversimplified or misrepresented partly because of his understanding of American freedom as expressed in acts of willpower and detached genius, an understanding that converges with individualist notions of sobriety and temperance.

Horton's works are often ambiguously appraised by critics and do not garner the intellectual engagement given to other African American or European poets. Keith Leonard, for instance, critiques Horton's "minstrel" oratory performances that merely "provided a mode of entertainment" to amuse white slaveholders. Leonard concludes that this predicament was caused by Horton's context and camaraderie with "pranking" college students, yet at the same time Leonard, like Sherman, recognizes Horton's self-characterization as "black bard" and devotes attention to the bardic tradition.[25] Horton, according to Leonard, failed to make the kind of poetic challenges that Phillis Wheatley did because he had not internalized the standards of European cultures.

The phrase "Fettered Genius," ironically the title of Leonard's book, comes from Horton's poem "The Poet's Feeble Petition," a petition handwritten on the backside of a letter to Horace Greeley in 1852 requesting $175 toward his freedom price. This letter remained in the private letters of university president David Swain, among other letters that Horton entrusted to Swain but never saw the light of day.[26] Oddly, Leonard does not highlight the fact that this poem never reached Greeley, and Horton's genius indeed remained fettered. In the poem, Horton characterizes himself as a "Bard" in line 7, and the final stanza reads as follows:

> *Then listen all who never felt*
> *For fettered genius heretofore—*
> *Let hearts of petrifaction melt*
> *And bid the gifted Negro soar.* (ll. 13–16)[27]

Leonard comments, "Horton has agency . . . no matter the material effect of the poem, a capacity to participate somewhat in the construction of the identity in his culture. All African American abolitionist poets used a version of this early-modern construction of the individual to make claims upon society through the mastery of its social codes of imaginative and moral personhood."[28] Although I share Leonard's concern with showing that those who were enslaved were not socially dead and did have "agency," I challenge his characterization of Horton's sense of "genius" or "distinction" as simply another variant of the romantic individual and his dismissive interpretation of Horton's performances as mere "entertainment" for white audiences. Rather, these performances were essential to the public space, the temperate and intellectual "home," that Horton craved.

While Horton's appeals for help to obtain his outward liberty from chattel slavery never succeeded, even as a slave he negotiated a relative freedom and public persona. Significantly, he contributed to the meaning of culture at the university through his public performances and poetry. James Horton, his second owner in the Horton family, "did not want to part with his dithyrambic plough-boy."[29] Not only did Horton bring some money to his owners by hiring out his time and through the sales of his poetry, but he also gained some prestige as "poet Horton," or "the black bard," at the university. Even while a slave he was invited to give two Fourth of July commencement speeches;

the first was only five minutes long, but in 1859 he was not so reserved.³⁰ His "Address to Collegiates of the University of North Carolina: The Stream of Liberty and Science" runs for twenty-nine pages. It was performed orally, transcribed by the male students, and preserved at the University of North Carolina archives.³¹ For students who considered Horton merely a buffoon, they did put notable effort into transcribing this address. His oratorical skills and public performances while he remained enslaved suggest more than a desire to acculturate to a community. More significantly, his works show a longing to reshape the very meaning of American freedom through the creation of a temperate public space. In other words, although Horton has an ambiguous reputation as a drunkard, or "buffoon," who struggled with both inward and outward freedom, his interweaving of the rhetoric of temperance reform and of neoclassical, republican, aristocratic virtue prominent in the culture of the University of North Carolina at the time reveals a complex meaning of freedom.

When Horton gained his legal freedom at the age of sixty-eight, he traveled to Philadelphia where he hoped to be recognized as a poet, meeting with the well-known teetotalers of the Benjamin Banneker Institute. However, he did not make any long-term literary contacts there. Reginald Pitts speculates that Horton's negative reception by the African American elite of the institute may have had two main causes. On the one hand, he may have "fortified himself with a drink of liquor."³² On the other hand, Horton had spent his lengthy life in a "generation of captivity," to use Ira Berlin's phrase, and the freeborn blacks of the Banneker Institute looked down on those who too strongly represented the "peculiar institution" of Southern slavery.³³

The details of Horton's life after being finally "freed" are vague. Reginald Pitts argues that Horton connected with the Pennsylvania Colonization Society and finally repatriated to Liberia.³⁴ Others, such as M. A. Richmond, think Horton probably died alone, perhaps drunk in Philadelphia; still others, like Walser, mused that Horton found his way "home" to Chapel Hill, North Carolina, realizing that he was better off as a slave.³⁵ It is believed that Horton died in 1883, but this claim is also uncertain.³⁶ We do not know where, when, or how he died, and no one has discovered a marker for his grave.

Though Horton desired liberty and freedom, such qualities entailed for him more cosmopolitan and cultural exchange than liberty of movement or inward freedom would provide. There seems to be some basis for Saunders Redding's claim that an egotism emerged in Horton's poetry: "What seemed to anger Horton most was not the existence of slavery, so much as that a genius like himself was inconvenienced by it."³⁷ Sherman and Richmond present Horton as consistently longing for liberty, liberty as a law of nature, the kind that informs American romantic and rationalist beliefs in independence and self-sufficiency. But Horton was a man who spent more than sixty years as a slave, and he carved out the meaning of his life in an entirely different context: as a slave, yet performing poems for the boys at the University of North Carolina and longing to be recognized by his peers. Like them, he understood freedom through the discourses of his time, particularly through anxieties around drink, slavery, and temperance. He participated in the ideals and practice of temperance but, unlike many free temperance activists, he enacted a meaning of freedom that did not directly oppose itself to his immediate environment. His poetic freedom did not conform to the inward and private modes of liberty that suited many temperance reformers.

The reform movements of abolitionism and temperance overlapped, as scholars have made clear in, for instance, the essays from *The Serpent in the Cup*, which assesses the interplay between temperance, slavery, race, and freedom. For instance, John W. Crowley's "Slaves to the Bottle" hypothesizes that the temperance literature and popular novels in the 1840s may have had a "subtle bearing" on the slave narratives that developed at the time.³⁸ In a similar vein he considers how the trope of freedom from British tyranny and references to the American Revolution influenced the temperance novel and the shape of freedom it desired.³⁹ Crowley uncovers an interplay between temperance writings, with their metaphors and rhetoric of overcoming an inward "slavery to the bottle," and slave narratives. Nothing, however, intensified the meaning of reform as an inward purity as did the presence of chattel slavery in a "free" republic. Indeed, many of the essays in this collection highlight "dark" metaphors and the overcoming that accompanies the passage to purity and, presumably, whiteness in temperance literatures of recovery. Levine's analysis of Brown's *Clotel*, for example, unravels the problematic continuity between "blacking," bondage, and inebriety—as well as the way the excessive power of plantation owners was often associated with inebriety.⁴⁰ Elsewhere, Levine has brought to light the interplay between the rhetoric of temperance reform, abolitionism, and racial uplift and the values of thrift, self-reliance, and industry.⁴¹

For many antebellum reformers, the impact of legalized chattel slavery on the American cultural meaning of "freedom" expressed itself ambiguously within a "progressive," civil space and rhetoric. The "pursuit of happiness" emphasized freedom as self-mastery, sobriety, self-control, and restraint, and always sat uneasily next to any semblance of dependency. However, while inebriety was conflated with slavery and freedom with sobriety, few published authors were enslaved both as chattel and to the bottle. George Moses Horton's peculiar situation provides us an imaginative and performative interpretation of a less detached form of temperate freedom.

Though Horton was portrayed as the stereotypically "blackened" and "drunken" slave poet, longing for temperance and liberty, his work offers another experience of captivity and bondage. He expressed an alternative meaning of "temperate" freedom as spontaneous action expressed in public performance. His poetry and speeches beg for a reassessment of dichotomies of drunken and pure, master and slave. Horton's particular situation of slavery in North Carolina, and his attempts and failures in poetry and oratory, identify a desire for a republican and performative freedom lacking in discourses of purity and self-restraint used by temperance reformers in North Carolina and, later, in Philadelphia.[42] Throughout his captivity and even in his eventual but precarious "freedom," he kept striving for a public space in which the inner freedom of self could meet an outward freedom of performative expression.

Generally, within the American republic—particularly in the antebellum period—slavery had taken on two distinct meanings. In the first instance, it meant legalized ownership of other human beings (primarily Africans) through the institution of chattel slavery. The other meaning that became prominent during the Second Great Awakening referred to the bondage of the will to alcohol or any addictive substance or habit that prevented the free and independent exercise of one's faculties. The metaphor of being a "slave to the bottle" was popular with both Northern and Southern reformers. Frederick Douglass and other black abolitionists agreed that bondage to King Alcohol was as damaging, maybe more so, than the outward bondage of chattel slavery. According to Douglass, "It was about as well to be a slave to *master*, as to be a slave to rum and *whisky*."[43] However, while both Douglass and Horton confronted problems with the discourse and actions of temperance societies, Douglass turned to individualistic, progressive, self-reliant, and moral virtues oriented toward industry and work ethic to an extent greater than Horton, who remained enslaved.

One can witness a different attitude toward the idea of humans possessing a transcendent, individualist, or sovereign nature, for instance, in the attitudes toward animals and the land presented by Douglass and Horton. To justify enslavement, many slaveholders compared slaves with animals who lacked the capacity for "genius" or intellectual development. Aristotle even defined "natural slaves" as subject to the passions: "Other animals do not recognize reason, but follow passions. The way we use slaves isn't very different."[44]

American slaveholders' identifying Africans with the passions coincided with the argument that they were more susceptible to debauchery and alcoholism. Douglass, as David Brion Davis comments, characterized his rare leisure time on the plantation as spent "in a sort of beast-like stupor, between sleep and wake, under some large tree." Many writers following Douglass noted that the legacy of slavery contributed to the "animalization" of African Americans.[45]

Douglas and Horton differ in their appraisal of the relationship between humans and animals, and in the extent to which animals are objectified in their association with materiality and passion. Douglass, imbibing the negativity associated with animals, displays a more detached and hierarchical view toward animals than does Horton. Douglass's comparison between slaves and livestock implies that it is ridiculous to provide so much care for animals when slaves are treated as livestock, or worse. For instance, Colonel Lloyd is immediately presented as a brutal (and insane) master because he lavishes care on his horses and whips his slaves for the slightest imagined mistreatment of them.[46] The classic example of slaves' dehumanization is Douglass's comparison between enslaved children and pigs. He writes, "Our food was coarse corn meal boiled. This was called *mush*. It was put into a large wooden tray or trough, and set down upon the ground. The children were then called like so many pigs, and like so many pigs they would come and devour the mush."[47] It goes without saying that slaves should be treated as equal human beings. However, the comparison to pigs stirs the audience's sympathies because pigs are often viewed as dirty and, presumably, well adapted to eating corn meal because they are slaughter animals for human consumption.

In contrast, Horton commonly compared himself to animals in a positive manner by neither "animalizing" himself nor personifying them with "rational" qualities; he presented with integrity the situation and the indignities that animals suffered. Horton's perspective may be indicative of his situation within a transcultural moment in which he was not always primarily preoccupied with overcoming slavery or protesting his condition in the name of Enlightenment progress and freedom, as was Douglass. Rather, he was also concerned with relationships, with humans and the animals to which he compared himself—like the plough horse, the dog, and the bird. His failure to fit within the paradigms of private and public, of passion and reason offered by temperance and abolitionist reformers of the time, does not suggest that he was a pathetic victim who drank himself to death in despair.

If Horton expresses an elitism in his claims to "genius," he equally sees value in the land and the animals around him. Animals are given an inherent worth, suggesting Horton is unable to transcend the material environment in an individualist fashion that would separate him from the animals. Horton's 1845 poem "Division of an Estate" captures the separation of kin on the auction block, an issue so well presented in abolitionist literature as unjust.[48] Yet Horton focuses not only on the enslaved people but on the animals—and not simply as personifications for the "poor vassals" (l. 34). He writes:

> *The flocks and herds*
> *In sad confusion now run to and fro,*
> *And seem to ask, distressed, the reason why*
> *That they are thus prostrated. Howl, ye dogs! Ye Cattle, low! Ye sheep,*
>   *astonish'd, bleat!*
> *Ye bristling swine, trudge squealing through the glades,*
> *Void of an owner to impart your food.*
> *Sad horses, lift your head and neigh aloud.* (ll. 7–14)

Like the vassal, the animals must leave "home" and follow the dignity of the "trav'ling sun" that ends "his journey" "with tears" (ll. 19–20). Horton uses the rhetorical device of the command to plead with the animals to protest; he commonly employs this neoclassical approach to create an empowered speaker. The swine, notably, are not presented as filthy, but squeal their lament through the more romanticized "glades" rather than a dirty swamp.

Horton seems to hold a belief in the reasonableness of nature, and his attention to animals could support his belief in the republican and revolutionary natural law of liberty. His 1828 poem "In Hope of Liberty" was reprinted in the *Liberator* as "On Liberty and Slavery." Written in the common meter of the hymn, the final stanza ends with an apostrophe to "Liberty," whose "sacred sun" "we crave ... to rise," "the gift of nature's God!" Sherman claims that Horton's poetry presents the theme of "natural rights" promoted by Jeffersonian proclamations of "life, liberty, and the pursuit of happiness." To be sure, liberty is presented; life and the pursuit of happiness, however, are not themes I find asserted in his poetry. Sherman equates the "poet's sacred muse" with "benign nature," but justice and even vengeance seem more common themes, and they go hand in hand with the denial of a sacred law of liberty.[49] Nature's law was often not contrary to slavery. Moreover, in Enlightenment circles such as Jefferson's, benign nature presented itself as hierarchical. Such a view of nature is uncharacteristic of Horton's poetry, which commonly places animals on equal footing with humans.

In essence, Horton did not seem to share in the rhetoric of progress, the detachment from others, or the individualism that many reformers presupposed. The situation of temperance reform in many parts of the South differed from that of Northern reformers, who linked abolition with freedom from slavery and laissez-faire progress. Southern reformers were reluctant to equate temperance goals of purity and Christian virtue with opposition to slavery, a point that makes Horton's use of temperance rhetoric even more complicated. Black temperance lodges, such as the Templars with whom Brown was associated, would obtain charters during Reconstruction in the late 1860s and 1870s, though white Southern Templars would not recognize them.[50] Such forms of temperance associated with black freedom were not prominent in Horton's milieu. As a matter of fact, white Southerners often viewed slavery as necessary for maintaining order and black sobriety. Sherman quotes Thomas Ruffin, chief justice of North Carolina's Supreme Court from 1853 to 1861, who defended slavery for its effects on "the moral and social condition of each race." Sherman explains: "Blacks, he said, are physically suited to labor, and if freed they would soon sink into drunken, debauched savagery," much like animals.[51] Nonetheless, Southern temperance did early on share an association with antislavery efforts in the North. Rather than equating evangelical conversion and evangelism with republican ideology, however, Southern temperance leaders adapted the discourse of purity and reform to suit a "hortatory moralism, whose aim was not to abolish slavery but to operate it in a moral manner."[52] As such, Horton's writings about temperance and slavery were complicated because his ambiguous public appearance in the South would still be, disappointingly, as a temperate, moral slave, rather than as a free man. Furthermore, while he often depicted drink as leading him to many vanities, it ironically was also his first introduction to some minimal camaraderie, and a sense of social identity, with his masters and with students.

This ambivalence comes to the fore in his 1845 autobiographical preface to *The Poetical Works*.[53] Horton claims to support the values of temperance, having outgrown "the moral evil of excessive drinking."[54] Note that here he qualifies his critique of drink with "excessive" and does not imply total abstinence. Temperance was legislated at the university in 1837, and the students had formed societies throughout the 1830s.[55] Horton wrote several poems on the issue: "The Tippler to His Bottle" in *The Poetical Works* and "Songs of Liberty and Parental Advice" and the "Intemperance Club" in *Naked Genius*. "Intemperance Club" begins:

> *On smiling wealth, intemp'rance war began,*
> *Away young heath and mother genius flew;*
> *And when from [health] the child and parent ran*
> *In stepped Dyspepsia belching, how do you do?* (ll. 1–4)[56]

The poem continues in an exaggerated and parodic rendition of temperance literature of the time, with its focus on sensational themes of domestic violence and financial ruin.

In the earlier 1845 poem, "The Tippler to His Bottle," Horton asks his bottle:

> *Often have I thy stream admired,*
> *Thou nothing has availed me ever;*
> *Vain have I thought myself inspired;*
> *Say have I else but pain acquired?*
> *Not ever! No, never!* (ll. 6–10)

Horton may have come across Poe's "The Raven," which was also published in 1845, or Poe may have come across Horton's poetry, given that Poe has continually been accused of plagiarizing parts of "The Raven."[57] Horton shares not only Poe's penchant for repetition and refrain but also his ambivalence toward temperance and strong spirits. Most significantly, Horton points toward a desire for material, outward freedom rather than the false inner freedom that both the bottle and temperance, in its focus on inner purity, offered. In Poe's poem, the refrain "nevermore" becomes an intensified echo of "nothing more" from the first few stanzas. The language shifts from "Perched upon a bust of Pallas just above my chamber door / Perched, and sat, and nothing more" (ll. 43–44) to "Tell me what thy lordly name is on the Night's Plutonian shore! / Quoth the raven, 'Nevermore'" (ll. 49–50).[58] Similarly, Horton's first three stanzas end with "Not ever! No, never!" and the last two reply "more, never!"

Horton's "tippler" speaks to his bottle, and though he asks some rhetorical questions, as in Poe's poem, the speaker turns more immediately accusatory, with exclamatory refrains aimed at the bottle. However, though Horton turns away from his bottled "false friend," there is an allure in the relationship that parallels the attraction he felt when reading his verses to the young white boys at the university, even if he was ridiculed. Both the bottle and the students inspired the initial genius and creativity, the passion and sensuousness that stirred the imagination. Sherman notes the ambiguities in Horton's interaction with the students: despite having been humiliated, in his 1859 commencement speech "he called himself 'your sable orator' and 'your poor orator'" and seemed to "cater ... to UNC students' whims."[59]

The camaraderie and drinks he was "privileged" enough to have shared with the students gave him a compensatory freedom at first, and also gave him the flowing verses. He writes in "The Tippler":

> Power from my tongue flows like a river,
> The gas flows dead I'm left behind,
> To all that's evil down confined,
> To Flourish more, never! (ll. 17–20)

He, like Poe, was addressing a limit to the human attempt to obtain transcendental perfection, such as offered in the egotistical sublime or Emersonian romanticism. The bliss or altered state is a "gas" that "flows dead" now. The ambiguous positioning of "I'm" in the middle of the sentence can either be read as qualifying the word "dead" or as requiring a pause between "flows" and "dead." The ambiguity is significant: in the first reading, Horton would mean that while the gas flows, he is left dead now; the spark of truth that the bottle often inspires has now run dry. In the second reading, the gas is no longer flowing and he is left speechless or tongue-tied, "to all that's evil down confined." In the second reading, he has never left the bottle but has, rather, simply run out of rum.

The lack of drink may have been one problem for Horton, since he was, after all, a slave. Though he certainly could acquire alcohol, it was possibly more difficult for him to obtain vast quantities. The poem thus had asked, "What has thou ever done for me?" and later responds "Flows from thy fount thou cheerful giver, / From thee affluence sinks to stealth" (ll. 12–13). Whatever "affluence" Horton could have obtained from selling his poems, though quite a boon for him, would not have been enough to buy his freedom or pay his way to Liberia.

Clearly, Horton came to recognize the so-called evils of excessive drinking, but none of the critics who mentions Horton's love of the bottle seems to believe he stayed sober. Although we can view him as "backsliding," perhaps he had another, less purified conception of the temperate personality. In his 1845 autobiographical preface, he recounts his introduction to drink and characterizes the people who gave him alcohol: his owner and the students. The students had "flattered [him] into the belief that it would hang [him] on the wings of new inspiration, which would waft [him] into regions of poetical perfection."[60] The pursuit of sublimity and private, vain genius occurs for Horton throughout his writings in his differentiation of the private and public modes of "genius." He recognizes here, just as he will warn the students later in his

1859 address, that drunkenness can be—most significantly—a cause of public embarrassment rather than a moral sin.

Horton's plea for "temperance and regularity" in 1845 runs counter to an inward discourse of self-restraint and an inner freedom found in self-possession or rational control.[61] His first introduction to alcohol with his owner functioned like the "safety valves" that Frederick Douglass spoke of in his autobiographies—attempts to make an unbearable situation bearable and to curb potential rebellion by deadening the mental capacities necessary for revolt.[62] According to Horton, "Often has he [his owner] called me with my fellow laborers to his door to get the ordinary dram, of which he was much too fond himself; and we, willing to copy the example, partook freely in order to brave the storms of hardship, and thought it an honor to be intoxicated. And it was then the case with most of the people; for they were like savages, who think little or nothing of the result of lewd conduct."[63] Here, Horton reverses the fears of Judge Ruffin, quoted earlier, that blacks would fall into "savagery," showing instead how dishonorably the master race behaves. But Horton's goal, unlike Douglass's, is not to take back that self-control and act as if he were in full possession of his will and private faculties. On the contrary, true "temperance" is to be expressed through participation in a public culture—the true public honor that Horton sees disguised in drunken camaraderie. For instance, in his comments about his master's drinking, he complains that the master when drinking excessively did not handle his affairs in a "cultivated" manner, a value that will become increasingly important for Horton's sense of temperance and public freedom.

In the preface, Horton "lamented" the fact that he "was raised in a family or neighborhood inclined to dissipation," which served to "stifle the growth of uncultivated genius." He describes his "old master" as "an eminent farmer," possessing "prudence and industry." However, problematically, his master "did not descend to the particularity of schooling his children at any high rate; hence it is clear that he cared less for the improvement of the mind of his servants."[64] Of course, Douglass and other abolitionists promoted a form of republican education, but not quite in the same sense as Horton. Horton does not conflate the metaphor of "slavery to the bottle" with the system of chattel slavery; thus, he presupposes a middle ground between slavery and freedom, drunkenness and purity. Reformers often tended to present extreme dichotomies between purity and sinfulness and between freedom and slavery. Ironically, this stance led many to give freedom an inward, moral locus. Douglass tended to use intemperance to describe the overseers, to show how "the power to enslave intoxicates (and thereby degrades) the slave owner and their hirelings."[65] Horton's criticism of the master's inclination toward "dissipation" is much different than the demonization of the slave system and alcohol's sinfulness advanced by abolitionists who propounded temperance. He notes that his master possessed qualities of "prudence" and industry—these are not impeded by the slave system or alcohol—but he lacked culture, honor, and other rather aristocratic virtues (similar to those Brown seemed to admire). Horton criticizes not so much the excess as the manner in which inebriety sacrificed public virtues for an individualistic locus of freedom. In contrast, Douglass, looking back, characterized excess and drink as indicative of slave power that inhibited the individual faculties and industry, power that could be overcome through singular intellect and will.

For a person like Horton, enslaved for more than sixty years, temperance posed a contradiction or at least a decided and intense ambiguity: if an enslaved person were addicted with his will in bondage, through temperance he would be able to free the will from bondage yet would remain enslaved with no proper arena to exercise a free will. While Horton lamented his enslaved condition and continually struggled for his freedom, his poetry thematically emphasized public space and virtue and set critical limits on individual liberty as the hallmark of freedom. Through his poetic expression and public performance he refused to identify the fundamental meaning of human freedom with the institutions of the society that had enslaved him. Like those communities of enslaved Africans who expressed alternative meanings of freedom using the rhetoric of the Bible, Horton refused to make freedom a purely futuristic project of moving from slavery to freedom or from inebriety to sobriety.

A PUBLIC PERFORMATIVE SPACE FOR "GENIUS" TO SHINE

In his poetry and orations, Horton was influenced by neoclassical rhetoric and transposed it to Southern soil. He most commonly used heroic couplets, ballad forms, hymnal meters, blank verse, and many classical images that made his poetry similar to that of white Southerners of the time.[66] The Greco-Roman images, however, were consistently applied to Horton as an enslaved person—Southerners liked to consider their slave society as sharing many features with ancient slavery. Indeed, his patron Caroline Lee Hentz originally portrayed him in her novel *Lovell's Folly* as having, "instead of the broad smile of the African . . . the mild gravity of a Grecian philosopher."[67] And in his 1859 Fourth of July address he praises the eloquence of the "orators of Greece,

Athens, or Rome," suggesting that he is an "intended Washington, an expectant Napoleon," but "deplor[ing]" his "lot" to be in "the fields of uninterminable labor rather than in a repository of Belle Letters."[68] While such rhetoric can entail aristocratic hierarchy, Horton's use of neoclassical and revolutionary meanings of temperance as indicating the "golden mean," rather than inner purity and virtue, brings to light connections between the word "temperance" and the idea of keeping time. In other words, this understanding of temperate freedom—of keeping time with others—requires a public space in which his oratorical and poetic genius can shine. Such a space would limit what Horton sees as the dangers and the vanities of "abounding exalted faculties" associated with the solitary egotism of excessive drink.[69]

Horton's tendency to situate freedom and genius in his present, bounded space should indicate that genius is not simply "natural" or based on the faculty of will. For instance, Horton defended nativist "American" "genius" in response to the visit of the Hungarian revolutionary leader Louis Kossuth to the United States: "I am for developing our own resources, and cherishing native genius.... As a North Carolina patriot, I ask, Why leave our own to stand on foreign soil?"[70] Sherman and Richmond see Horton's call to acknowledge "poetry of native growth" as consistent with the Emersonian call for cultural nationalism. Again, Horton's conception of "genius" and public recognition are opposed to a cultural nationalism based on individual or private creative power. In his initial response to Kossuth's visit, Horton's championing of a European revolutionary shows his awareness of revolutionary action—the freedom of American slaves was one issue raised by the Revolutions of 1848. Moreover, Horton clarifies that he is a "North Carolina patriot" and situates himself in a much more local model of democratic republicanism than Emerson would have. Horton evidently longed for his poetry to "be circulated throughout the whole world," but his notion of genius is not solitary, transcendent, or metaphysical.[71]

On the contrary, genius is derived from the labor required of an artificial craft and needs the public and the "world" to endure. As Horton puts it in "The Art of a Poet," one of his later poems from *Naked Genius*: "The diamonds water lies concealed, / Till polished it is ne'er revealed / Its glory bright to show" (ll. 16–19).[72] Moreover, his concept of "native talent" does not stress the prototypical Emersonian disdain for European models of art as if he were calling for an "American poet," breaking with European forms. Rather, in its appeal to a "poetry of native growth," Horton's sense of "genius" was bound to public acknowledgment and performance in North Carolina, and particularly at the university. As a corollary, Horton's "public" itself was also far different from the emerging "voluntary" societies that were developing in parts of New England and the North; his public was founded on aristocratic hierarchies that situated genius as an issue of honor and appearance rather than an idealistic and transcendent will. Horton's particular republican background helps us understand available notions of public freedom beyond temperance and mainstream abolitionism.

Horton's milieu was suffused with the Jeffersonian idea of a natural aristocracy of geniuses, whose talents echoed classical statesman and philosophers.[73] The anonymous author of the introduction to Horton's *Poetical Works* certainly acknowledged, almost as a direct response to Jefferson's dismissal of "African" genius, that Horton's poetry should "remove the doubts of cavilists with regard to African genius."[74] Whereas the anonymous author is careful to note that Horton is not actuated "by a desire for public fame," Horton in fact consistently expressed such a desire.

The University of North Carolina, however, was considered a "poor relation" of the Jeffersonian neoclassical and Enlightenment ideals that founded the University of Virginia.[75] Though the students were "sons of wealthy planters," the general population of North Carolina was uneducated and illiterate. Moreover, the dominant agricultural setting differed from the larger Virginia or South Carolina plantations; Horton, for instance, initially worked as a farmer, a "cow-boy," alongside his master's sons. Horton felt—despite laws to the contrary—that he was an unacknowledged but essential part of the family of his first master, William Horton, such that upon William's division of his estate, Horton writes not that he was bequeathed to James, but that "James fell heir to me."[76] Horton's relative liberty, compared to those enslaved on larger plantations, resulted from being raised in a family that owned fewer slaves, as was typical in North Carolina.[77] Despite the laws that forbade slave literacy and hiring out, Horton was allowed to hire out his time and to read without being viewed as a threat by his owners. Possibly his owners did not value an aristocratic "culture" or share the idea that revolt might result from literacy.

While Horton always desired to be legally free, his situation of relative liberty and literacy occasioned deeper reflections on the meaning of genius, public appearance, and freedom of movement and expression. In his preface to *The Poetical Works*, Horton criticizes the students for belittling him and for desiring him to "spout" or give an extemporaneous oration on various subjects. At first, Horton was "inspired" and felt an "enthusiastic pride," which he equated with a "vain egotism, which always discovers the gloom of ignorance, or dims the luster of popular distinction."[78] He is aware of the difference between his private and privative egotistical "genius" and false flattery, on the one hand, and public and institutional recognition of "distinction," on the other—in other words, between the inner and outer worlds of freedom.

Horton occasionally dreamed of liberty of movement and voluntarism, as in his 1829 poem "On Liberty and Slavery" in which he first appeared in the persona of a bird, pleading to "Now bid the vassal soar" (l. 20). However, I am more concerned with appraising the "space" of slavery that Horton inhabited, a space that gave birth to his notion of "popular distinction," which became "public distinction" in his 1859 address. This space was theatrical in several senses. American slavery as an institution might be seen as tragicomic. Though slavery was legal, blessed by most of the founding fathers, neither "slave" nor "slavery" is mentioned in the U.S. Constitution.[79] Slavery somehow seemed "necessary" to the meaning of "freedom" in the first modern nation born of a democratic revolution. This fundamental contradiction evokes a certain sense of theatricality. Moreover, George Moses Horton, a literate enslaved African American, spent most his time as servant, poet, and companion with the young white college students at the University of North Carolina, earning money by writing acrostics they presented to their ladies as their own productions. As Richmond notes, "The story of a black man supplying the language of passion for courtship of white young ladies by white young gentlemen is enough to trigger a mind-blowing Freudian excursion."[80] And, finally, the space of Horton's slavery becomes even more audacious when he is called on to deliver two commencement addresses to his "companions" on the Fourth of July. From this perspective we can understand Walser's characterization of Horton as "jester" or "buffoon." Horton himself realized he was often playing the "buffoon" for the white students. As he implies in his autobiographical preface, written in the 1830s, he knew the difference between true genius and buffoonery: "But I soon found it an object of aversion, and considered myself nothing but a public ignoramus. Hence I abandoned my foolish harangues, and began to speak of poetry."[81] The contradictory modes of the theatrical would evaporate into the ephemerality of the odd if we left things there and did not situate Horton within the totality of his context.

I interpret the facts of Horton's life symbolically as a "body of time," a notion partially derived from his poetry and performances. From another perspective, this notion of a "body of time" can situate Horton methodologically within what Mary Louise Pratt has referred to as the transcultural situation. For her, contact zones are spaces of colonial encounter in transcultural situations where persons of different backgrounds, possessing different valences of power, are in relationship.[82] She foregrounds the interactive, improvisational dimensions of these encounters and sees them as copresent and interlocking understandings and practices. A great deal of interaction exists between the colonizers and the colonized or, in this case, between the slave owners and the enslaved, but in most cases it is the colonized or the enslaved who are able to admit the full meaning and human dimensions of the situation and from it undertake self-conscious creative expressions. Horton is able to enact multiple, interlocking perspectives: he is neither this nor that (neither socially dead, nor free) and thereby becomes a hybrid subject that partakes in multiple cultural positions, similar to the hybridity described by postcolonial thinkers like Homi Bhabha. From the totality of Horton's "body of time," he expressed the meanings of performance, memory, and freedom as the complex nexus of discourses and experiences of slavery materially present in his life.

Horton professes a desire to be remembered for the rhythmic enactment of voice within a public space of his peers. This classically derived Roman republican ideal permeates his poetry and orations. Horton claims that the "acrostics I composed at the handle of the plough and retained them in my head (being unable to write) until an opportunity offered, when I dictated whilst one of the gentlemen would serve as my amanuensis."[83] As a result, we have access to Horton's earliest writings primarily through Hentz's transcriptions. While writing became important, he continued an oral and performative mode. Such performance brings to light the public and situational context of Horton's identity—how he was perceived in relationship to his own desires.

In the 1859 address, transcribed by students, his tone throughout is commanding, and he chastises the students, asking them, "Have you any regard for public distinction?"[84] He propounds Christian and republican "virtue," "civilization," "reason," and "temperance." In the case of temperance, Horton seems less concerned with the idea of inner purity than with the idea that "habitual atrocities" such as intemperance might lead to "public disgrace" and the "frowns of disgusted parents."[85] He finds a "diplomatic grace" in temperate appearance, drawing on an older sense of temperance as moderation and the "golden mean" between extremes in all public behavior.[86] He appeals as a "sable orator" to the college graduates to "applaud the memorable deeds of your dead forefathers" and warns them not to forget the promise of revolution for liberty and freedom.[87] He also recommends that, rather than criticize, they should acknowledge the "mental eminence . . . in one of low birth [and] expand the narrow circle"—that is, their Christian-republican institutions—"in which he stands."

Though this address is transcribed and difficult to read, the tenor is one of empowerment. The overarching mode of address is the command in the subjunctive mood, quite common in neoclassical appeals to the muse, God, or the public. As he commands the students, "You should endeavour more faithfully to enlarge the base of the pyramid of your independent republic which has stood the test of almost a century now tottering beneath the burden of the treacherous pillars of chance."[88] His wish is that they

> *Let no time pass idly by*
> *With no needful service done.*
> *Seize the moments as they fly*
> *And count them life as dearly won.*[89]

The use of the command form, which relies on the conditional and the subjunctive mood, corresponds with a situation of rupture and liminality as theorized by Victor Turner in his discussion of social drama, rites of passage, and theories of performance. Turner points out that the liminal is the state of being between a past that is no longer and a future that is not yet. The revolutionary possibility of an enslaved person delivering a Fourth of July commencement address to those who would enslave him is such a liminal occasion. More generally, liminality has been applied to the negotiation of the binary subjectivities of oppressor and oppressed, or fugitive and free, master and slave. In this performative moment, according to Turner, there can be a "doffing of masks, the stripping of status, the renunciation of roles, the demolishing of structures." Horton seems quite conscious of the revolutionary and ritualistic nature of the performance, taking the carnivalesque to the subjunctive mood in which, Turner points out, new "structures are then generated, with their own grammars and lexica of roles and relationships."[90]

The constructed, rather than natural or metaphysical, nature of freedom as expressed in public performance and memorialization comes through in Horton's poetry as well. In "Memory," written in 1845, and "What Is Time?" written in 1857, Horton stresses the uncertain nature of this worldly temporality; the latter poem forwards a "carpe diem" motif, concluding with the command to "Improve while ye may." However, the choices posed for "improvement" do not suggest a concern for the individualistic modes of self-reliance and purity that had become the traditional carpe diem of romantic love. Horton was married, but he never referred to his marriage and, by all accounts, his slave marriage seemed an unhappy one. Rather, Horton calls for a public space to be established in the moment, the spontaneous time of individual melody and freedom, followed by public harmony and aesthetic beauty. Horton ends with a call to follow "the eagle's wing," a major symbol of American identity.

According to the speaker, the choice of flight in this instant, in this world, is "either languish or to sing. / To sink or to ascend."[91] This freedom entails no simple or willful escape, no act of self-control.

Through memory and imagination, Horton had recourse to the neoclassical Roman republican tradition—the same one used by the Founding Fathers to legitimate their illegitimate democratic republic. Horton had the courage to forge an "other" meaning of freedom from this tradition while yet enslaved. In so doing, he undercut the prevailing meaning of temporality assumed in a situation of domination. In situations of this kind the enslaved are supposed to occupy a "time of anticipation," for "real time"—the time of the existential "now"—is possessed by the masters and the owners. Through his notion of performance and the arena of public space, Horton created a time for the free exercise of public virtue.

Horton took seriously a particular time of republican freedom understood as revolutionary time, an in-between moment of presentness and possibilities. To be sure, Horton's poems that deal more directly with time, such as "What Is Time?" and "Imploring to be Resigned at Death," show that he did not understand time in the sense of progress or as an arena for the "pursuit of happiness." Both poems highlight the present moment and the full character that the republican performer must display to be honored and remembered at death and to receive Christian salvation; the latter poem wishes for a "martial distinction" to be "display[ed]" and commands

> Let me die, and my worst foe forgive,
> When death veils the last vital ray,
> Since I have but a moment to live,
> Let the last debt I pay,
> Go chanting away. (ll. 21–25)[92]

The refrain throughout the five-stanza poem is the single line "Go chanting away." Like his bird of freedom and also like the public bard, he understood the full public character as revealed in the moment of performance. As the meter slows down through pause and repetition, Horton's refrain becomes an enactment of public freedom in communal song and chant rather than a future wish.

While self-mastery, freedom of the will, and progress seem the goal for many Northern abolitionists and temperance writers, Horton turns to ancient cultures and Southern ideals of republican virtue. Part of the reason for this might be the odd predicament of hiring out through selling one's poems. Most slaves who hired out would work in trades such as blacksmithing, on ships, or doing other odd jobs; poetry and the performance of poems was a different matter. Horton dictated and performed much of his poetry to young students. In other words, his developing sense of independence was less connected to individual freedom as a structure of inwardness than to the freedom to perform.

Culture for Horton was a public matter, but seen from a twenty-first-century perspective, his perspective may have had a hint of snobbery and elitism. Indeed, Horton seemed to share a disdain for the illiterate condition into which he, as a slave, had been thrown. He, rather than his masters, held an elitist ideal of culture, and he looked down on them for their lack of interest in poetry or public speaking. It was common for Southerners to disapprove of the rising popular culture and the materialist and individualist values propounded by Northerners. But such criticism does not entail maintaining or reverting to the hierarchies of the "peculiar institution."

In contrast to the ideals of self-improvement, which put forth a progressivist and instrumentalist ideology of the work ethic, Horton applauded the dignity of work and economy while expressing an aesthetic freedom as the beautiful in the present time. The time of freedom for Horton was momentary yet eternal; it was the fullness of the present and the expression of the individual in a public space. All the contradictions expressed in Horton's life defined another body of time—a time in between. This time, full of the faith evoked by imagination and memory, recognizes human finitude and bans questions concerning the future. It unleashes the desire to express the "whole duty of humanity" in manifesting the glory of God through free performance.

This desire for a worldly and performative role in public space is expressed in Horton's 1865 poem "One Generation Passeth Away and Another Cometh." Ironically and sadly, the fear of public obscurity Horton expressed in this poem would come to pass, even after Horton was "free" and made his way North, "without a stone to show his grave" (l. 20). The title of the poem itself asserts the transitory and momentary state of the present generation. Taken from the Psalms, the maxim indicates the presumed wisdom of King Solomon that all is vanity and that there is nothing new under the sun. By implication, Horton's "genius" might have nothing novel to offer the world. Indeed, Horton's bird resurfaces as a "vain bird":

> Vain bird, a while think what am I,
> Here entering 'mid a hawk-like throng;
> Quickly hatched out, as quick to fly,
> And dare not tarry long. (ll. 13–16)[93]

At first, he asserts disdain for the novel as mere egotistical vanity, and the bird of hope appears as "quickly hatched out, as quick to fly." But there is a longing for public glory and fame and a sense of despair when he asks if it is true that "the mighty and the stout / who lived this fading world to crave" (ll. 17–18) might be "Left forever gone without / A stone to show their grave" (19–20).[94] Horton finds his idea of freedom in public fame and the memorialization of his public character. Again, this expression of freedom as public memory harks back to the Roman character of slavery. As Hannah Arendt pointed out, referring also to Barrow's discussion of slaves in the Roman colleges, "The curse of slavery consisted not only in being deprived of freedom and of visibility, but also in the fear of these obscure people themselves 'that from being obscure they should pass away leaving no trace that they have existed.'"[95]

Horton began by turning to the dignity of a memory in the "fading world," and he framed the poem with the carpe diem motif: the actors in his world must "Break into time to gather fame," even if they "pass at once again" (7–8).[96] While his time is transitory, the fullness of his public character should be eternally memorialized; implicitly, he moves away from the individualist and private locus of freedom that often led reformers to neglect the splendor of the public realm that might be valuable for a "genius" of Horton's sort emerging from slavery. He departs from the evangelical distrust of worldly pleasure and from the recommendation of willpower and inner restraint to remove sin. The reformed and pure body was an instrumentalist ideal that mastered time in its progressivism and excluded a sense of heterogeneity; a heterogeneous and enlarged public space was also necessary for harmony, beauty, and distinction to shine.

George Moses Horton defines a strange position in early African American literature. While most of the literature of this tradition was created by free blacks and could be placed within the stylistics of abolitionism, his meaning of freedom as performance was not exhausted by the inwardness of moral purity nor expressed in the sinister sobriety of instrumental rationality. Horton inhabited a "contact zone" defined by slavery. Rather than seeing his owners and masters as exemplars of freedom, he sought through his "performances" and his writings about the public performative act to express a "body of time" out of which a meaning of democratic and republican freedom, a cosmopolitan exchange, could be wrought within the very heart of slavery.

His cosmopolitanism was not disinterested but remained attached to the land and region while longing for intercultural exchange in restrained performative dialogue. His final publications express uncertainty, however, about the prospects of being a "stranger nowhere in the world" at his advanced age without friends, homeland, or public space and community.⁹⁷ As Sherman points out, after the end of the Civil War, when Horton was almost seventy, he journeyed with Captain Banks and the Ninth Michigan Cavalry Volunteers from Raleigh to Lexington and back again; he "walked almost 300 miles and had lived precariously in army camps in the heat of May, June, and July." He composed more than ninety poems for his last book, *Naked Genius*, and continued writing acrostics for the young men in the cavalry to give to their girlfriends. Undoubtedly tired from the journey, he looked forward to traveling to Philadelphia for a new life but may have realized that his opportunity to "shine" and be recognized in a cultural exchange had passed. According to Sherman,

> The "unfettered" slave surely enjoyed his freedom to versify, but many poems in *Naked Genius* suggest how difficult Horton found these months on the road among strangers. After a lifetime in bondage, for him a restrictive but protective environment, Horton may have missed the familiar small world of the Chatham farm and the eight miles of countryside to Chapel Hill. Many poems in *Naked Genius*, like "The Southern Refugee," express longing for home, family, and friends in the voice of the poet himself, or voices of soldiers displaced by war; the word "home" appears in the titles of seven poems.⁹⁸

His economic and social dispossession in "freedom" and his disappearance at the end of his life may make recent characterizations of cosmopolitanism based on marginality and "refugee" status more appropriate in this final journey north. Horton looked forward to "freedom," but his sense of freedom never involved the rootless travels of borderless privilege. His poem "The Southern Refugee" (1865) suggests the cost of losing his "native home" and of replacing the internal, if ambiguous, possibilities for intercultural exchange at the university and in his region with the uncertain "roaming" of a detached, "unfettered" cosmopolitanism. In this poem, "my native home" is the refrain throughout, and the location of home seems to be the South:

> *I trust I soon shall dry the tear*
> *And leave forever hence to roam,*
> *Far from a residence so dear,*
> *The place of beauty—my native home.* (ll. 25–28)⁹⁹

In spite of, or perhaps because of, the speaker's position as "refugee," he does not romanticize slavery or the South, and the "tear" is faithfully dried. As Faith

Barrett points out, many of the poems from *Naked Genius* express ambivalence toward the place of his "native home" and, indeed, even the identity of the speaker of the poem.[100] They certainly cannot easily be conflated with the performative minstrelsy of a nostalgic longing for "Dixie," just as Horton's performances for the students should not be interpreted as such. Horton's longing for civil, temperate space for "genius" remained rooted in a locus of intimate performativity that suggested the reconstructed possibilities for a republican culture, a "home" created in exchanges.

CHAPTER 4

Frances E. W. Harper's Black Cosmopolitan Creoles
A Temperate Transnationalism

In Frances E. W. Harper's 1892 novel *Iola Leroy*, in a discussion of the development of "civilization" in the United States, the protagonist Iola offers a vision of national foundations to her uncle Robert and her would-be suitor, Dr. Gresham. The nation should be "'Not simply,' says Iola, '... building up a great material prosperity, founding magnificent cities, grasping the commerce of the world, or excelling in literature, art, and science, but a nation wearing sobriety as a crown and righteousness as the girdle of her loins.'"[1] This passage alludes to ideals of Christian universalism in Isaiah (11:5), temperance, "commerce," empire, and civilization. Though Harper's criticism often focuses on ideals of female and racial uplift, it is nearly impossible not to notice these other themes in her work. For example, Minnie Le Grange, the narrator of *Minnie's Sacrifice* (1869), "felt it was no mean nor common privilege to be the pioneer of a new civilization."[2] Neither Iola's nor Minnie's ideals of civilization, however, are complicit with the imperialist capitalism that often accompanies the rhetoric of Christian universalism. Harper consistently opposed the rise of consumer capitalism without abandoning her Christian orientation. Her discourse of civilization was grounded in temperance, restraint, duty, and self-sacrifice, with faith in women's rights and racial progress. Such a discourse is not easily conflated with the more popular individualist focus on purity of race and asceticism often promulgated by white temperance activists and women's rights advocates, particularly those in the Woman's Christian Temperance Union (WCTU). Indeed, Harper's literature often responds to their racism. Harper, like Brown, conceived of temperance as a founding discourse of a modern democratic civilization that challenges the nationalist ethos of American individualism and progress. The type of civilization that emerges in her work was also a creolized and cosmopolitan space of exchange that challenged antimiscegenation within the WCTU and beyond.

Harper's temperance position and activism is well-known and appears in much of her fiction, poetry, and speeches. Regardless of whether temperance is the main theme of a particular work, as it is in *Sowing and Reaping: A Temperance Tale* (1867) and "The Two Offers" (1859), all of Harper's protagonists are temperance proponents. Harper was also a popular speaker and author. After moving to Philadelphia in 1871, she joined the WCTU, serving as superintendent of the Pennsylvania "colored" chapter for seven years and superintendent of the national "colored" division for five years.[3] Harper, like many African American reformers, equated slavery to alcohol with chattel slavery.[4] Rather than reducing alcoholism to an internal and individual moral impurity, Harper represents slavery to drink as a continuation of the political and social oppression manifest in the excesses of chattel slavery and capitalist greed.

Prior to the Civil War, Harper delivered speeches on the abolitionist lecture circuit, and she also showed her commitment to temperance early on in her poetry. Harper was a well-known poet; evidence suggests that a slim volume titled *Forest Leaves* was published in 1845, and *Poems on Miscellaneous Subjects* was published in 1854.[5] She began writing fiction in the late 1850s and continued into the Reconstruction and post-Reconstruction periods. She spent much of her later life in the North, in Maine and Pennsylvania, but she was born free in Baltimore in 1825 of uncertain patrimony and resided there until the Compromise of 1850 forced her family to leave.[6] She was raised by her aunt in a prominent free black family. Her uncle, the Reverend William Watkins of the African Methodist Episcopal (AME) Church, founded the school she attended until the age of thirteen and became one of the more vocal abolitionists and reformers from the area until he immigrated to Canada.[7] Harper was active in the Underground Railroad and was close to William Still, who published a biographical sketch and parts of her letter to him in *The Underground Railroad* (1871), his famous collection of accounts from escaped slaves and activists.[8] Harper toured parts of Southern Ontario on the transnational abolitionist circuit and visited fugitives in 1856; she was one of the only black women at the time to make a living as a lecturer and author.[9] She moved to Ohio in 1850 to become a schoolteacher after her family left for Canada.[10] Like many of her fictional characters, she committed herself to educational reform, working and lecturing on the issue in the Southern states during Reconstruction. She remained active in reform, particularly temperance reform, and continued to publish poems and essays until her death in 1911.

To call Harper cosmopolitan runs counter to most scholarship about her, which commonly—and correctly—situates her as committed to racial uplift but critical of upper-middle-class wealth, excess, and elitism. Harper used serial publication through the *Christian Recorder* to challenge the sense of audience as lowbrow, middlebrow, or highbrow, as Carla Peterson explains.[11] Following the Civil War, many women who witnessed the negative effect of the masculine culture of drinking on the domestic realm, Harper among them, felt compelled to become involved in the temperance movement. For Harper, like Brown, intemperance encompassed a total corporeal and spiritual healing and entailed broader meanings of freedom connected with the refounding of civilization and culture. As Peterson comments, "In *Minnie's Sacrifice* and *Sowing and Reaping*, she offered readers a program that promoted the self-disciplining of both individuals and a society rendered intemperate not only by drink but also by the elite's accumulation of wealth and consumption of a cosmopolitan high culture that was finding its way into the new monthlies."[12] While I agree with Peterson's interpretation of Harper's program of recovery, Harper does not emphasize individual willpower or "individual moral responsibility" as the primary solution to intemperance.[13] Indeed, temperance was a larger societal problem and, like slavery, it would not be solved by individual moral responsibility alone. A public civil society, one committed to freedom and justice, was needed to shape an individual sense of responsibility in the first place.

Nor was Harper's understanding of "cosmopolitan" strictly an elitist orientation. After all, cosmopolitanism entails restraint from the passionate frenzy Harper associates with clannish behavior. Her sense of cosmopolitanism is also evident in her use of creolization and her firm opposition to the pervasive antimiscegenationist sensibilities and laws during slavery and following Reconstruction. However, Peterson views Harper's literary use of creolization, and especially the creolization evoked by the presence of Haiti in Harper's fiction, as a sign of excess and negativity that contrasts with the Northern ideals that she views Harper as supporting. In her words, "In Harper's literary imagination, southern slaveholding culture has its origins in the foreign Creole culture of prerevolutionary Haiti and is characterized by ostentatious displays of wealth and moral self-indulgence. It thus stands in negative contrast both to the many accounts of the independent black Republic of Haiti published in the *Recorder* and to Harper's visions of the North as a site of industrious free labor."[14] Creole culture and identity is not "foreign" to the United States or the "Americas" for Harper but is firmly enmeshed in the history of Louisiana— although in *Minnie's Sacrifice* the links to Haiti appear mainly through the

Haitian Revolution. In addition, Harper's definition of creole is not limited to wealth or self-indulgence. Rather, she suggests the possibility of a cultured and temperate "American" creole character to challenge the narrow individualist "pride" of the Anglo-Saxon culture that continued to enact racist policies while opposing "Southern" slavery.

A rooted and anti-elitist cosmopolitanism is Harper's corollary to Iola's vision of a temperate nation and empire. Moreover, *créolité* becomes a cultural episteme for understanding the origins of the American hemisphere and how it can be healed. The challenge to ethnic or national interests—that is, "local color"—was characteristic of much American literature at the end of the nineteenth century and in the context of Reconstruction. From the position of a white European privileged cosmopolitanism, Henry James depicted the petty nationalist and materialist interests of Americans in *The Gilded Age* (1873). In *The Innocents Abroad* (1869) the "cosmopolitan" Mark Twain mocked American tourism and the nationalist attitudes of Americans who remained unchanged by their travels to Europe or the Holy Land.[15] And most important, perhaps informing Harper's depiction of Louisiana, Southern writers in the postbellum era wrote "local color" literature, such as Kate Chopin's "Desirée's Baby" (1893) and "La Belle Zoraide" (1894) or George Washington Cable's stories in *Old Creole Days* (1879) and his novel *The Grandissimes* (1880). Cable and Chopin confronted racial intermixtures in the identities of "white" creoles in Louisiana, but their stories were often set before the Civil War.[16] For Harper, these hidden intermixtures, though indicative of a history of violence, led to the possibility of a new race of African American creoles who possessed the hope of healing the intemperate excesses of slavery and building a new cosmopolitan civilization. Harper, like Brown, imaginatively used Haiti to frame the beginnings of "black" or creole cosmopolitanism and the pan-African and international affiliations that united the diaspora.

At the end of the nineteenth century, in a context of ongoing discussions about how to acknowledge and include former slaves as citizens in a democratic republic, African Americans like Harper and Brown questioned the nature of cosmopolitanism and the national ethos. For example, at the end of *Iola Leroy*, Iola's spouse, Dr. Latimer, who, like Iola, is a black creole who looks outwardly white, and with whom she has her ever-desired "spiritual affinity," is upheld as "a true patriot and a good citizen."[17] He is a consummate temperance reformer and a "leader" working "for the benefit of the community." While he exemplifies American patriotism, the narrator remarks, "his patriotism is not confined to race lines. 'The world is his country, and mankind his countrymen.'"[18] Seemingly an American, yet also a cosmopolitan "citizen of the world," the "Good Doctor" Latimer is a Christlike figure with a gentle effect on the South like the "influence of the sun upon the earth." He possesses the ability to heal the "old animosities of slavery into the new community of interests arising from freedom."[19]

Being a "citizen of the world"—that is, being "cosmopolitan"—has since the Enlightenment often implied an open and liberal character. The initial expression by Diogenes the Cynic was, however, not so affirmative. Because the Greeks valued belonging to a political community, the city-state or polis, Diogenes's expression "was intended to be a snub, an insult to all forms of civility, not an expression of universalism," and "as late as the first century C.E. the idea that one could be a citizen without a city was, for the Greeks, still unimaginable."[20] Harper emphasized the need for local "communities of interest" for citizenship, and she also echoed the language of liberal and Enlightenment thinkers who discerned promise in "society" rather than in a community based on hereditary, biological, or ethnic-national precapitalist structures.[21] In the language of Ferdinand de Tonnies, *Gesellschaft* (or civil society) is consistent with the Enlightenment's "cosmopolitan" communities of shared interests; he coined another term, *Gemeinschaft*, to describe traditional community values rooted in a hereditary sense of shared destiny, kinship, and origin. Though Harper's writings suggest otherwise, theories of cosmopolitan "communities of interest" commonly place little emphasis on intimacy, reciprocity, or ethical collaboration, becoming instead a corollary of the larger artificial, abstract, and ephemeral society. In the late nineteenth century, the North might be construed as a cosmopolitan *Gesellschaft* while the South retained values based on a white racial heritage of blood and privilege. Harper's "community of interest" implied something more innovative than that represented by either the North or the South: that the values arising from democratic freedom could bring together a diverse cosmopolitan society governed by ethical and politically binding communal interests emerging from the culturally, geographically, and racially uprooting experience of transatlantic slavery. Harper continually criticized Northern capitalism and its racist modes of societal organization, alerting the reader to an understanding of freedom different from the individualist or capitalist-progressive versions often associated with "uplift." Yet, she certainly could not be called nostalgic for the Southern tradition of "white" blood kinship with its materialist excesses and aristocratic antebellum heritage. That in-between position informs Harper's creole and temperate cosmopolitanism. Iola asks Harper's question: "To whom to-day is the world most indebted—to its millionaires or to its martyrs?" She continues:

"The leader of a race to higher planes of thought and action, to teach men clearer views of life and duty, and to inspire their souls with loftier aims, is a far greater privilege than it is to open the gates of material prosperity and fill every home with sensuous enjoyment."[22]

In both *Minnie's Sacrifice* and *Iola Leroy*, Harper criticizes the excesses of Spanish and French Catholic creoles, but also of Northern capitalism and racism. Her opposition to the excesses of capitalism and her recognition that the modern Western world was founded in the transatlantic slave trade do not lead to simple acquiescence to a Northern Anglo-Protestant work ethic or ideology. On the one hand, the criticism of wealth resounds through all her works and indicates a departure from laissez-faire universalism or detachment. Universalist bourgeois cosmopolitanism of this sort drew on but diverged from the initial Enlightenment cosmopolitanism articulated by Immanuel Kant. According to David Harvey, "As Kant pointed out, a certain kind of cosmopolitanism necessarily follows on the material spread of trading and commercial relations between peoples. This underpins the bourgeois cosmopolitanism that Marx and Engels evoked in *The Communist Manifesto*. Yet, as Marx and Engels also concede, there is something positive and constructive about the bourgeois construction of the world market."[23] Harvey asks a question Harper might have pondered from a different location and time: "How can a more far-reaching and progressive cosmopolitan project—such as that of universal communism—be constructed on the ruins of the bourgeois order?"[24] Harper imagines cosmopolitan "communities of interest" as foundational for a transnational creolized American identity in the Reconstruction era. Additionally, her involvement in temperance movements led to a conviction that a temperate practice of restraint, self-denial, and sacrifice should be the basis for a new type of creole, cosmopolitan, and transnational civilization to oppose the rise of clannish forms of community, consumerism, and bourgeois excess.

Harper's work explored the history of creole cosmopolitanism as a first step toward tempering an increasingly Anglo-Saxon national American identity. Yet, she also surveyed diasporic and black nationalist forms of democratic community. In a discussion of Harper's posthumously published "Fancy Sketches," Carla Peterson contends that Harper's "self-conscious literary nationalism . . . distinguished her from . . . other black women activists," and a commitment to "maroonage," particularly in the "Palmares community," presented Harper with "an ideal form of government."[25] Peterson's argument situates Harper's focus on "racial uplift" in a transnational and diasporic context, but the debate over Harper's commitment to a black nationalist racial identity continues.

In *Minnie's Sacrifice* and *Iola Leroy*, Harper's protagonists are white enough to pass and are raised ignorant of their African blood. Iola discovers her origins under circumstances that echo the tragic mulatta motif: her white creole father dies of yellow fever and her white racist creole uncle, who vehemently opposed the marriage between Iola's parents, finds a way to nullify the will that would have left Iola, her siblings, and her "quadroon" mother (whom she believes to be white creole) free and wealthy. However, neither Iola nor Minnie become victims but instead challenge white supremacy by refusing to "pass" even when they could and by dedicating their lives to their "people" as educators. Though Minnie is lynched in the end, her death is viewed as a holy "sacrifice" for her race. The powerful gesture of refusing to pass has led many critics to situate Harper within a black nationalist and racial uplift discourse. Leslie Lewis concludes that Harper's use of "biracial characters" culminated in a powerful choice: "a rejection of whiteness and an affirmation of blackness as a racial identity."[26] Other critics note the ambiguity of the outwardly "white" characters' rejection of "passing": such descriptions might indicate a commitment to racial uplift, an acceptance of one-drop racial categories, or an attempt to mollify the white readership.[27] Harper's commitment to recovering an "African" diasporic identity rooted in the raced experience of transatlantic slavery is undeniably a thread throughout her work. However, her attention to *créolité* as creating racial ambiguity—black creole or white creole—emerged as a counterpoint to one-drop racism in the United States in her effort to reimagine a hemispheric identity.

In *Minnie's Sacrifice*, *Iola Leroy*, and much of Harper's temperance fiction, allusions to her characters' origins in New Orleans and their creolized identities suggest a new temporality and a new geographical setting from which to imagine a trans-American identity tempering an increasingly Anglo-Saxon narrative of laissez-faire cosmopolitanism. While some critics argue that the setting of *Iola Leroy* is vague—and this is partly true—the novel requires significant geographical repositioning as the narrative shifts in time from before the Civil War to the Reconstruction present and in space from one location to another.[28] Unlike Chopin and Cable, Harper is not a landscape writer and often indicates place names using dashes. However, *Minnie's Sacrifice* and *Iola Leroy* possess clear indications of their characters' general locations, beginning with Haiti and New Orleans, and Harper does not situate recovery as a placeless utopia. Temperance is crucial to Harper's new temporality and American space that opposes the association of excess with creole and resituates creole as a possible site for reconstruction and recovery.

AMERICAN CREOLIZATIONS: NEW ORLEANIAN AND HAITIAN COSMOPOLITES

When reflecting on William Wells Brown's creole stylistics, I employed Edouard Glissant's discussions of creolization as a cultural and linguistic process resulting from the slave trade and characteristic of the signifying structures of Caribbean and particularly Martiniquean "transplanted" peoples.[29] Whereas it is used in linguistics for specific practices, the word "creole" is commonly used now, as Ralph Bauer points out, "to denote a 'black' person or a person of mixed racial heritage." The modern usage derives from "a semantic shift that took place only in the context of the nineteenth-century post-colonial United States and Caribbean, primarily Haiti."[30] The meaning of the word varies according to the geographical and historical context. Bauer explains that prior to the nineteenth century, the "imperial world" used the word in a "broadly *geographic*" register to connote an inhabitant of a "European territorial possession outside Europe, either of European or African descent," who had been born in the colonies rather than in the mother country. The term likely comes from the Latin "*creare*, to make, to create, i.e., something new" and was first used in "Western languages as a Portuguese neologism (*crioulo*) in a colonial New World context—to distinguish Black slaves born in the Americas from those brought from Africa." In the Spanish register, the designation more commonly described colonial "settlers of European ancestry."[31]

In Europe the process of "creolization" was usually "evidence of a cultural 'degeneration'"—that is, becoming like the "Indians."[32] John Stewart points out that for the Spanish, though creole originally "referred to those born of Old World parents in the colonies," the connotation changed as a result of the racial intermingling of Spanish, native islanders, and African slaves.[33] Bauer shows that for the Old World, this "darkening" led to the idea of cultural degeneration based on "humorial theory" conjoining cultural and physical development with climate. "White" European creoles, usually French or Spanish, strove to distance themselves from any association with Africans, though their authority in the eyes of many Europeans residing in Europe was already in doubt because of the belief that spending time in the American lands would taint one's intellectual capacities.[34]

Because of the whitening of "creole" by those European Americans who defensively clung to the remnants of white Europeanness, African Americans outside of Louisiana have viewed the appellation with a hermeneutics of suspicion. Many understandings of the term still operate from the "one-drop" theory of white racial superiority. This means that intelligence and the panoply of "civilized values" accrue to the white race, and any approximation of these values is presumed to derive from the amount of white blood possessed. In addition, creolization too often fails to acknowledge the racial sexual terror committed on enslaved women forced to become human breeders and to bear children who would be human commodities owned by slave masters. This point seems to direct Carla Peterson's interpretation of "foreign creoles," such as the white creole who raped Minnie's mother in *Minnie's Sacrifice*. In light of this history, however, Harper disrupts a foundational meaning of white superiority in the United States by undermining the meaning of "white" creole. "One-drop" theories dissolve through imaginative representations of ambiguously white/black creoles and through a reformed creole cosmopolitanism.

The Louisiana Territory, where the language and practice of creolization has a long history, serves as the setting for many of Harper's novels. This place is prominent in *Minnie's Sacrifice* and *Iola Leroy*, but in other novels this geography's residue surfaces in characters' names and in the ambiguities around cultural and racial identities. Despite this, the cultural ambiguity of her characters, which unsettles readerly assumptions about racial and ethnic background, has been largely overlooked in criticism of Harper, though there is no dearth of discussion on race. New Orleans looms large in many of Harper's works, and in *Minnie's Sacrifice* we learn that slaveholder Bernard Le Croix owns a plantation on Red River near New Orleans.[35] Addressing the racial intermixtures in New Orleans, John W. Blassingame notes, "By the time Reconstruction began, miscegenation had been going on for so long that more people of both the 'white' and 'Negro' populations in New Orleans had ancestors in the other race than did the residents of any other city or state in America. In fact, the population was so mixed that it was virtually impossible in many cases to assign individuals to either group."[36] By making New Orleans the originating locale of her novels, Harper implies that the meaning of America as a cosmopolitan civilization should not be limited to New England or the Northern metropoles, nor even to a thriving Southern port such as Charleston, but equally and especially should include the one place in the United States that possessed an acknowledged tradition of creolization. While her novels deal with empirical issues of race mixture, Harper's uniqueness lies in her suggestion that creolization is a major source of cultural knowledge.[37]

Thus, although there is an affirmation of African American identity and the "race" in Harper's works, the extent of her narrative sympathies with racial and cultural indeterminacy has not been fully considered.[38] As Julie Cary

Nerad contends, "Rather than assuming that the child Iola is black passing as white, ... if we disregard U.S. racial logic, then the adult Iola is as likely to be passing as black."[39] Nerad argues that Iola makes a choice to be black and that the ideology of racial uplift has skewed our perceptions of racial identity in Harper's work.[40] Though I disagree that race could ever be viewed as a "choice" within the structural and legal context of one-drop racism, I share her sense that the focus on uplift has overshadowed many subtleties, such as cultural ambiguities and transnational forms of identity.

While supporting aspects of Northern Anglo-Protestant ideology (self-reliance in particular), Harper criticizes the specific racism conjoined to an "Anglo-Saxon" identity. She suggests that white creole and black creole heritages of the South may be a positive source of identity and cosmopolitan "civilization" if white creoles acknowledge slavery and Africa as sources of their identity. Her fictional works, including both the later *Iola Leroy* and some of her early, racially neutral literature, challenge readers to consider transnational cultural identities as points of contact in reconstructing an America unbounded by the discourses of race that often accompany nationhood.[41] The early Louisiana Territory and the history of New Orleans and Haiti shape the names and cultural identities of Harper's characters, who are predominantly French, Spanish, and African creole emigrants from Haiti. As such, her reflections on Reconstruction return to the origins of "American" identity in a hemispheric context. The historical backdrop of Haiti and New Orleans suggest cultural and racial ambiguities informing a limited and rooted cosmopolitanism: limited by the mark of *créolité* and the excesses of the slave trade and rooted in the interested community of recovery and temperance.

New Orleans has long been imagined in literature, culture, and politics as transnational and cosmopolitan. In 1803, Jefferson's Louisiana Purchase doubled the size of the United States, and the diversity of the region derives from both its French and Spanish origins, initially through French colonization and then through the Spanish claim on the territory from 1763 until 1800. Its inhabitants had African, indigenous, Spanish, French, Canadian, Acadian, and Mediterranean backgrounds. The vast territory would become crucial to national expansion and imperialism, shaping the meaning of American civilization. Without the success of the Haitian Revolution and French preoccupation with the island, Napoleon would not have abandoned the claim to Louisiana and his dreams of a North American empire. French and Catholic rule influenced the nature of slavery in the Louisiana Territory. Some of the racial and cultural intermixtures resulted from the fact that under the prerevolutionary

Black Codes, the "Code Noir" of Louis XIV, slaves were permitted to "purchase their freedom."[42] Rather than legitimating revolutionary freedom, Charles H. Long points out, Jefferson's purchase and "the Americanization of the territory was synonymous with a commitment to the extension of African slavery as a fundamental institution of American society."[43]

One can witness the Americanization of New Orleans in George Washington Cable's fiction, which is set in the time of the Louisiana Purchase. In his novel *The Grandissimes* (1880) he is critical of the white French and Spanish creoles in New Orleans and attentive to the racial intermixtures inherent—but often denied—in their identities: "Those Creoles have such a shocking way of filing their family relics and records in rat-holes."[44] Cable clearly shows the impact of Americanization in 1804 and the fear of the Haitian Revolution. Racial tensions and claims to whiteness by creoles increased: the one-drop rule and the expansion of slavery led families to examine racial identities previously left ambiguous. The novel addresses this through the white creole Honore Grandissime's attempt to achieve restitution for his mixed-blood half brother. As patriarch, Agricola Fussilier, Honore Grandissime's uncle, raves:

> The smell of white blood comes on the south breeze. Dessalines and Christophe have recommended their hellish work. Virginia, too, trembles for the safety of her fair mothers and daughters. We know not what is being plotted in the cane-brakes of Louisiana. But we know that in the face of these things the prelates of trickery are sitting in Washington allowing throats to go unthrottled that talked tenderly about the "negro slave"; we know worse: we know that mixed blood has asked for equal rights from a son of the Louisiana noblesse, and that those sacred rights have been treacherously, pusillanimously surrendered into its possession.[45]

The narrator tells us that Agricola, though appearing to be white and believing he is white, descends from the Aztec "Indian Queen" Lufki-humma. Rather than acknowledge his mixed blood, Agricola "whitens" as a result of the Haitian Revolution and the Louisiana Purchase, after which Spanish and French creoles lost their sense of authority and legitimacy. Creoles increasingly reacted violently toward and distanced themselves from the (outwardly) mixed-blood siblings they had previously tolerated. Cable's creoles are examples of the complex system of racial intermixture and concubinage. Cable describes increasing tolerance in New Orleans, though racism continues, and he specifies Haiti's significance in the region. His characterization of white creoles also parallels Harper's in many respects.

In the Reconstruction period, Harper would have been familiar with Cable's popular writings, though *Minnie's Sacrifice* (1869) was written before Cable's works, which were published in the late 1870s and 1880s. Cable's stories and novels implied "that Creoles are racially as well as nationally indeterminate."[46] This intermixture of French, Spanish, African, and Native identities contrasted with the "cultural homogeneity" of his "U.S. characters," who "are rigidly Anglo in cultural and racial origin.[47] Jennifer Greeson argues that this depiction of "a creolized and historically liminal Louisiana thus illuminates what Sandhya Shukla and Heidi Tinsman recently have called the 'transnational process of domination.'"[48] Reconstruction was a crucial turning point in the expansion of the United States and the beginning of its imperialist ethos, against which Harper attempts to revise the nature of American civilization and temper the excess of both Southern creole racial aristocracy and Northern Anglo-Saxon Protestant racism.

Cosmopolitanism, transnationalism, and creolization predominate in discussions of New Orleans in hemispheric American studies, challenging the centrality of New England as the epistemic center for the foundation of the United States. Matthew Pratt Guterl comments that in the mid-nineteenth century "travel accounts often explicitly set New Orleans in a hemispheric—and not a nationalistic—milieu, especially when the subject was related to trade or slavery, or when the focus was on polyglot populations and multicultural lifestyles."[49] The southern Louisiana region also presented the racial and cultural ambiguity of "creole" to the American imagination as the country attempted to consolidate a Northern and predominantly Anglo-Saxon vision of its racial-national identity. Cable shows how "white" creoles attempted to assert their own cultural distance from African heritage, often denying their genealogies. In effect, "creole" came to mean a Louisianan of white European (French or Spanish) derivation. In contrast, when speaking of those with African blood, the racial classifications of "quadroon" or "mulatto" are used. Although Harper follows the normative use of "creole" and employs prominent theories of natural history, her discourse undermines claims of whiteness on the part of creoles and places European "white" creoles and African "black" creoles on the same level because so many of her characters are of one-eighth African blood but pass as white creole. In other words, she counters the central national-racial vision of the reconstructed United States. The Louisiana Territory, and New Orleans in particular, becomes the locus for this possibility because of its diversity, its history as a central trading port, and its role as the site for colonial powers to present competing meanings of "civilization."

In fact, the reader is often unclear about the racial background of Harper's characters when she disturbs the presumed Anglo and clearly "white" or "black" racial dichotomies by turning to creolized cultures. For example, in *Trial and Triumph* (1888–89) the protagonist has the French name Annette Harcourt, but she is clearly black in appearance—her entire family is described as such. Given this, one assumes that her fiancé, Clarence Luzerne, is also African American. Toward the end of the novel this racialized assumption is momentarily troubled—perhaps mainly for North American readers who might not expect such subtle attention to cultural distinctions—by the appearance of Marie Luzerne, who identifies her heritage as "creole." Marie, Clarence Luzerne's long-lost wife, resurfaces just as he is to wed Annette Harcourt. In Marie's words, "I was born . . . in New Orleans. My father was a Spaniard and my mother a French Creole."[50] Creole here indicates racial intermixture: Marie claims that though the Catholic Church will recognize the marriage with a Spanish Catholic husband, her mother could not "contract a civil marriage, which would give her the legal claims of a wife," presumably because of her African ancestry.[51] Harper creates ambiguity by writing "French Creole" without intending the European colonial born. She also suggests a stronger possibility for equality within the Catholic Church than within American civil society—departing from her pronounced Protestant affinities.[52] Harper furthers this ambiguity in *Iola Leroy* when she disturbs the whiteness associated with "creole." Foreshadowing events later in the book, Camille comments to Louis Bastine, an attorney who has come to Ohio to capture Iola, "I always feel sorry . . . when I see one of those Creole girls brought to the auction block. I have known fathers who were deeply devoted to their daughters, but who through some reverse of fortune were forced to part with them."[53] In other words, Iola is "one of those Creole girls."

In *Iola Leroy* the "white" meaning of creole as of European descent is normative; this is clear because the white slaveholders Eugene Leroy and Alfred Lorraine are creoles. They are "of French and Spanish descent," and Eugene Leroy is "the only heir of a Creole planter."[54] As Iola tells the story of her history, the reader learns that the Leroys were from New Orleans, although Eugene moved his racially intermixed family to a Mississippi plantation and still took the children to the Catholic church in New Orleans.[55] Early in the novel, when Eugene (Iola's father) announces to his cousin Alfred that he is to be married, Alfred replies, "Is it one of those beautiful Creole girls who were visiting

Augustine's plantation last winter?"[56] We know "creole" in this context means being of European descent, particularly when Eugene Leroy remarks, "The wedding is to be strictly private. The lady whom I am to marry has negro blood in her veins," to which Lorraine replies, "The devil she has!"[57] This presentation of creole as white European may imply that Harper has accepted racial binaries of black and white or, perhaps, that her white Protestant audience would not be as attentive to the subtle ambiguities throughout the narrative that result in the progressive destabilizing of whiteness.

To be sure, for Harper's white Protestant readers, "creole"—and its associations with Catholicism, diversity, and non-Anglo heritage—may also suggest a disposition prone to excess and lack of restraint, but the concept is more than this. Eugene Leroy, an orphan with "vast possessions" and "without the restraining influence of a mother's love or the guidance of a father's hand," often squandered his "abundant leisure" in his youth, indulging his "unsettled principles, and uncontrolled desires" in the pursuit of "ease and pleasure." Yet, countering the suggestion that Catholicism in the South leads to creole excess, his luxury entails attending "watering places in the North."[58] Notably, Harper balances potential stereotypes by remarking that the North encourages intemperance, even if Leroy's creole, motherless, and wealthy background may have contributed.

In the earlier text *Minnie's Sacrifice*, also set near New Orleans, the word "creole" is not used, but creoles are main characters. Bernard Le Croix is a white Spanish and French creole and the presumed father of Louis, a black creole enslaved through hypodescent. Louis, ironically, is outwardly white and can pass. The ethnic, cultural, and racial irony emerges when Louis is eventually sent to the North to attend school after Le Croix's daughter, Camilla, rescues him from slavery by persuading her father to let her "bring him up as a white child."[59] A few pages later the narrative implies that Bernard is Louis's father and that adopting him and sending him North to be educated "suited him; for then he could care for him as a son, without acknowledging the relationship."[60] Louis Le Croix is so white that in response to her father's query "Who ever heard of such a thing as a Negro being palmed upon society as a white person?" Camilla exclaims, "Negro! Pa, he is just as white as you are, and his eyes are as blue as mine."[61] Indeed, unaware of their implied biological relation and the indeterminacy of creole identity, Camilla raises him as a white creole brother. Additionally, Minnie Le Grange is whiter than the "whites" in the area. Like Louis, she is born of concubinage, from Haitian creole refugee descendants. So white is Minnie that Le Grange jokingly reassures his white friend Josiah Collins, who is taking her North to live with a Quaker family, "The child is whiter than you are, and you know you can pass for white."[62]

As levels of creolization—whether of transplanted Europeans or through racial intermixture—unravel in the novel, so does the U.S. national story and the fictions of whiteness and Anglo-Protestant origins. Bernard Le Croix "was the only son of a Spanish lady, and a French gentleman, who were married in Hayti a few months before the revolution."[63] The narrator is sympathetic toward the Haitian Revolution, "which gave freedom to the Island, and made Hayti an independent nation."[64] Of course, not many Anglo-American writers would have commended the revolution; the United States did not officially recognize Haiti as an "independent nation" until 1862. As the central origin for these creole characters, Haiti also suggests another revolutionary beginning for "American" identity during the Reconstruction period. Haiti, as I pointed out in the discussions of Delany and Brown, was a *lieux de mémoire* for many African Americans. Haiti represents the first modern black republic and is part of the broader transatlantic revolutionary ethos; furthermore, like New Orleans and southern Louisiana, it counters the white narrative of U.S. national history. In Haiti, systemic slavery had ended, a grave contrast to the U.S. situation in which, ironically, slavery remained essential to the foundation of the republic.

Like many Haitians, the Le Croix family was drawn to Louisiana: "Preferring a climate similar to his own, he bought a plantation on Red river, and largely stocked it with slaves."[65] Harper's attention to the climate insinuates the theme of natural history. Debates over the climate and the development of culture existed from the classical era forward, and in the revolutionary age, Thomas Jefferson in his *Notes on the State of Virginia* challenged this European view of the American climate and natural history as potentially having degenerative effects on white European creoles. On the other hand, Jefferson also used the Enlightenment discourse of race to elaborate the presumed reasons African slaves could not excel in intellectual, cultured, and literary pursuits on the new continent. Jefferson praised the oratory and the potential capacity for civilization and genius of Native Americans. But when he considers Africans in the New World, Jefferson argues that their race—their "nature"—has made them unsuited for intellectual pursuits. In Bauer's words, "If the American environment did not have a degenerative influence on human culture . . . but African American creoles were obviously (to Jefferson) inferior, it must be that Africans had arrived in the New World already as a distinct 'race.'"[66] According to Bauer, debates over creolization placed a new focus on "nineteenth-century scientific debates about race."[67] Of course, Harper's works were written long after Jefferson's, but ideologies of natural history and scientific racism had not disappeared. By presenting the main families of *Minnie's Sacrifice* as Haitian refugees who bring their slaves to a semitropical climate similar to that of Haiti, Harper implies that the abilities and talents of African creoles and European creoles are equivalent. Many writers presented the transition in Reconstruction as "from European to U.S. rule." Cable simultaneously presented the Louisiana region as a tropical scene of degeneration: "The 'Creole' locals of tropical America are not able to transform their own colonial way of life in order to participate in historical progress and develop their own territory."[68] Again, in this period the climate is often viewed as nurturing shiftlessness and lack of initiative. Nonetheless, Harper criticizes Northern Anglo-Saxon "progress." Indeed, the North commonly appears with ambiguity, even when fighting for the end of slavery; as Iola's Uncle Robert remarks, "I think that some of these Northern soldiers do two things—hate slavery and hate niggers."[69] And Iola and Minnie are both prevented by Northerners from attending school or workplaces once their African blood is discovered. In other words, while Harper clearly admires certain ideologies and character traits of Anglo-Saxon Protestantism, she depicts Northern racism as consistent with asceticism, individualist detachment, and "pride."

For instance, in *Minnie's Sacrifice*, Harper contrasts Anglo asceticism with the lifestyle of European white creole Bernard Le Croix. While wasteful, he is also a literary and cultured character: he "devoted himself to poetry and the ancient classics; filled his home with the finest paintings and the most beautiful statuary, and had his gardens laid out in the most exquisite manner."[70] He is also more sympathetic to Louis's plight than the average white slaveholding father would be, even though we are aware at the opening pages that he had likely taken Louis's mother "Agnes, fair, young and beautiful . . . with not power to protect herself," as his concubine.[71] His refined and sympathetic disposition derives from the fact that, as the narrator notes, "being a member of two nations having a Latin basis, he did not feel the same pride of race and contempt and repulsion for weaker races which characterizes the proud and imperious Anglo-Saxon."[72] His Latin identity poses a greater sense of possibility in this earlier novel. Surely Harper also agrees with Iola's white creole and cosmopolitan father, Eugene Leroy, when he offers a defense of African historical genius to his wife, Marie:

For years, when I lived abroad, I had an opportunity to see and hear of men of African descent who had distinguished themselves and obtained a recognition in European circles, which they never could have gained in this country. I now recall the name of Ira Aldridge, a colored man from New York City, who was covered with princely honors as a successful tragedian. Alexander Dumas was not forced to conceal his origin to succeed as a novelist. When I was in St. Petersburg I was shown the works of Alexander Sergevitch, a Russian poet, who was spoken of as the Byron of Russian literature, and reckoned one of the finest poets that Russia has produced in this century. He was also a prominent figure in fashionable society, and yet he was of African lineage. One of his paternal ancestors was a negro who had been ennobled by Peter the Great. I can't help contrasting the recognition which these men had received with the treatment which has been given to Frederick Douglass and other intelligent colored men in this country. With me the wonder is not that they have achieved so little, but that they have accomplished so much.[73]

After sending his children to Ohio for their education, Eugene Leroy had hoped his children would travel to France, where they would not suffer from the same "caste feeling" and would be able to participate in "the best circles of art, literature, and science."[74] Harper also shares Eugene Leroy's valuing of an interracial aesthetic. Yet, challenging Leroy's cosmopolitan character, she promotes a more pragmatic and rooted sense of cosmopolitanism grounded in a moral duty to redeem the history of slavery and the colonization of "America." Her characters would not run to France or pass as white (creole) European.

Though Harper is often viewed as championing almost exclusively Northern virtues, such as industry, thrift, and self-reliance, *Iola Leroy* and *Minnie's Sacrifice* offer contrary visions of transnational development that consciously revise creole cosmopolitanism to place aesthetic and cultural openness within rooted communities. Bernard Le Croix's virtues are his creole identity and literary aesthetics, as well as his striking lack of self-reliance in some matters. The narrator tells us that he was in fact quite dependent on his daughter, Camilla, after losing his wife: "He superintended the education of his daughter, because he could not bear the thought of being separated from her."[75] Not every white Creole in Harper's work developed the dignified cosmopolitanism of Le Croix; Minnie's white creole father, for instance, presents an image of shiftlessness and excess: "Le Grange, like

Le Croix, was of French and Spanish descent and his father had also been a Haytian refugee. But there the similitude ends; unlike Le Croix, he had grown up a gay and reckless young man, fond of sport, and living an aimless life." He pursues the "beautiful quadroon named Ellen."[76] Again, the racial demarcation of "quadroon" rather than creole implies that creole is a white European transplanted identity. Her daughter Minnie, however, would be closer to "white" in appearance, and thus more proximate to "creole." Clearly, Harper is not pursuing a racial ideology stemming from the superiority of white blood and appearance. She seems more interested in the liminality afforded by creolization.

Bernard's daughter, as Leslie Lewis indicates, presents a possible point of healing and understanding between the races.[77] Camilla Le Croix, despite being "petted" and smothered by her father, lacks "female relatives to guide her." This lack of a white creole mother places her in even closer contact with the influences of the plantation: "She had no other associates than the servants of her household, and the family of Mr. Le Grange. Her mother's nurse and favorite servant had taken the charge of her after her death, and Agnes had been her nurse and companion."[78] Camilla is even closer to blackness than the average prototypical white woman, and she becomes an abolitionist sympathizer: "She had lived so much among the slaves, and had heard so many tales of sorrow breathed confidentially into her ears, that she had unconsciously imbibed their view of the matter; and without comprehending the injustice of the system, she had learned to view it from their standpoint of observation."[79] While Camilla does not quite arrive at the position of the "other," we are left wondering about her pure whiteness as much as we are about Minnie Le Grange's. By acknowledging her "blackness," Minnie sacrifices not only her privileged place within white supremacy but also her life, when she is lynched by the Ku Klux Klan while teaching the former slave children in the newly freed territory.

Nevertheless, the problematic negative rhetoric of natural history and the potential limitations of the climate persist. Later in the novel, after participating with the slaves in the Civil War, Louis assumes his position as leader of "our race" during Reconstruction and speaks with a Union soldier, who announces his lingering racism by stating, "As to intermarrying with them, I am not prepared for that."[80] Louis, a product of interracial union, says that marriage "and social equality among the races will simply regulate itself."[81] This resonates with the claim Harper made in speeches that the newly emancipated were not seeking "social equality" but rather "Christian affinity." Indeed, in an 1888 speech she criticized Southern women in the WCTU for conflating the two issues, thus appealing to their sense of Christian duty to override their racism.⁸² An irony, to be sure, is that that all her characters are creole and socially equal in some respects, but actual social equality entails a long battle to overcome "custom and education." Louis, nevertheless, enunciates views on the climate that indicate natural differences between races and cultures: "I believe that what you call the instincts of race are only the prejudices which are the result of custom and education, and if there is any instinct in the matter it is rather the instinct of nature to make a Semi-tropical race in a Semi-tropical climate."⁸³ It is unclear whether the narrator entirely agrees with Louis's climatological interpretation, but the idea that natural history need not justify social inequality based on race reappears in Harper's later work.

Toward the end of *Iola Leroy*, and in a tense Reconstruction environment, an intellectual discussion raises issues about the benefits of African colonization and the development of American "civilization." A *"conversazione"* is organized for "thinkers and leaders of the race to consult on subjects of vital interest to our welfare."⁸⁴ Through the dialogue, Harper touches once again on notions of natural history and intellectual development. As these thinkers debate the merits of colonization, Miss Delany rejects the idea of going to Africa: "'America,' said Miss Delany, 'is the best field for human development. God has not heaped up our mountains with such grandeur, flooded our rivers with such majesty, crowned our valleys with such fertility, enriched our mines with such wealth, that they should only minister to grasping greed and sensuous enjoyment.'"⁸⁵ The character's name might be an ironic allusion: it is well known that after the failure of Reconstruction, Martin Delany returned to support emigration even as he criticized colonization organizations organized by white abolitionists.⁸⁶ Her name could also be an allusion to Lucy Delaney from St. Louis, who was no supporter of colonization and whose autobiography and petition for freedom—she argued for the enforcement of the law of matrilineal descent—was published in 1891, a year before *Iola Leroy*.⁸⁷ Harper's Miss Delany touches on the crux of a problem when she notes the "Semi-tropical" region's "fertility" and the widespread "grasping greed and sensuous enjoyment" dominating the area during Reconstruction and after. The discussion continues: "'Climate, soil, and physical environments,' said Professor Gradnor, 'have much to do with shaping national characteristics. If in Africa, under a tropical sun, the negro has lagged behind other races in the march of civilization, at least for once in his history he has, in this country, the privilege of using climatic advantages and developing under new conditions.'"⁸⁸ However, several participants counter the view that climate leads to racial degeneration.

For instance, the Honorable Dugdale reminds the group of a key passage from Song of Solomon: "I am black, but comely; the sun has looked down upon me, but I will teach you who despise me to feel that I am your superior."[89] These lines recur elsewhere in Harper's work and indicate her connection to African American Christianity, particularly the AME Church.[90]

The use of climatological references in Harper's works, then, seems to be directed primarily to entertain the ideals of a variety of readers who would be familiar with the racial and geographical associations. While not precisely mollifying an audience who shares in these stereotypes, Harper does not simply acquiesce to the idea that Louisianans must possess a "Semi-tropical" inclination to dissipation (and "Africans" an even worse predisposition to shiftlessness). Notably, at the end of *Iola Leroy* all the remaining members of the Leroy family, along with Dr. Latimer, Iola's husband, settle in North Carolina—which, though "Southern," seems to represent a liminal point between the plantation culture of the South and the extreme individualism of the North.

The characters in *Iola Leroy* depict some common readings of the South and particularly Louisiana as a racially and culturally degenerate area in desperate need of Northern education, industry, and progress. The typically Northern concept of self-reliance emerges, but in Harper's work it entails communal commitment and integrity.[91] These ideals are presented along with a transnational vision to promote a rooted cosmopolitan identity, bound through slavery, rather than a narrowly defined nationalism or laissez-faire cosmopolitanism.

FROM THE EXCESS OF CREOLE SLAVERY TO TEMPERATE COSMOPOLITAN CIVILIZATION

The meaning of cosmopolitan identity and creolized space in Harper's fiction counters the more abstract universalism common in Enlightenment ideals of the "citizen of the world," who could be viewed as rootless and privileged, even if tolerant.[92] Harper's cosmopolitanism applies to those who recognize the role of slavery in shaping the American character and understand that temperance is needed to redeem the modern world from the excesses of its founding. In her novel *Trial and Triumph* (1888–89) slavery is used as a metaphor that speaks to the structure of democracy in the Reconstruction South, in particular the reliance on "social customs" and public opinion. Sounding like Alexis de Tocqueville, who repeatedly criticized the tyranny of public opinion as a main problem with American democracy (and whom Harper had read), Mr. Thomas states, "I think there never was slave more cowed under the whip of his master than he is under the lash of public opinion. The Negro was not the only one whom slavery subdued to the pliancy of submission. Men fettered the slave and cramped their own souls, denied him knowledge . . . and the Negro, poor and despised as he was, laid his hands on American civilization and has helped mould its character. It is God's law."[93] Achieving social equality or changing public opinion, Harper understood, was not a practical goal in her immediate environment. As Louis noted in *Minnie's Sacrifice*, "I want to see this newly enfranchised race adding its quota to the civilization of the land. . . . We demand no social equality, no supremacy of power. All we ask is that the American people will take their Christless, Godless prejudices out of the way, and give us a chance to grow, and opportunity to accept life, not merely as a matter of ease and indulgence, but of struggle, conquest, and achievement."[94] The "ease and indulgence" was not only associated with white creoles and chattel slavery, but also with many white women, North and South, as well as Northerners driven by capitalist and intemperate profit during and after Reconstruction.

While Harper's temperance fiction sometimes places faith in women's desire to protect the domestic realm and achieve "enlightened motherhood," she was not convinced that white women's views, white women's voting rights, or public opinion more generally would challenge racial oppression. In her 1866 speech to the WCTU, titled "We Are All Bound Up Together," Harper remarks, "Talk of giving women the ballot-box? Go-on. It is a normal school, and the white women of this country need it. While there exists this brutal element in society which tramples upon the feeble and treads down the weak, I tell you that if there is any class of people who need to be lifted out of their airy nothing and selfishness, it is the white women of America."[95] While Harper's comments here are directed at the racism within the women's movement, the points could be extended to the WCTU, to which Harper nevertheless remained committed.[96] Harper's temperance fiction, while seeming to be racially neutral, also destabilizes the nature of racial identification. She presents creole characters, making it difficult to assign the stereotypes often promoted in white temperance literature linking inebriety to blackness or black *créolité* and racial contamination through the slavery to the bottle metaphor. In doing so, she undermines the white center, or racial purity, of the audience and its presumed racial neutrality.

For Harper, chattel slavery was intertwined with American civilization to such an extent that its aftereffects—"recklessness," indulgence, and "selfishness"—affect the possibility for temperate cosmopolitanism. Recklessness, such as that expressed in intemperance, and violence, such as that enacted in lynching, were conjoined: "'Slavery,' said Mrs. Leroy, 'is dead, but the spirit which animated it still lives; and I think that a reckless disregard for human life is more the outgrowth of slavery than any actual hatred of the negro.'"[97] Toward the end of the novel, the hero and cosmopolitan creole Dr. Latimer claims, "We have had two evils by which our obedience to law has been tested—slavery and the liquor traffic. How have we dealt with them both? We have weighed in the balance and found wanting. . . . The liquor traffic still sends its floods of ruin and shame to the habitations of men, and no political party has been found with enough moral power and numerical strength to stay the tide of death."[98] A few pages later, he concludes, "In civilized society . . . there must be restraint either within or without. If parents fail to teach restraint within, society has her check-reins without in the form of chain-gangs, prisons, and the gallows."[99]

Dr. Latimer, like most cosmopolitans of the Enlightenment ethos, expresses concern with "restraint either within or without," paralleling what Norbert Elias called the "psychogenetic" and "sociogenetic" processes of civilization. The concept of civilization is Eurocentric, and even if the oppressed countered that vision with alternate models of African civilizations, its emergence depended on the opposition to "primitives." As Elias points out, civilization began to correspond to "civilized behavior" particularly during the French Revolution, but the concept was later used to describe and justify the process of colonialism throughout the West.[100] It had broadly transnational implications, though it could also correspond to specific national, religious, or political visions. Latimer recognizes the need to control affect, drinking, and other intemperate and excessive behaviors on the psychogenetic and sociogenetic levels.

Harper's vision of a creolized and cosmopolitan civilization is a reminder of the heritage of slavery and of the need for restraint and temperance in civilization. Nonetheless, discourses of temperance and "civilization" often run counter to the indeterminate, open modes of identity suggested by a creolized space. To be sure, racial intermixture often converged with alcoholism and was equated with cultural and national degeneration of the body politic. Walt Whitman vividly depicts this process of mental, racial, sexual, and national deterioration in his early temperance novel *Franklin Evans; or, The Inebriate: A Tale of the Times* (1842), which in 1888 he "vehemently disavowed," remarking that he only wrote the popular novel for "profit" rather than any support of temperance, though he was an earlier member of the Washingtonians.[101] His protagonist's descent into inebriety and insanity is interlinked with racial intermixture. As Debra Rosenthal points outs, Whitman "exploits the indeterminacy and flexibility of language to advocate racial temperance in a liquor-temperance tract. . . . Miscegenation, like alcohol, is a dark blot on the U.S. character and a threat to a healthy U.S. C/constitution."[102] In much temperance literature, the inebriate is imagined as one who has "literally lost his whiteness," and in *Franklin Evans*, the protagonist's demise is paralleled by his "change of skin color."[103]

Whereas Harper uses Haiti and black creole identities as potential sources of strength, critique, and transnational identity, Whitman does the opposite. Franklin marries a "Creole" slave woman named Margaret, with "a complexion just sufficiently removed from clear white, to make the spectator doubtful whether he is gazing on a brunette, or one who has indeed some hue of African blood in her veins. Margaret belonged to the latter class." Franklin's marriage with Margaret occurs "under the influence of the liquor" and in "drunken vagaries . . . quaffing bottle after bottle with the planter."[104] When he sobers up, he is filled with "disgust" and begins to "hate her."[105] Margaret eventually becomes a demented, vindictive murderer, killing Mrs. Conway, the white woman Franklin Evans marries after abandoning Margaret. We are also told that Bourne's father, Evans's Southern "drinking buddy" and fellow bachelor, "had come over from France, during the troublesome times there, in the latter part of the last century."[106] The implication is that he is "perhaps a slaveholder originally from Haiti."[107] State-level reform triumphs through the signing of the temperance pledge, and in his "'mania' abstract whiteness is the solution to the nation's internal flaws. . . . As a banner in Franklin's imagined city declares, 'The Last Slave of Appetite is Free.'"[108] This problematic desire for "purity" seemed to preoccupy much of temperance movement.[109] Alcoholism and race, though long explained by scientific theories, became even more subject to medicalized discourses in the postbellum period: the disease concept of alcoholism became more pervasive and ethnology more popular in explanations of insanity and criminal predispositions. Harper may have been trying to avoid conflating inebriety with either blackness or the "reckless" white or black creole when she identified the blue-eyed, blond African creole and cosmopolitan Dr. Latimer as the healer of intemperate slavery.

By addressing the process of creolization in shaping New World civilization, Harper undermines the equation of temperance with white purity and inebriety with blackness. Indeed, Northerners in a rush to profit from establishments like the "grog-shops" in *Iola Leroy* were responsible for many of the problems with Reconstruction. As Aunt Linda says to Robert, "Dem Yankees set me free, an' I thinks a powerful heap ob dem. But it does rile me ter see dese mean white men comin' down yere an' settin' up dere grog-shops, tryin' to fedder dere nests sellin' licker to pore culled people. Deys de bery kine ob men dat used ter keep dorgs to ketch de runaways. I'd be chokin' fer a drink 'fore I'd eber spen' a cent wid dem, a spreadin' dere traps to git de black folks' money."[110] As with chattel slavery and kidnapping runaways for profit, "Yankees" continue to be complicit with racial oppression in their individualist concern for profit. When Robert tries to understand the problems with white Northerners and racism by querying whether "the temperance people want colored people to vote the temperance ticket," Aunt Linda comments that yes, but "culled people gits mighty skittish ef dey tries to git em to vote dare ticket 'lection time, an' keeps dem at a proper distance wen de 'lection's ober. Some ob dem say dere's a trick behind it, an' don't want to tech it. Dese white folks could do a heap wid de culled folks ef dey'd only treat em right." Aunt Linda—and Harper—views the alcoholism of former slaves as resulting from not having many other options; liquor is cheaper than other forms of entertainment: "I beliebs we might be a people ef it warn't the mizzable drink."[111] Indeed, Harper supported prohibition and, though she did promote self-reliance and self-respect, indicated that alcoholism needed to be addressed on a larger societal level as part of the "inherited sin" of slavery and the implicit creolization of America.

In her fiction, this recovery entailed at least two processes. First, prohibition was necessary, as indicated by Aunt Linda's predicament in *Iola Leroy* and Dr. Latimer's condemnation of the liquor trade. Second, support groups countered the idea that the passions could be controlled by a simple act of self-control; self-reliance and control may emerge from group support, but it does not originate on its own. In the temperance novel *Sowing and Reaping*, Charles Romaine has little self-control, nor can he acquire it without support and a temperance group pledge of abstinence: Romaine is a "confirmed drunkard."[112] He is, from Harper's perspective, accurate in his criticism of his father: "'To-day,' he said to himself, 'he resolved to cut loose from me apparently forgetting that it was from his hands, and his table I received my first glass of wine. He prides himself on the power of self-control, and after all what does it amount to? It simply means this, that he has an iron constitution, and can drink five times as much as I can without showing its effects, and to-day if Mr. R. N. would ask him to sign the total-abstinence pledge, he wouldn't hear to it.'"[113] Full of denial, Romaine Sr. offers Charles a drink, even after he knows his son is an alcoholic, an act that leads to Charles's relapse and subsequent death.

In fact, everyone surrounding Charles is complicit with and enables his inebriety. Jeanette, unlike Belle, chooses to marry him even though she knows he has a problem: "True to her idea of taking things as she found them, she had consented to be his wife without demanding of him any reformation from the habit which was growing so fearfully upon him. His wealth and position in society like charity covered a multitude of sins."[114] Charles Romaine is still regarded as a "victim." And even in light of the wealth and indulgence that is his birthright, he is unable to take individual responsibility without a larger community intervention. Individual responsibility in recovery from alcoholism, as in recovery from other forms of slavery, must be accompanied by "communities of interest" and widespread social support. To be sure, Paul Clifford, Belle's suitor, is a successful temperance reformer largely because his mother recognized the propensity to inebriety in their genetic history (his father was an alcoholic). She was "fearful that the appetite for strong drink might have been transmitted to her child as a fatal legacy of sin." From that awareness of inherited and generational sin, she made sure her son inculcated the virtues of "self-control" and knew of the "horrors of intemperance."[115] Clifford's mother recommends self-control, but this form of restraint does not depend on the individual aloof from social and inherited attachments. She acknowledges that alcoholism, like slavery, is not the fault of the victim, and that a much larger network of support is needed for healing.

In Harper's text the links between slavery and inebriety are clear when Belle Gordon, the protagonist of *Sowing and Reaping*, asserts, "I don't know; there are two classes of people with whom I never wish to associate, or number as my especial friends, and they are rum sellers and slave holders." Belle defends her position to her naive and vain cousin, Jeanette Roland, the soon-to-be-wife of Romaine the drunkard, by claiming that, like a "pirate," "they are both criminals against the welfare of humanity. One murders the body and the other stabs the soul."[116] One is condoned by the "law," and the other is "outside" of it. Belle describes a scene in Tom Anderson's saloon: one man says he "feels that [he is] a slave," even though he thinks at some point he "could have broken [his] chain." As with his poor son Charley, "liquor was his master."[117] By Harper's time the slavery metaphor had been applied to a number of social maladies, including inebriety, but it permeates all her work. In her 1888 speech "The Women's Christian Temperance Union and the Colored Woman," Harper wrote, "Victor Hugo has spoken of the nineteenth century as being women's era, and among the most noticeable epochs in this era is the uprising of women against the twin evils of slavery and intemperance, which had foisted themselves like leeches upon the civilization of the present age."[118] Notably, the AME Church's publications were centrally concerned with the historical meaning and mission of Christian "civilization" as it related to

Africa's role, slavery, and the impact of intemperance in the formation of the modern economy.

Harper's novel understanding of temperance and freedom draws on Africanist understandings of slavery's impact on intemperance to challenge those propounded by the WCTU, which tended to highlight a pure white identity as the basis for a sober Anglo-Protestant Americanism. For example, even Frances Willard, the well-known daughter of abolitionists and left-leaning president of the WCTU, found herself succumbing to American racial strictures when she indicated in an interview with Lady Somerset that "illiterate" and "shiftless" blacks might be responsible for the failure of prohibition in the South. Ida B. Wells famously responded to this remark and noted that Willard had never opposed segregation in general, lynching, or segregation in the WCTU.[119]

Racial tensions within the WCTU coincided with the end of Reconstruction, but Harper supported many of its social and political reforms. In 1877 the WCTU had publicly renamed itself the "Home Protection Movement."[120] Such a public goal of protecting the home was, to say the least, ambiguous for many African American members. As Glenda Elizabeth Gilmore notes, many white temperance reformers, including a large number of Southern white women in the WCTU, still considered slavery to be a "civilizing" force: without slavery, they argued, the African population might be extinct within a generation or two, presumably because of a proclivity to inebriety. And, given that one drunken incident involving a black man might invoke an "'I-told-you-so' editorial in the local white newspaper," African American women involved in temperance reform "worried not just about the pernicious effects of alcohol on the family but also about the progress of the entire race."[121]

The protection of the nuclear American family meant creating a space apart from the public and, of course, a space of white purity not to be contaminated by surrounding racial degeneration and inebriety. Harper's works "promote the norms of domesticity, but in so doing deconstruct the conventional binaries of masculine/feminine and public/domestic."[122] For displaced African Americans, civil public space and private domestic place could never be neatly divided. One's entire social and corporeal self had to be integrated into the public and vice versa, whether at home, at the dinner table, or in political space. For the WCTU, the home became a place to "protect." This desire can be seen in some of Harper's temperance fiction, but for Harper the home was also opened up to public discussions and debates, as is shown is the *"conversazione"* toward the end of *Iola Leroy*. Her independent women also challenge the norms of heterosexual union and women nurturing men as the way to fulfill ideals of domesticity. As Belle Gordon comments, "It is better and wiser to stand alone in our integrity than to join with the multitude in doing wrong."[123] The tyranny of public opinion, even within groups, however, had taken the place of the "communities of interest" and debate that Harper viewed as crucial to racial recovery and Reconstruction.

Harper forcefully addressed the faulty reliance on social customs and the tyranny of public opinion in her 1888 speech on the WCTU. She did not mince words in "We Are All Bound Up Together," the speech given more than twenty years earlier, in which she confronted white feminists in the audience for their racism: "You white women speak here of rights. I speak of wrongs. I, as a colored woman, have had in this country an education which has made me feel as if I were in the situation of Ishmael, my hand against every man, and every man's hand against me."[124] Even so, Harper's fictional temperance writings and her work in general are sometimes conciliatory, particularly because they seem to address a white audience.

The racial identities of Harper's protagonists are often not brought to the fore. And even when it is clear, as in the cases of Iola Leroy and Minnie Le Grange, that the characters are "black," they are not, as they have been passing as "white" for much of their lives. In Harper's temperance fiction, as Debra Rosenthal argues, "this tension between Harper's career, which was devoted to black distinction, and the racelessness of 'The Two Offers' and *Sowing and Reaping* questions the relationship between writer and reader. If author-audience ties abide by affiliations of race, then color may determine who reads and misreads the texts. Possibly Harper modulated her stories to suit her audience."[125] The audience for those "deracialized" stories published in "Afro-Protestant" presses was largely African American.[126] Because she was speaking to a predominantly "black" audience, Harper may have encouraged an empowering vision of "moral reform" through temperance within the black community without feeling the pressure of placing questions of race to the fore.[127] Rosenthal contends that Harper's temperance fiction presents "deracialized," racially indeterminate characters. So neutral are the descriptions that they "could be black," but their "middle-class" lives seem "indistinguishable from those of white Americans." Rosenthal understands this as inculcating a sense of "dignity" in the audience because the characters have the same "entitlement and ability as whites to circulate in brilliant society and be concerned with moral reform."[128]

Building on this interpretation, DoVeanna S. Fulton suggests that "temperance transcends racial categorization" and that Harper was writing for "multiple audiences," especially those who were "familiar with the historical and contemporaneous circumstances of the mainstream temperance movement and social reform in general."[129] Fulton follows P. Gabrielle Foreman in considering the "histotextuality" of Harper's writing, a process that presents homonymical associations between characters and other historical figures to which particular readers would be alert. Clearly, by naming her main character Iola Leroy, Harper employed, in Foreman's words, "the noted pen name of the fiery radical activist, Ida B. Wells." Wells and Harper shared much in common, and the use of the name Iola may "associate" Harper with Wells without calling to mind Wells's forceful condemnation of lynching and tendency to draw attention to details of sexual abuse and violence."[130] Fulton makes the interesting homonymical association of Josiah Gough, a reformed inebriate in Harper's *Sowing and Reaping*, with the well-known Washingtonian John Gough and suggests that the white reformer's histotextual appearance "destabilizes" readerly expectations of "racial categorization," making it "moot."[131] Rather than being "moot," Harper's temperance fiction displays traces of creolized cultural (and racial) meanings that have all but been elided in favor of racial uplift and the idea that temperance transcends race.

For example, in *Sowing and Reaping*, despite the lack of specific geographical setting, Harper's characters all have French or creolized names that complicate their racial and cultural positioning. In light of the creolized names in *Minnie's Sacrifice* and *Iola Leroy*, it seems logical to suggest that the names in her "deracialized" fiction are also creole. (One might also notice the French derivation of Minnie Le Grange and Iola Leroy.) The use of the shortened French "Belle" Gordon as the protagonist's name presents a cultural ambiguity, as does her cousin's more obvious French name, Jeanette Roland.[132] John Anderson (a very British name) is the saloon keeper, a figure who plays the villain in most of Harper's fiction, thriving on excess, beauty, and luxuries for the "price of blood." Anderson thought he would make a fortune by ensnaring "misguided slaves of appetite" to his "palace of sin." Paul Clifford, Belle's suitor, has a more ambiguous name.[133] Charles Romaine, with an unmistakably French creole name, is the main drunkard in the novel.

Romaine was originally Belle's suitor, but she rejected him because of his intemperance. Her cousin Jeanette, however, acquiesced to Romaine's behavior even though Belle forewarns her, "He is a slave who does not be, in the right with two or three [drinks]."[134] It was, in Belle's view, Jeanette's womanly responsibility to discourage Romaine from drink and to refuse a domestic union without reform; indeed, part of her domestic duty is to reform, though Harper does not place domesticity as the ultimate goal of womanhood. (This point comes to the fore in "The Two Offers." Janette, the protagonist, thrives without a man and is not afraid of the societal stereotype of "old maid." Belle is not afraid to remain as such either.)[135] Charles Romaine eventually succumbs altogether to the demon drink when he slips on ice in a drunken stupor and is unable to save himself, despite his earlier efforts to moderate and control his "appetite."[136] Appetite can be compared to the passions, and the visceral inability to restrain the passions is triggered in slavery to drink. While Harper may be suggesting a predilection to drinking and excess as specific to the creole, others are equally affected by drink. Being unable to restrain the passions and denying the problem seem to be criticisms directed at the Romaine family.

While the race of the characters remains ambiguous throughout the novel, toward the end Belle says to her mother, "I have often heard papa say that you were the first to awaken him to a sense of the enormity of slavery. Now mother if we women would use our influence with our fathers, brothers, husbands, and sons, could we not have everything we want?" The passage seems to imply that Belle is a white person or an elite free black person—or, more likely, creole—and the audience appears to be white women who, the mother explains, need to have even more "influence" than the desired "vote" can bring. They need the "sense of responsibility which flows from the possession of power"—"an enlightened and aggressive power."[137]

Likewise, her temperance story "The Two Offers" (1859)—though published in the *Anglo-African*, a periodical "designed to educate and to encourage, to speak for and to black Americans"—presents as its protagonists Janette Alston, a "pale intellectual woman," self-made and recognizing the meaning of sacrifice, and her cousin Laura Lagrange, the "only daughter of rich and indulgent parent."[138] One might assume that Laura's indulgent past and her resulting lack of discernment in marrying a "vain and superficial" inebriate is a corollary to her creole character and name. It seems unlikely, however, that a white Northern audience would assume these characters were black creole. Moreover, the subtleties in background would have to be gauged by a culturally and racially astute audience, particularly because French creole names in racially unmarked fiction might imply white characters to many audiences comfortable with black and white binaries. Nonetheless, Harper's temperance fiction suggests the predilection toward unrestrained appetite in creoles and emphasizes the need for community to cultivate the self-reliance and cosmopolitanism manifest in the black creole Dr. Latimer of *Iola Leroy*. As with chattel slavery and racial intermixture, denial is at the heart of alcoholism in the Romaine family. For white Northerners, individualist greed detached from community allows for profit from racism and intemperate consumption of alcohol and other luxury commodities.

Though she did not self-identify as creole, Harper was often characterized as such, and early in her literary career Harper was questioned about her identity. As Foster points out, "Commentators often mentioned her color. One described her as 'a red mulatto,' and reporter Grace Greenwood volunteered that she was 'about as colored as some of the Cuban belles I have met with at Saratoga.' Harper's own letters note that members of her audience often debated whether she was an African-American or 'painted' to appear as one."[139] Baltimore, where Harper spent the first twenty-five years of her life as a "free" black, was part of a slave state but also a cosmopolitan port city shaped during Harper's lifetime by the Haitian Revolution.[140]

Creoles in parts of the world that have undergone colonization and domination in the modern period define the formative site for a cosmopolitanism that would prevent the erasure of the colonial experience. Creolization becomes a precise critical stance for a total transition and transformation. The meanings of "creole" during the nineteenth century vary—from stable European transplanted identities to racially and culturally intermixed identities. However, some, such as those with "white" creole, cosmopolitan identities, deny their cultural and racial ambiguity through claims of white superiority. While Harper consistently declares a commitment to the "race" in her life and through her characters, she equally attends to an imaginative possibility for transnational creolization, temperance, and an acknowledgment of slavery in the foundations of an American identity. The recklessness and indulgence of some white creole Europeans suggests a tendency to succumb to a pursuit of pleasure and excess unleashed by their rootless creole identities in the New World. Women were never immune to this critique; both Marie Luzerne and Laura Lagrange from "The Two Offers" are spoiled and pampered members of the cosmopolitan leisure class who see little need for restraint and have little awareness of their enmeshment in the inherited sin of intemperance and slavery. This same disposition led Bernard La Croix in *Minnie's Sacrifice* to his "reckless" concubinage of Minnie's mother. The denial of that inheritance would likely have led Minnie and Iola Leroy to the same fate, but they refused to "pass" in the name of white purity—and its intemperance. Harper showed that without recognizing that the transatlantic trade and *créolité* inaugurated modern exchanges between nations and thus needed to be brought to bear on any cosmopolitan sensibility, an "unsolved American problem" would remain.[141]

CHAPTER 5

"The Quintessence of Sanctifying Grace"
Amanda Smith's Religious Experience, Freedom, and a Temperate Cosmopolitanism

> And then I knew how sensitive many white people are about a colored person, so I always kept back.... I was something like the groundhog; when he sees his shadow he goes in; I always could see my shadow far enough ahead to keep out of the way.
>
> There has been no attempt to show a dash of rhetoric or intellectual ability, but just the simple story of God's dealings with a worm. If, after all, no one should be brought nearer to God, and to a deeper consecration, I shall be sadly disappointed; for my whole object and wish is that God will make it a blessing to all who may read it; and with this desire and prayer I send it forth to the world.
>
> —AMANDA SMITH, *An Autobiography*

BEGINNINGS OF A TEMPERATE COSMOPOLITAN FAITH

After returning from her missionary travels abroad from 1878 to 1890 under the auspices of the Methodist Episcopal Church, a primarily white denomination, Amanda Berry Smith published her autobiography, *An Autobiography: The Story of the Lord's Dealings with Mrs. Amanda Smith, the Colored Evangelist; Containing an Account of Her Life Work of Faith, and Her Travels in America, England, Ireland, Scotland, India, and Africa, as an Independent Missionary* (1893). The demonstrative title reveals much about her life while raising many queries. For instance, what are the resources for the several ventures of her life—being a "colored" woman in the latter part of the nineteenth century? What are the primary purposes of the life story? The text, more than five hundred pages long, only partially answers these questions. The spiritual autobiography is structured recursively and often in diary form, recounting seemingly minor events from specific days and moments in her travels rather than revealing a direct path to a sublime resolution: her account is "the simple story of God's dealings with a worm," not a hagiography. Nevertheless, Smith felt she performed her part in promoting the ongoing experience of God's manifest holiness. Smith wrote the autobiography to raise money to support her plans for an orphanage for African American children in Chicago. The struggle for money (whether to provide for herself, her travels, or others), which she also characterizes as a struggle with the devil, was ever present as she developed the meaning of faith and sanctification. Economic support was, however, only one of the ambiguities that plagued her life.

Smith's life and evangelist work is a testament to a novel form of restrained and "temperate" cosmopolitanism holiness. This is partly because Smith came from a generation that continued to feel rooted in the experience of slavery, because she traveled, and because she redefined the issue of temperance as an expression of freedom and grace. Smith was involved with the Woman's Christian Temperance Union (WCTU) from the early 1870s onward and would even become a national evangelist for them in 1893. But her commitment to temperance was foremost an article of faith linked with the gospel temperance evangelism that was key to the initial development of the organization, which was rooted in Methodist theology and the Holiness movement. Over time, in its "Do Everything" ideology, the WCTU would shift away from its roots and instead infiltrate institutions and politics.[1] In addition to differing religiously from other temperance activists, Smith continually endured racism and racial tensions. Smith shows in her autobiography how she shrewdly negotiated with white women reformers and with those reformers who viewed themselves as superior as a result of white supremacist ideology.

Even more than Harper, Smith was circumspect and nuanced, "something like a groundhog" in addressing these issues publicly. She often used creolized diversion as a literary strategy, shifting topics and undermining the authority of white reformers and their desire that she present her life as a moral exemplum. Instead, she offered many possible paths to temperance and freedom. Contrary to Harper's more literary and fictional writings, Smith's public performances and creative writings were nonfictional enactments of grace as an evangelist and preacher of the Holy Spirit. Harper's works not only promoted ideologies of racial uplift but also explored a radically imaginative creolized space for a cosmopolitan, trans-American experience based in temperance. Likewise, Smith's temperance and Holiness faith does not easily fit into discourses of racial uplift, economic success, and liberal individualism. Her very identity as an evangelist, as well as her motive for writing a spiritual autobiography, only secondarily promoted a doctrine of economic advancement or liberal progressive theology. Still, she obviously desired that those suffering from the effects of slavery, colonialism, and poverty in West Africa and in the United States would become self-sufficient and empowered to participate in international exchanges. Moreover, Smith's evangelical form of temperance was bound to the construction of free spaces for conversion. She caught glimpses of those in her childhood through sanctification and in cosmopolitan exchange with others as she traversed the continent and the world.

Religious experience and the camp meeting environment affected Smith's actual freedom and her developing sense of freedom as rooted in community. Smith was born into an enslaved family in 1837 in Long Green, Baltimore County, Maryland, but she was freed by the age of three. According to her account, her parents experienced a relatively lenient form of slavery. The Greens were "a good master and mistress, as was said" (18). (Notably, Smith qualifies the phrase "good master" as someone else's perspective.) They allowed her father, Samuel Berry, to buy his freedom by raising money hiring out his time to perform odd jobs in the area. By 1840 he purchased the freedom of his wife, Mariam Matthews, and his five children who were born in slavery (18). The Greens were willing to free the family because one of their Presbyterian daughters, "Miss Celie," attended a lively Methodist camp meeting and experienced conversion; the awakening led her to desire even more lively services and to "go to the colored people's church" (20). Shortly after her conversion she became ill and died but not, however, without requesting—indeed demanding for three days prior to her death—that her parents let Smith's father purchase his family (21). This early moment in Smith's autobiography frames the meaning of conversion as antislavery, and Smith consistently drew attention to cultivating interracial fellowship and overcoming racism as essential to conversion. The divine experience of "sanctification," or "enduring grace," that she learned through the Holiness movement led to her ongoing commitment to missionary travels and enacting the cosmopolitan blessings of the Holy Spirit.[2]

While Miss Celie's experience of conversion led to antislavery views, Smith later implies that sanctification might not immediately end a racist disposition.

She notes that at a Holiness meeting in 1878 at Horton Street in Philadelphia one woman told her that she used to "dislike" Smith for being "a colored woman." But once "God saved her He took it all out, and now she loves me as a sister and thinks I have a beautiful color! Of course, I call that a good conversion to begin with." Smith continues, "Some people don't get enough of the blessing to take prejudice out of them, even after they are sanctified" (226). Given Smith's emphasis on faith over works, achieving a normative morality was secondary to the cosmopolitan disposition that might result from faith in God through conversion, inspiring openness to others of various colors and cultures. While the Methodist and African Methodist Episcopal (AME) churches denied the possibility of sanctification, the manifest presence of the Holy Spirit, Smith and other African American female evangelists risked alienation by declaring they were sanctified, directly opposing the hierarchical and patriarchal scriptural authority of the church.[3] Essential to sanctification was the ability to overcome "intentional sin," and that seemed like an assertion of purity. However, as Smith makes clear in her autobiography when she recounts her many failings and the degrees of sanctification, both the "blessing" of sanctification and the actions that constitute sin are often ambiguous. Moral norms, for her, are negotiated in relationship with others through trial and error, with the goal of cultivating an egalitarian community free of racial oppression.

Smith's first conversion experience occurred at the age of thirteen at a Methodist church while working as a servant for a white family in Maryland, but she recounts having lost the gift of grace soon thereafter (29). Smith also had a vision while deathly ill as a result of a difficult childbirth while married to her first husband, Calvin Devine. She describes this "trance" lasting "about two hours"; it begins with "a most beautiful angel" appearing to her and "motioning" her to "go back." She descends to "a great Camp meeting" where she preaches to "thousands of people" who are "slain right and left" (42). The vision of camp meeting materializes in her call to preach. Later introduced to the Holiness movement, she experiences "heart purity" and sanctification while living in New York and hearing a voice that directs her to attend the Green Street church of revivalist and Holiness minister John Inskip.[4] Her "enduring grace" in 1868 inspires a persistent cosmopolitan belief that the blessing of the Spirit is meant to overcome racial categories—though she does not succumb to an enlightened color-blind universalism.

She describes her initial revisionary interpretation of scripture in the following passage:

> Somehow I always had a fear of white people—that is, I was not afraid of them in the sense of doing me harm, or anything of that kind—but a kind of fear because they were white, and were there, and I was black and was here! But that morning on Green Street, as I stood on my feet trembling, I heard these words distinctly. They seemed to come from the northeast corner of the church, slowly, but clearly: "There is neither Jew nor Greek, there is neither bond nor free, there is neither male nor female, for ye are all one in Christ Jesus." (Galatians 3:28.) I never understood that text before. But now the Holy Ghost had made it clear to me. (80)

The text from Galatians indicates Smith's rejection of a worldly disposition. Yet the holy message is one of achieving openness and tolerance in human interactions, not simply the adoption of the liberal progressive ideology that became prominent in many abolitionist and temperance reforms.

Few if any Protestant denominations of this period ordained women or allowed them to preach, but one of hallmarks of the Holiness tradition was its espousal of woman preachers. To be sure, the tradition of Christian perfectionism attributes its origins to Charles Grandison Finney, the great revivalist and first president of Oberlin College, a school that admitted African Americans and women. Though they hewed to a conservative theology, the Holiness perfectionists were more likely than not to be abolitionists during the antebellum period. Slavery was denounced not because it was un-American and unconstitutional but because it was ungodly.

Though Smith crossed racial and cultural boundaries in the Holiness movement and the Methodist Church, she retained a significant sense of home in the African Methodist Church.[5] Following a "missionary" path and what I characterize as a cosmopolitan path of freedom, grace, and movement, Smith traveled as part of her conversion as an itinerant preacher at camp meetings and as an international missionary from 1878 to 1890 in the United States, England, India, and West Africa. Smith was among the few women—and even fewer black women—who were evangelists and ventured abroad at the end of the nineteenth century.[6] While she maintained her membership in the AME Church, she struggled as a woman to be legitimated. Her public accomplishments empowered black women, and she was likely the main reason the AME Church changed its policies on female ordination.[7]

Early on, Smith was attracted to temperance as an article of faith, but she did have personal experience with addiction: she describes her first husband's problem with drinking, but she omits mentioning her brother's alcoholism.[8]

She began her preaching career at camp meetings throughout the Midwest and became a member of the WCTU in 1875 as she formed affiliations through the Holiness movement and one of its most prominent founders, Phoebe Palmer. Invited as a result of her connection with Mary Coffin Johnson, national secretary of the WCTU, Smith traveled to England in 1878. The WCTU later appointed her to the position of national evangelist; she declined the offer in 1892 because she was completing her autobiography, but in 1893, with the impending publication of her book, she accepted.[9] To be sure, Smith had many predecessors—she was not the only female African American itinerant preacher to challenge the patriarchal structure of the AME Church or to affiliate herself with the Holiness movement.[10]

GOSPEL TEMPERANCE AS A MODE OF GRACE AND CHARITABLE EXCHANGES

Although the WCTU was initially associated with the evangelism of "gospel temperance" and the Holiness movement, as early as 1876 it publicly renamed itself the "Home Protection Movement." As I noted when discussing Frances Harper, such a public goal of protecting the home was ambiguous for many of the organization's African American members. Temperance, for many African American reformers, encompassed a moderate, antihierarchical redemption of "civilization" and civil behavior—not simply a moralistic reform of family structure. At times Smith promoted norms of Victorian domesticity, and she reluctantly criticized aspects of the WCTU and other white reform organizations. Nevertheless, by preserving God as the external source of charity and the limit of the individual will, she departed from their sensibilities to reimagine the exchange structures of laissez-faire and individualist Protestant theology.

Smith retained deeper ties to gospel temperance than did many members of the WCTU, and this influenced her missionary activity. Gospel temperance focused on saving drunkards and converting them, and it is tempting to view this conversion process as depending on the power of the individual will. However, humiliation before God is much less individualistic than is the restraint negotiated by the liberal subject bereft of an outside limit. Addiction as a matter of individual choice resolved through self-control and the will to purity suggests a cosmopolitanism consistent with the restraining Kantian subject of liberal individualism. In contrast, William Wells Brown's use of restraint was predicated on a liminal, creolized discourse complemented by a sociogenetic emphasis on reforming civil behavior. While not evangelistic like Smith, Brown limits the value of individual willpower in his modified notion of restraint.

The secular programs of temperance promoted by groups like the Washingtonians relied on a certain voluntarism. This contrasted with a view of alcoholism as an original sin or as a disease beyond one's control, a view that developed later. As Katherine A. Chavigny points out, for groups like the Washingtonians, the Good Templars, and the Sons of Temperance, with whom Brown was involved, inebriety was viewed not as a sin but rather as a character defect that could be reformed through sympathy. Many gospel temperance reformers shared the focus on sympathy but were dissatisfied with the refusal of many temperance reformers to call drunkenness a moral or inherited sin that required conversion to evangelical Christianity. During the 1850s, gospel temperance attracted many Protestant converts with widespread revivals, and prayer meetings became more popular in urban environments: "Reforming individuals continued to resonate with evangelical Christians, who believed that social change must begin with a change in an individual's convictions and behavior. By the mid-1850s, the nation was reeling from sectional strife over slavery, controversial prohibition laws, and an economic depression."[11] Gospel temperance as an article and demonstration of faith for those who converted to evangelical Christianity remained popular through the end of the nineteenth century.

While Chavigny suggests that gospel temperance relied on a voluntary change of conviction and character for conversion to sobriety, this is a somewhat general interpretation of religious experience. Many gospel temperance proponents—Smith, for example—knew that simple willpower would not solve addiction without the grace of God. Protestant reformers since Calvin have emphasized that conversion does not result from anything the sinner may do: justification is by faith alone. Smith followed a strong theology of captivity and original sin—founding her persona as a lowly "worm"—that viewed sanctification not as a matter of works but as a matter of faith, humbling the individual will to God and the Holy Spirit's presence. Yet, some individual effort and assistance from other people and institutions were required.[12] Smith consistently opposes voluntarism and accomplishes a creolized cosmopolitan faith contingent on the revelation of God's Word. Though alcoholism is not viewed as an incurable and overdetermined "disease," it is rooted in deeper transatlantic exchanges that Smith as a missionary in Liberia and Sierra Leone worked to reform.

Brown criticized the reliance on voluntarism, sympathy, and affected performances by some Washingtonians, like John Gough; his commitment to temperance was deeply invested in reforming civilization to create a creolized civility and to promote restraint through cosmopolitan association. Membership in many African American temperance associations did not depend on having a drinking problem. Temperance for many African American reformers provided a much-needed civil association that was ecumenical and that promoted a cosmopolitan and restrained character. Nonetheless, as noted in chapter 1, the secrecy of the Masons, the Sons of Temperance, and other temperance associations could be used to exclude and to promote elitism rather than to establish political and economic freedom or to construct a temperate cosmopolitanism and public exchange with others.

Smith repeatedly notes her discomfort with secret societies. Beginning with her second marriage to James Smith, when she moved from Philadelphia to New York in 1865, Smith felt the pains of exclusivity. James was a "Master Mason" and wanted her to participate in "high-toned" clubs. She assumed she might fit in because, after all, she "was high-toned in spirit,—always had been; I think I took after the white folks I lived with; they were aristocratic. So I thought that is a good idea and I will get to know all the nice people; so I joined three different societies" (62). She became "greatly disappointed in the spirit . . . manifested among members." To please her husband she even joined the "Heroines of Jericho," a society for the "Master Masons' wives and daughters" with "flashy times" and "tinsel regalia," but Smith never adjusted to their mentality. After she was sanctified, she experienced the "folly" of these clubs (62). Yet, even in Liberia in the 1880s, Smith had to contend with the club spirit subsuming what she believed was the true sense of sanctification and gospel temperance. According to her account, new immigrants in Sinoe County, Liberia, formed temperance societies like the Daughters and Sons of Temperance, which she felt detracted from gospel temperance and the ecumenical focus:

> March 6. In the afternoon I went to Mrs. Morgan's to meet the lodge of Good Templars, and Daughters of Temperance. It is perfectly wonderful how all these old societies, which had once flourished, but had well nigh died out, began to be revived all over the republic as soon as I had begun the Gospel Temperance work among the young people and children, so that when I asked for co-operation and help, I was told that they belonged to this society, and to the other society, it had gone down, but that they were going to commence again. So to show them that I was with them in anything that was for the well-being of the people, I joined them, and helped what I could. But, Oh, how hollow, and empty, and unreal. After

all it is not the tinsel and show, but it is the real heart work for God and souls that Africa needs, especially. (355)

Smith worked to end the importation of alcohol and the alcoholism of the native Liberians and black immigrants.[13] Her autobiography describes the people's poverty and lack of education, which were only exacerbated by the "liquor trade" and the colonial powers.

Her experience with racism and slavery necessarily affected the way she understood temperance, salvation, and freedom—and the possibility for "home" in the United States or as an international missionary. Rather than redoubling her commitment to the WCTU, Smith's temperance sensibility encouraged alliances with other nondenominational temperance organs in West Africa. She confronted the damaging consequences of the liquor trade in Liberia as the settlers attempted to form a viable republic after being freed or escaping slavery. In 1885 William Taylor, the Methodist bishop in Liberia, "credited her with whatever limited success temperance and holiness enjoyed in Liberia." In 1888 in Philadelphia he commented in a speech, "She went there and throttled the thing—took the lion by his beard in his own den, and on the line of holiness and temperance brought about . . . wonderful change, illustrating what can be done in that line by intelligent, earnest missionary effort."[14]

In contrast, temperance societies often segregated and excluded, making them complicit in the economic, social, and class disparities that Smith highlighted in Liberia. Protecting privacy and civil liberties was more popular than emancipating the oppressed and achieving political freedom through acts of free association in public spaces, such as those enacted by "secret" and private societies. Though seemingly far removed from Brown in her missionary practices, Smith also mobilizes temperance as a cosmopolitan movement that allows her to associate with organizations and people throughout the world. Smith's involvement with gospel temperance and the WCTU demonstrated an awakening from the intemperate commodification of enslaved Africans and African descendants to build a cosmopolitan civilization.

Many problems in Smith's life and her willingness to be the subject of intense scrutiny and criticism by both whites and blacks stemmed from what she prized most highly: her faith in God and the sanctifying grace of her conversion. Her refusal to accommodate to the domestic roles provided for black women at the time and her faith in sanctification provoked her to live without self-righteousness and moral ambiguity. Still, Smith submitted to and perhaps shared many traditional white Victorian values held by the upper-middle-class women with whom she associated. At times, she seemed to long for a similar bourgeois respectability, and she repeatedly expressed her anxiety over public appearances and "propriety."[15] This is understandable given that she was a public figure subject to racialized and gendered gazes. Her reticence may also have arisen from the worldliness involved in a public role as preacher—and the worldly temptations such publicity brings.

For instance, Richard Douglass-Chin highlights Smith's concern about her appearance as indicative of her concern with bourgeois aspirations. In particular, her Quaker-styled bonnet seemed to cause her much anxiety when she became aware that many in Britain only felt it appropriate that Quakers dress in the Quaker style. Smith, however, like many African American female reformers in the nineteenth century, had always worn the dress as a mark of simplicity rather than as an expression of religious affiliation or fashion.[16] Sojourner Truth famously wore the Quaker bonnet and plain dress, as did Zilpha Elaw and other female itinerant preachers: "The plain dress of Amanda Berry Smith and Sojourner Truth and the respectable dress of Frances Harper and Ida B. Wells may have conveyed different religious messages, but their insistence on entering public, white-dominated space as ladies led to at least one similar ordeal—they were all driven from trains, streetcars, or churches because they were black, regardless of what they were wearing."[17]

Other middle-class anxieties plague Smith, but her bourgeois aspirations were not their source. For example, in her autobiography she recounts being anxious about her inability to pay the mortgage that had been secured with the "charitable" help from her white friends, but she never wanted to be a homeowner in the first place. She writes, "I was ashamed to tell anyone, it would look to white people like bad management on the part of those who were my friends. Then I knew what some of my own people would say, and had said already, that I was a kind of a 'white folks' nigger,' and I knew they would say, 'That is just what I told you it would all come to, can't tell me about white folks.' They wouldn't see God in any of it" (232). Notably, Smith is anxious about the response of both the white community and the black community, and, in the end, she is pleased to be rid of the house. The "burden" placed on her by white charity disappears when she departs for England and embarks on her journey to be a missionary to India and West Africa: "So I wrote to Brother Robinson, 'I can't come, but sell the house or give it away, I don't wish it, get your money out, I don't want any.'" She continues, "I was sorry for the good people who had given the money, but could not help it" (233). Her criticism of "charity" was part of her attempt to redefine the exchanges she negotiated with white patrons.

Although performing charitable acts generally was considered evidence of faith rather than earned salvation, many Protestants viewed their performances of charity as warranting some admiration from the receiver (or victim) of such acts. Smith was keenly aware of her position as a charity case and continually thwarted the givers' egotism by attributing all acts to God and God alone.[18]

Of course, the equal economic exchanges of a modern capitalist economy did not exist for black missionaries or preachers of the Methodist Church. As Smith remarks, "I suppose no church or society ever gave a salary to a colored man, no matter how efficient he was, as large as they give to a white man or woman, no matter how inefficient he or she may be in the start; and I think they are generally expected to do more work. This I think is a great mistake." The lack of salary for black missionaries speaks directly to the question that people asked her: "If I think that missionary work in Africa prospers and develops better when under the entire control of colored people, or do I think it is better under the control of white people." She explains that white missionary activities have had greater success than when natives have been left in charge without any financial support. Contrary to Douglass-Chin's suggestion that Smith is "advocat[ing] the preferability of white to black missionaries in Africa,"[19] Smith remarks, "I do not attempt to make any explanation of this; I simply state the facts as I met them" (423), and then comments that the black missionaries are not paid. She leaves it to the reader to discern why white missionaries may have greater success.

Her economic situation and her relationship to white patrons were always tenuous; though an itinerant missionary affiliated with the white Methodist Church, she was not officially funded. She went to Liberia in 1879 without the support of the church, and though some "friends sent sporadic contributions," "the annual sum of about twenty pounds that an Irish woman collected and sent her constituted her only regular income." Notably, most missionaries received five times this amount.[20] This precarious situation is an example of the ambiguous independence and cosmopolitan freedom that characterized her life.

SANCTIFICATION, SPIRITUAL AUTOBIOGRAPHY, AND CREOLIZED PATHS

The independence to live between racial and religious communities as a widowed and single African American woman—and to travel without any significant backing to Great Britain, India, and West Africa—cannot be attributed simply to a willful ego. On the one hand, its basis can be located within the Holiness tradition. On the other, Smith strongly desired independence because she was enslaved as a child and witnessed her mother's determination to achieve individual and communal freedom. While Smith's autobiography may parallel slave narratives, many of the postbellum slave narratives written by men focused on achieving a type of freedom that promoted the Protestant work ethic, individualism, and capitalist values. Following many abolitionists, Smith also promoted conversion and temperance, but for her, temperance was a consequence of holiness and sanctification—freedom—and her autobiography sharply diverges from the success story characterized by Booker T. Washington's *Up from Slavery*. According to Francis Smith Foster, many of the post-Reconstruction autobiographical works "did not dwell upon the horrors of their writers' past conditions of servitude but were instead cheerleading exercises to urge continued opportunities for integration of blacks into American society or to depict black contributions to the Horatio Alger traditions."[21]

Departing from the individualist stance of Washington and others, Smith was sustained by the early depiction of community rooted in her mother's strength. Smith's parents hid escaped slaves as part of the Underground Railroad. During this time, her mother was feared by slave catchers for having once threatened them with a cane when they came by the family home looking for runaways. As Foster comments, "Smith tells us that slavecatchers would come to their house with search warrants but refuse to enter saying to her father, 'We have heard your wife is the devil. . . . You know, Sam, we don't want any trouble with her, you can tell us just as well.'" Foster concludes that many "slave women saw themselves as working toward the progress of their race."[22] Yet, while Smith may be motivated by a rootedness and interdependence inherited from her mother, her sense of journey and mission are also grounded in a cosmopolitan Holiness.

This rootedness to her mother and the Holiness tradition contribute to the creolized style of her autobiography, which in turn parallels the creole and cosmopolitan exchange inherent in her notion of sanctification as an ambiguous faith. Douglass-Chin, for example, notes the numerous slips into dialect, though he argues that Smith tends to repress such connections to the more vernacular black tradition.[23] But his argument presupposes an authentic blackness that becomes troubling in light the literary backgrounds and substantial education of many of the most prominent abolitionists and religious reformers. It is reductive to imply that they are all assimilationist or that their elitism is reflective of white liberal values. On the other hand, Katherine Clay Bassard disputes Smith's comfort with literacy and argues that many African

American female spiritual autobiographies, such as those written by Jarena Lee, Julia Foote, and Amanda Berry Smith, undermine the value of literacy that has been so prized as a path to freedom since Frederick Douglass. Indeed, spiritual autobiographies often approached language more circumspectly than did literary slave narratives. Early in her autobiography, Smith relays the dangers of literacy used by Satan to question God's grace.[24] She describes a book that presented an argument between "an infidel and a Christian minister" that the infidel wins with his relentless questioning. He also momentarily wins Smith's mind until her aunt reprimands her impertinence:

> Then I let out with my biggest gun; I said, "How do you know there is a God?" and went on with just such an air as a poor, blind, ignorant infidel is capable of putting on. My aunt turned and looked at me with a look that went through me like an arrow; then stamping her foot, she said: "Don't you ever speak to me again. Anybody that had as good a Christian mother as you had, and was raised as you have been, to speak so to me. I don't want to talk to you." And God broke the snare. I felt it. (29–30)

Smith's aunt reminds her of her mother's strength, and she "felt it" physically break the spell of sophistry and arrogance that sinful literacy could present.

Smith does not dismiss literacy or reading diverse literature entirely, but emphasizes that one must be cautious about "how" one reads.[25] The emphasis on method leads to a creolized relation to literacy in general, not simply from a religious perspective. The faith of Smith's mother allows Smith to feel rooted in a sanctified strength that counters Satan's consistent queries. Satan's voice constantly presents self-doubt to Smith, which parallels her anxiety in adopting the middle-class white values and judgments about domesticity for African American women. For instance, Satan's voice tries to dissuade her from attending the service of white Holiness minister John Inskip where she becomes sanctified. Not only this, but his voice also warns her not to "shout" and to conform to white values so as not to be excluded: "So when the Spirit came again I would shout; but before I knew it just as though some one threw a basin of water in my face, a great wave came and just as I went to say 'Glory to Jesus!' the Devil said, 'Look, look at the white people, mind, they will put you out,' and I put my hands up to my mouth and held still, and again I felt the Spirit leave me and pass away" (76–77).

The devil often promotes an ideology of white supremacy and patriarchy, not just antiliteracy, and Smith's arguments and faith present a creolized way to live with grace alongside the consistent self-doubt presented in the world. Indeed, Smith often uses a rhetorical strategy of creolization that bears some similarities to Brown's use of the "incidental" and anecdotal in his storytelling. As if to undercut the reader's expectation that important matters will appear toward the end of a religious reflection, Smith tells her audience of white liberal female activists a story about the big bonnet she often wore. Kelly Willis Mendiola notes, "These incidents also worked in a non-challenging way—through the retelling of Smith's own experience—to sensitize Smith's largely white audience to the inconveniences and pain of being black."[26] While the asides and diversions can function in this manner, they operate recursively. Recursion gives a reflective aspect of remembrance to the text, and this keeps Smith rooted to a past community while branching out to multiple stories and points of narration.[27] Moreover, like diversion, it limits the progression of the story, detracting from the main event and dispersing the centrality of one narrative.

As one example of Smith's diversionary style, the following passage shows her straying from the main purpose of relaying her singular path to sanctification and her journey as a missionary:

> How many mothers' hearts I have cheered when I told them that the blessing of sanctification did not mean isolation from all the natural and legitimate duties of life, as some seem to think. Not at all. It means God in you, supplying all your needs according to His riches. I return to my story. Thus as I thought, I asked again, "I wonder why the Lord did not sanctify me fully when he justified me? He was God, and He could have done it; He could have done it all at once if He had had a mind to." Then the question, "Well, why didn't He do it?" and I was blocked. I believe that question was from Satan. (103–4)

As I noted when discussing Brown, diversion functions as parallelism, which leads the reader away from one center or temporal movement to present multiple positions and a liminal, temperate status that refuses to succumb to the grandiosity of the sublime event or singular focus.[28] Smith's story of development is surrounded by the "mothers' hearts" and the remembrance of being bound, even as she moves forward to become an international missionary.

Though the undercurrent of abolitionism and interracial fellowship within the Holiness tradition attracted Smith, she gained strength through both the inner satisfaction and the spaces created through conversion and sanctifying grace. Through the love feasts and camp meetings she attended in the early

1870s, she developed a sense that "God is no respecter of persons."²⁹ Holiness sought not so much changes in the social order as changes to the inner self by achieving freedom from intentional sin and direct access to God's wisdom in the loving grace of Jesus Christ. Notably, Smith interprets American racism within the context of religious experience: "But if you want to know and understand properly what Amanda Smith has to contend with, just turn black and go about as I do.... And I think some people would understand the quintessence of sanctifying grace if they could be black about twenty-four hours" (116–17). She reminds white Protestants of the need to recognize slavery, the experience of being bound as property, as the most fundamental spiritual humiliation. In equating this humiliation with "sanctifying grace," and in expressing and reliving the anxiety of blackness when being viewed as a recipient of white charity, Smith implies (even if she does not always directly state) that holiness entails redeeming unequal exchanges. This is not to say that exchanges will be made equivalent as a quid pro quo, but that those who have been exploited will be recognized as possessing equal though diverse stories, gifts of the Spirit, and talents.

As a missionary, Smith was called by God to travel to West Africa, to the origin of the transatlantic trade (285, 337). Others who wrote letters on her account at the end of her autobiography testify that Smith performed her divine destiny in Monrovia as an evangelist for gospel temperance revivals to assist the newly freed African American Liberians in settling the republic and to convert the native West Africans. Notably, Smith also learns from them how to survive and thrive in the region.

She lived through a new form of exchange and salvation in camp meetings and love feasts, and in her journey to understand the traditions of other cultures while promoting her own orientation rooted in slavery, with a hope for love and mutuality, temperance, and civility. Smith took the Great Commission of the gospel recorded in Matthew 28:19 and Mark 16:15 not simply as Christian doctrine but as religious experience and as the pattern for her life. The Matthean account goes as follows: "Go ye therefore, and teach all nations, baptizing them in the name of the Father, and of the Son, and of the Holy Ghost: Teaching them to observe all things whatsoever I have commended you: and lo, I am with you always, even to the end of the world. Amen." Smith's early religious quest was to find a Christian community that would allow her to realize the meaning and nature of this command. The terrain of her career was literally and theologically the geographical world.

Sanctification and "enduring grace" oriented Smith to a sense of space as a missionary. She attends revivalistic spaces of exchange for conversion and

West African spaces of religious ceremony. When she is first called to Africa she is troubled by not understanding its geography. She recounts being overwhelmed when she first heard of the missionary work in Sierra Leone and Liberia: "I thought the next great qualification for African work, next to full consecration and sanctification, which I knew I had was to understand the geography, so as to know how to travel in Africa" (218). Indeed, she feels she is "too old to learn" to be in a new space and proposes to God that she will send her daughter in the future. Of course, she will come to view her work in West Africa as her primary role in God's plan.

THE TRANSRATIONAL AND THE TRANSNATIONAL: MOVEMENT AND MESSAGE

While Amanda Smith lived a relatively long life, from 1837 to 1915, during a significant period of American national history, none of the events that took place during this time became the identifying context for her life and thought. For example, although she lived during the Civil War and Reconstruction, she devotes hardly any attention to abolitionist movements. When she travels to England—a land well traversed by several famous black abolitionists of an earlier generation—no mention is made of them. And while she self-identifies as a Christian woman and feels particularly at home in Holiness meetings and Methodist churches, her sojourns were not sponsored by any church or denomination. Nor, indeed, does she place much emphasis or value in national identity as an American citizen.

Because Smith's identity is not strictly located within the structures of a stable institution, whether of marriage, church, nation, or ideology, it may seem difficult to discern a central frame for her life. Still, two interrelated expressions of selfhood dominate: her Christian vocation and her travels. She fits within a context described by Ira Berlin as the "freedom generation," for whom freedom was related to movement and travel. According to him, "The same spirit that pushed former slaves to take a new name sent them in search of a new residence." Given that slaves had been "bound" to plantations, with limited opportunity to travel freely except with passes, "the ability to move at liberty and to live in a place of their own choosing was one of the rights freedpeople identified most closely with their new status."[30] For Smith, travel was transformed into a mission to achieve the temperate, restrained cosmopolitan Christian salvation of the world. This form of cosmopolitanism denies neither real social injustices and inequities nor the social attachments that bind people to places and causes. Yet restraint and movement promote a faith in the new experience of grace created in civil exchanges with others in diverse locations and cultures throughout the world.

Smith's itinerant life, dedicated to promoting and creating sanctified communities, reconstructs a meaning of salvation, freedom, and "home" in response to the pressure of gender roles and domesticity for Victorian women. Indeed, the word "home" appears frequently through Smith's lengthy autobiography, whether in describing her home as a child, the homes she cleaned as a servant and "washerwoman," her home in New York, the home purchased for her by white members of the Methodist Episcopal Church, the homes she stayed at abroad, or the "native homes" she preferred to the hastily built "shanties" prominent among poor and newly freed settlers emerging from American slavery and immigrating to Liberia. That search for home as a new relation to the land through a cosmopolitan disposition toward transnational space directs Smith's pilgrimage and "mission" for temperance and salvation.[31]

The terms "transrational" and "transnational" clarify how Amanda Smith's cosmopolitanism is rooted in the restraint implicit in the meaning of temperance. These terms, Thomas J. Csordas explains, "point to the existence of modalities of religious intersubjectivity that are both experientially compelling and transcend cultural borders and boundaries."[32] Smith's Methodist and Holiness temperance mission directs the emergent space for religious and cultural exchange. Her intersubjective and transnational account of religious conversion, one deepened through involvement with native religions in West Africa, might also be specific to a former slave in search of "space" as home experienced through the Spirit revealed in presence with others, rather than a fixed, nationalist "place." Carolyn A. Haynes notes that Smith, as with other African American female evangelists, often seems subservient, but "instead of being subservient to whites and to men, [she] retranslated the term to mean utter submission to God."[33] However, Smith does not neatly follow the "politics of respectability" that seemed to empower many Christian women emerging from chattel slavery.[34] Instead, Smith emphasizes the phenomenological and ritualistic experience of sanctification. By acknowledging limit and human restraint in transcendence, Christian virtues like temperance are imputed as aspects of a converted disposition.

Smith was married and widowed twice, but these relationships were less than ideal. Her first husband was a "drunkard," and her second husband misrepresented his status as a minister, failing to provide economically and denying her the status of a minister's wife.³⁵ After the death of her second husband, following the path of domesticity was not her preferred method for achieving female virtue. In fact, Smith often struggles with a voice of Satan consistent with the traditional domestic expectations of late nineteenth-century Victorian society.³⁶ Toward the end of her life Smith cared for orphaned children, but throughout the most active part of her life she eschewed domesticity. Smith confidently battles and overcomes Satan's voice, which usually tempts her to perform such sinful duties as, ironically, "look[ing] for a husband."³⁷ For example, at one camp meeting where Smith only had two dollars, with which she was going to purchase new shoes for her daughter, she hears the Holy Spirit tell her to donate the two dollars to missionary work. Satan's voice intrudes: "Your child needs the shoes and you have no more. . . . Your first duty is to your child" (170). Smith continues: "Just then the Devil said, 'He that provideth not for his own household is worse than an infidel.' . . . I closed my eyes and lifted my heart to God and said, 'Lord, I don't understand it, but somehow I feel I have done right.' Then the Lord sent another shower of blessing to my soul. O, it went all through me like oil and honey!" (171). Soon after Smith gives the money, "three one dollar bills" appear under her plate, and she manages to support both her household and international missionary work. Smith's autobiography crafts space for a holy provider; indeed, direct monetary gifts from God facilitate her travels. Rather than seeking a husband and domestic life, Smith relates to God the Father as her home, her intimate other and spouse, and in the process transforms traditional female spaces of domesticity.³⁸ As Elkin Grammer argues, following her conversion and sanctification, Smith "made the most of this literary strategy of "'marrying' God and placing him at the center of her 'domestic' life in her *Autobiography*."³⁹ Although Smith criticizes moneymaking and domesticity, when necessary she adapts a Protestant ethic to help others build themselves economically and socially to enter the international stage.

Without sacrificing care for her biological children, the two children she adopted in Liberia, or those in the orphanage she strove to educate, she undertook a communitarian life as an itinerant missionary preacher traveling to the most faraway places in obedience to the gospel command to "Go ye therefore into the world." "World" for Amanda Smith possessed two interrelated meanings. While it is a geography she traversed in her peregrinations from the United States to the British Isles, India, and Africa, the world also carries a theological sense of the "worldly"—that is, the objects and modes of human life that reflect the prevailing society rather than God.

Her travels were not pilgrimages in any traditional sense and she did not understand them this way, as such rites have no legitimacy within the Wesleyan or Holiness traditions. It is even difficult to refer to them as a "mission" like the missionary ventures of Protestant denominations in which mission boards promulgated strategies, trained missionaries, and provided funding. Despite these demurrers, certain structural traces of both the pilgrimage and the mission arise in her journeys. One might find the inward orientation of Protestant pilgrimage beginning in the work of John Bunyan's popular narrative, *A Pilgrim's Progress*. Though Bunyan's work is from an English Nonconformist tradition, its allegorical and abstract structure and literary style do not match the personal testimonies and spatial experiences recorded in Smith's autobiography. What are the sustaining blessings, the surplus of wealth or grace, the divine excess to be derived from these travels for an evangelist missionary, an African American woman who was born a slave, referred to herself as the "washerwoman," and became an internationally recognized Holiness minister?

Given the lack of home in Smith's life, one might assume that the WCTU substitutes for a genuine home. This is not the case. As an itinerant who expands her "home" to encompass the "world," Smith departs from many of the values held by white women involved with the WCTU. While the WCTU was also rooted in the Holiness tradition and in Methodism, it turned more directly to political activism under the leadership of president Frances Willard. Moreover, such politicization advanced values of "home protection" and domesticity often bolstered by racist depictions of threats to the white "home"—inebriated black men, for example. Ida B. Wells famously criticized Willard in 1893 for comments made about black male inebriety and how the black male vote would threaten prohibition, remarks that were part and parcel of the lynching mentality. Smith was courted and recognized by the WCTU, but she was considered an exotic performer rather than an equal.[40] For instance, Willard recounted listening to the inspirational Smith sing in her rich and memorable contralto at the close of an 1875 camp meeting at Ocean Grove, New Jersey, which had become a Holiness resort where wealthy Methodists congregated.[41] Displaying a problematic "romantic racialism," Willard writes, "I shall never forget one Sunday evening and the surf meeting, of which she was the principal figure." The "African Sibyl" "took possession" of her, evoking tears and "beckoning [her] toward the ocean."[42]

Smith also eschewed ethnicity as a refuge or "home," either through an imitation of white culture or in some form of Afrocentric ideology. Though she valued relationships with white women, Smith criticized deference to white superiority when asked directly. As a black woman in the midst of white authority, she had reason to be concerned about the white response. At an Ocean Grove camp meeting in 1874, one white woman asked her, "I know you cannot be white, but if you could be, would you not rather be white than black?" Smith replied, "No, no... as the Lord lives, I would rather be black and fully saved than to be white and not saved; I was bad enough, black as I am." Smith recounted the woman's response: "How she roared laughing" (118). Using humor to deflect racial tension, she clarified that she was proud of blackness. While sharing many white American Protestant values, she also admired aspects of African-derived cultural practices, including shouting.⁴³ She located the meaning of sanctification and holiness in the experience of blackness and humility, though that experience is being lost, she suggests, by imitating white religions: "We colored people did not use to get up off our knees quick like white folks; when we went down on our knees to get some thing, we generally got it before we got up. But we are a very imitative people, so I find we have begun to imitate white people, even in that. The Lord help us" (162).

AMANDA SMITH'S AFRICAN "COMMUNITAS"?

At no point did Smith express a preference for the culture and manners of whites. While her ambiguous sense of "home" was arguably rooted in the AME Church, she evinces a special and sincere relationship to the indigenous people of West Africa. She admires the spontaneous expressive power of West Africans and of African American congregations, especially the ability to "shout" during worship services. Her concern for Africans and those of African descent acknowledges, on the one hand, her community of origin and intimacy and, on the other, a relationship that approximates what Turner has called "communitas."

Part of Smith's initial trepidation about traveling to West Africa stems from the picture books she read as a child that conjured visions of "a great heathen town. There were the great boa-constrictors, and there the great lions and panthers" (218). This attitude toward the heathen does not entirely disappear from Smith's work (though later, she also includes other Christians and classifies Catholics as heathens, given her evangelical Protestant orientation). For example, in Bombay, India, she remarked, "How sad to see the different idols they worship displayed on their flags and in every possible shape and way. My heart ached, and I prayed to the Lord to send help and light to these poor heathen" (300–301). Nevertheless, she maintained concern for the forms of community she observed, making note of how well the Africans in Liberia and Sierra Leone had adapted to the geography of the region in their buildings and cooking utensils—even recommending native buildings above European-recommended "shanties" that many immigrants from American slavery had the means to build.[44] Significantly, many forms of missionary endeavor—whether in the name of Christianity or secular democracy—neglect this attention to communal, social, and geographical spaces. As David Harvey points out, following World War II in Europe and the United States there are innumerable "examples of grandiose schemes that failed miserably because of a misreading of the geographical and anthropological circumstances. . . . The World Bank has, if the truth be known, a huge dossier of such failed projects in its archives."[45] In contrast, Smith stays attuned to every aspect of the geography to develop empowering relations in West Africa.

Leaving America meant letting go of conceptions of both its mission and its economic progress. Smith shares with many missionaries the goal of converting others to the Protestant faith. Yet her faith surpasses American nationalism and reaches broader Pan-African concerns. As William Walters points out, "Black missionaries also commonly quoted the Old Testament prophesy of David, that 'Ethiopia shall soon stretch out her hands unto God.'"[46] Smith repeats this passage when expressing wonder at her adoption of two West African children—Frances, a Bassa girl, and Bob, a Gredebo boy—who would travel with her back to England in 1889 and attend an English school (392). In her view, they would be future missionaries to the region (398). Ultimately, however, her travels to Africa strengthened her opposition to the liquor trade and commercialism in the region. Some black reformers, particularly those who promoted an emergent Pan-Africanism, challenged the more exploitative aspects of European colonialism. For example, Edward Blyden departed from an American nationalist emphasis or a simplistic acquiescence to Protestant capitalism, though his trust in European forms of government and training for Africans would result in self-government.[47]

While problematic, Smith's criticisms of non-Methodist religion and so-called superstitions, particularly sacred exchanges achieved through pilgrimage, fetish, or sacred space, are also driven by her background as a female formerly enslaved African American. Her choice to be free of worldly attachments is enmeshed in her personal history of being owned in slavery, suffering from racial poverty, and participating in two disappointing patriarchal marriages. She understands sacred value as achieved in conversion and faith—especially through the Holiness and Methodist camp meeting and love feast, rather than through a reliance on people or material objects.

Smith's sense of Christian civilization and conversion differs from that of many American and European Methodist missionaries. Her final reflections focus on the hypocrisy and racism inherent in assuming that immigrants to Liberia would be better equipped than native Liberians to practice Christian civil society. In her words, "I find that human nature is the same in black men, even in Africa, as in white men in America. It is the same old story everywhere: 'None but Jesus can do helpless sinners good'" (437).

In her account of the first Fourth of July she spent in Liberia, Smith indicates the type of Christian missionary she hoped to emulate. The Honorable H. W. Johnson delivered a speech (what she called a "tirade") in which he emphatically declared, "Liberia should be independent in her religions as well as her politics." According to him, the "foreign church" does not come with the "word of God." Rather, it comes with "some old pro-slavery traditions that assign all negroes to inferiority and eternal perdition. They come with all kinds of 'isms' . . . contentions that have caused rivers of blood to be poured out on the earth; contentions and doctrines which not only the people of Liberia do not understand, but which have never been understood by those who bring them to us. You may be sure that any religion that teaches the inferiority of the negro never came from heaven" (334–35). Smith remarks that she was "astonished by the speech," but all the "best people of the capital and of the republic" were present. Toward the end of her autobiography, Smith again expresses support of this critique of the hypocrisy of some missionaries in Liberia. Her religious values sought racial equality at a fundamental level. As part of the Methodist and Holiness ministry, Smith returns her readers and converts to the question of faith alone rather than works; temperance, too, she explained, was primarily accomplished through God's agency, not human effort.[48] Even though she maintained and even strengthened her connection with the WCTU, she only indirectly supported the values of domesticity and Anglo-American nationalism that became hallmarks of the organization.

That being said, Smith viewed most people as "heathen" if they were unconverted or uninterested in seeking sanctification through the practices of temperance and holiness. In 1885, Smith wrote a letter noting how difficult it was to implement temperance and holiness with the African American settlers of the colony and claiming that it would take "ages instead of years to get us out of the ignorance and superstition and everything else that slavery taught us. There is no use of hurrying in Africa."[49] In Liberia her criticism of the backwardness of indigenous Africans and of the former slaves who had immigrated to the colony is balanced by her criticism of the missionaries occupying the region. Indeed, "she encountered ministers and congregations who opposed holiness and temperance."[50] To be sure, temperance is not always viewed as an essential aspect of salvation, nor does it always entail total abstinence—yet it commonly did in Baptist and Methodist circles, particularly among those from the United States. In Smith's case, temperance as total abstinence from alcohol was a crucial expression of a converted and sanctified existence. Crucially, Smith views this opposition to temperance as a matter of Western Christians who "fall into all the customs and habits, and turn from Christianity easier than they turn the heathen from idolatry" (348). The vision of reform and "civilization" may enforce some "Western" values, but the self-critical engagement facilitates the ability of that religious disposition to provide modes of freedom other than individual purity or domesticity.

For instance, in writing about the Bassa in Cape Mount, Liberia, Smith is not entirely derogatory in her description of African religion as "devil worship" (382). Questioning African "superstitiousness" was, of course, not particular to Smith; as Walter Williams notes, "One thing that particularly bothered the Christians was the indigenous belief in witchcraft. . . . Amanda Smith prayed for a woman who was accused of being a witch, and who had to go through a trial by drinking toxic 'sassy wood.'"[51] Preceding the account of this incident, Smith writes:

> I am often asked, "What is the religion of Africa?" Well, where I was they had no real form of religion. They were what we would call devil worshipers. They say God is good; He don't make any humbug for them; so there is no need of praying to Him. But they pray, and dance, and cook large dishes of rice and fish, and set it out of a night so that the Devil can have a good meal. They think if they feed him well, and keep on good terms with him, he will give them good crops and good luck, and keep away sickness. If smallpox, or any sickness of that kind comes to their town, they say it is because somebody has made the Devil mad. (383)

While her characterization might be questionable, rooted in already established views of the Bassa as idolatrous and "fetish" worshippers, Smith's autobiography was dominated by the devil and Smith's own struggles to overcome him and his worldly orders.[52] Her criticism of the Bassa is not that the devil exists but that the devil is treated with such reverence and "idolatry" as master of a certain mundane suffering. In this regard, Smith articulates ideas similar to those of contemporary Catholic charismatics, who characterize the global situation as one in which the place or "legion" of evil has been destabilized.[53]

Perhaps more significantly, Smith is a sympathetic spiritual observer and participant in the witchcraft trial. She describes the case in which the king's wife is accused of witchcraft and, as a result, is made to undergo a test of drinking sassy wood to prove her innocence—if she is innocent she will vomit. The queen is vindicated by her vomit, but Smith awaits the verdict with trepidation; she is not preoccupied with criticizing any superstitions regarding the test but rather "pray[ing] for the poor, dear woman, that God would make her throw up" (387). Then she "trembled [and] said, 'Lord, do make her throw it up'" (388). This direct request to the first-person God is characteristic of Smith's religious disposition. So involved is Smith in the ritual process that one cannot sense her judging a "superstitiousness," but she wants to thanks the Lord for the queen's vomit: "Well, I could have shouted. I said, 'Thank God.' But I didn't say it very loud, for those fellows looked vengeance, and I was afraid they would drive us away. Then she drank the second basinful, and then the third, and threw it up, and she was victor. My! Didn't I come home out of that place jumping? I cannot describe how I felt" (368). Smith does criticize the gender bias of the process of communal judgment and the queen's relative powerlessness, but she also criticizes Christians for similar behavior on other moral questions. In Smith's interactions with native Liberians, she is able to let go of "America" and home-as-place in a transrational and transnational gesture, as she commented the Lord would want her to do. In doing so, she embraces the space of religious and cultural exchange and affects the dispositions of those around her as they affect hers.

Undeniably, white middle-class women in the United States, England, and the British colonies in Africa and India sustained Smith's work with their financial resources and companionship. Yet, while Smith does not deny the relationships, she does not bond with them through communitas—that is, through sharing a common basis for the relationship, especially related to domesticity as the basis for the accumulation of capital and respectability.[54]

In addition to tempering her praise of white folk with reminders of the "quintessence of sanctifying grace," Smith challenges the idea that she is receiving charity or support from white patrons, thus denying intimacy or community. In essence, she deflates the ideals of Northern philanthropists and subtly undermines interpretations of her missionary goals as coequal with Americanism and the Protestant work ethic. In empowering gestures and allusions Smith carefully adapts scripture, particularly lines from Matthew: "Seek and ye shall find" and "All things whatsoever ye ask in prayer believing, ye shall receive" (285). Her use of Matthew leads her to view money and fortune as aspects of a sacred exchange—and she clarifies that she would "never tell people [her] need" but rather make it "known directly to God." She would then pray that God "put it into the head of some of [her] friends" to assist her with money, and it would appear (335–36). Ultimately, it was not the agency of white friends that helped her; rather, she remarks, "God showed me when I had learned to let go of human help and expectation, and trust in Him alone, that He could take care of me without America if He wanted to, for He had sent me to Africa Himself and I must trust Him to see me through" (335). It is clear that Smith has a special regard for the cultures she related to in West Africa—one that almost constitutes a "communitas."

Initially oriented toward salvation and healing, Smith's modified pilgrimage allows for the formation of communitas (and home) along the journey. Communitas, to follow Victor Turner, occurs because of the liminal, in-between status of pilgrims who open themselves to novel experiences in leaving home. Smith's itinerancy is an expression of "homelessness," and female itinerants, particularly those who are African American, depart from the typical domestic sphere.[55] The Holiness tradition with its sanctifying grace as the inward site of God's presence provided an ontological and theological space for being-at-home. In addition, it provided them with a purpose—a divine reason for being in the world as purveyors of the gospel of Christ. For her, the theological norm was religious experience and not a racial designation; God and God alone remained the space and place of home.

HOME, FREEDOM, SALVATION: A RELIGIOUS COSMOPOLITAN IDENTITY

Contemporary discussions of cosmopolitanism hark back to Kant's famous 1784 essay "Idea for a Universal History with a Cosmopolitan Perspective."[56] In it Kant shows how peaceful exchanges and commerce among nations are related to the possibility of peace and the cessation of violence. He probes the sources of discord and the manner in which rationality based on observing nature and societies could bring about a peaceful state of affairs within the international community. Contemporary proponents of cosmopolitanism, even when critical of Kant, however, often overlook the much earlier cosmopolitanism inherent in the religious orientations of Buddhism, Christianity, and Islam.

Kant is attempting to make a case for the establishment and maintenance of peace between institutional forms of human society, whether tribes, states, or races. Diagnosing the "law of nature" through the practice of reason, Kant problematically attributed violence in human society to a state of savagery and heathenism—the lack of the use of reason in human affairs. If this was viewed as true in Kant's time, it has surely proven untrue since then. The nation-state, which Kant viewed as necessary, became the epitome of civilization; it was supposedly based on reason yet has been the source of increasing violence in the modern world. The American republic, the premier democratic nation-state of the modern period, legitimated slavery in its founding constitution. The nation-state has impeded the movement of persons across borders by emphasizing loyalty to a single society over against the universal bonding of humankind.

If the word "cosmopolitan" generally connotes being a "citizen of the world," Smith's life—as a formerly enslaved, noncitizen of the United States who was not even officially supported as a missionary—is a testament to a novel form of cosmopolitanism. She is from a generation that continued to feel rooted in the experience of slavery, who traveled and promoted—and would later redefine—temperance as a global missionary expression of a public religious freedom. Such freedom, an emergent attempt at transnational religious and cultural exchange, allowed for ritualistic and charismatic performances of conversion. For Smith, this temperate and open disposition was nourished in the early experience of free grace; yet the threat of enslavement loomed in her childhood, and even after "freedom" her economic security remained precarious.

The concept of religious pilgrimage illuminates dimensions of Amanda Smith's life. Her journey was, however, accompanied by a simultaneous denial of her travels as pilgrimages—a "revelatory evasion." Indeed, Smith criticized Catholics for attachment to sacred material space, idols, and fetishes. At St. Peters, before journeying to Africa, she criticizes pilgrimage directly, pitying Catholics who come to St. Peter's statue and kiss the foot, "cross themselves and pray, 'That is all they get in return for their long pilgrimages, and their prayers and tears.' How sad! How glad I am that the lines have fallen to me in a more pleasant place, and I have a goodly heritage. Praise the Lord!" (291). Pilgrimage also concerns the healing invoked by the religious encounter with a sacred space, such as St. Peter's. This understanding of the inherent sacred value of material space, even the land itself, is contrary to Smith's Protestantism but also to her sense of relying entirely on the invisible agency of God—beyond national or familial attachment. Notably, Smith is similarly disgusted with an African Christian preacher's hidden possession of "cowries" under his robe, as well as with the Hindi worship of deities of the land (409). This response to pilgrimage is ambiguous; Smith, though a missionary with a goal of saving the "heathen," and one who sees Africa as having an essential role in the development of Christian civilization, seems to be on her own pilgrimage, at least of the sort that Victor Turner described.

Turner highlighted the importance of the empirical and symbolic meaning of "home" in religious journeys. Pilgrimages operate within a dialectic of structure and antistructure. "Home" and "being at home" define the empirical and symbolic structures of stasis and order; in leaving home, the pilgrim disrupts home's stability. While the pilgrim breaks with the order of home, the ultimate goal is to influence the structure of home with new energies and possibilities. Such expectations are an integral part of the structure of most pilgrimages.[57] A sacred space is traversed in the act of pilgrimage. For Smith, "home" has an ambiguous meaning; it does not define a fixed place. She moved through space not to visit some holy site, as with most pilgrimages, but to find human souls in need of the gospel. In her case, sacredness was transferred to an inward religious experience and expressed in the power of the Word of God through the voice of a sanctified messenger. Her movement through space revealed the blessing that God is no respecter of persons or spaces.

In Smith's understanding, "sanctification [was] an instantaneous experience, rather than an ongoing process."[58] Sanctification, conversion, and temperance were the impetus and originating experience, and thus not "home" as a structure of stability and intimacy, that set her on her journey. She discerned very early how this religious experience was based on a biblical foundation, on the Gospels and on the New Testament in general. Three biblical passages, all from the Gospel of Matthew, illustrate the nature and meaning of antistructure as religious experience. First, the Great Commission, "Go ye therefore, and teach all nations, baptizing them in the name of the Father, and of the Son, and the Holy Ghost" (Matthew 28:19), formed the pattern of Smith's life. Second, the situation of her life is almost exactly described by Matthew 8:20: "The foxes have holes, and the birds of the air, nests; but the Son of Man hath nowhere to lay his head." Finally, her radical independence is based on Matthew 6:35: "Therefore I say unto you, take no thought for your life, what ye shall eat or what ye shall drink; nor yet your body, what ye shall put on. Is not life more than meat, and your body more than raiment?" To live out one's faith in this way required temperance and independence from the structures, forms, and conventions of "the world."

Smith's career was independent, utopian, and otherworldly. She was an almost perfect example of life as antistructure rather than life as conventional and institutional. Her critiques were never launched because she had been excluded from some conventional institutional form of culture. Perhaps coincidentally, when she returned to the land of her birth, she went to Chicago to raise money for an orphanage for African American children. In the face of powerful institutions, economic structures, governments, and nation-states, she retreats but remains in the shadowy antistructure to remind humans that they are creatures made in the image of and dependent on God.

Though Smith describes herself as "something like a groundhog," staying out of the way of white people when necessary, there is little denying that she spent much of her life in association with white people and white women's organizations, particularly the WCTU.[59] But to understand this association as simple acquiescence to whiteness or longing for whiteness or money disparages the sheer length of time spent in movement, pilgrimage, and missionary modalities, exploring and testing various forms of "home" and religious exchange between races, religions, cultures, and national ideologies. Indeed, one must pause on the irony of a former slave, washerwoman, enthusiastic missionary, and Holiness preacher spending the end of her life ferreted away in central Florida in a cottage built by a wealthy white landowner and "china manufacturer" who converted at one of Smith's camp meetings and love feasts in Ohio. Living on the periphery of the town George Sebring built, Smith was generally accepted and had a "home" for the final few years of her life before dying of a cerebral thrombosis in 1915.[60]

Epilogue
Tempering and Conjuring the Roots of Cosmopolitan Recovery

> Mars Whiskey wuz right dere an' Mars Marrabo wuz a mile erway, an' so Ben minded Mars Whiskey an' fergot 'bout Mars Marrabo.
>
> —CHARLES CHESNUTT, "LONESOME BEN"

Appetite—restraining and controlling it, or unleashing it through the wild "savagery" of passion—was an intense American problem through the nineteenth and early twentieth centuries. A lack of self-control and a pursuit of excessive passion were often pathologized as illnesses from which the poor, particularly poor races, and "primitives" suffer. Yet, the Declaration of Independence proclaimed "life, liberty, and the pursuit of happiness" as the tenets of faith in a free democratic American identity. The authors addressed in this book criticized the legacy of that pursuit: consumerism, greed, individualism, and objectification of others. Despite this, the promise of freedom has, for many generations, proven intoxicating.

While the freedom found in drinking, excessive consumption, and recreational drug use may be enticing for some, alcoholism and addiction have rarely been associated with pleasure. Jennifer L. Fleisner notes, "Addiction is frequently portrayed as related more to pain than to pleasure, insofar as it is organized around an idea of loss and necessary repetition—an unshakeable longing or craving—rather than the homeostatic ideal of fulfillment."[1] She identifies this pain of addiction in Chesnutt's conjure tale "Lonesome Ben" (1897) and the phenomena of "earth-eating," which eventually kills Ben in the story—as it did many slaves in the African diaspora.[2] Notably, poor whites also engaged in earth-eating, but the white medical institution pathologized the slaves' behavior as an addiction, a further example of the inability to restrain the appetite. Curiously, earth-eating was also considered symptomatic of extreme "nostalgia" and melancholia.

Ben's nostalgia for a homeland is the root of his excessive consumption of clay. African American religion and culture at the end of the nineteenth century can be understood through the use of conjure in Chesnutt's tale.

Chesnutt's portrayal of conjure could be read as another expression of the tempered creolization process traced in different ways throughout this book. Many African American reformers experienced a position of in-betweenness that touches on aspects of excess and moderation, cultural and racial creolization, and the need for restraint in recovery from slavery. While Chesnutt does not literally travel to other continents, he imaginatively explores flight and settlement, excess and limitation, and temperance and conjure. As a lawyer and one of the most well-known African American writers in the postbellum era, Chesnutt presents a creolized and Africanized cosmopolitan religion. In a historical moment of increased violence and lynching following slavery and the failure of Reconstruction, his imaginations of conjure suggest a religion and cosmology replete with transformative metamorphoses. Conjure echoes the longing for a healing relation to the land and the materiality of bodies that traversed the continents in the aftermath of slavery.

According to Yvonne Chireau, conjure could be used to heal or harm, to protect, and to challenge injustice.[3] Reformers promoted healing and challenged injustice through a temperate cosmopolitan disposition, one that emerged alongside European forms of temperance and cosmopolitanism but possessed creolized expressions in bodies, home, and the land. Chesnutt's revisions of conjure show that creolization and cosmopolitanism arising out of the excesses of slavery and colonization can also result in tragedy. The land itself becomes a conjured and consumptive force in "Lonesome Ben," one of the "nonconjure" conjure tales—these are the stories published after *The Conjure Woman* that are narrated by Uncle Julius, like the others, but lack a conjure woman or conjure man. In Chesnutt's world, "conjuring" describes the processes and expressive meaning of a diasporic African American cosmopolitan ethics of restraint, temperance, and limit.

"Lonesome Ben" reveals a complex nostalgia for home and a reciprocal relation to the land in the compulsive addiction to earth-eating. The medical nostalgia manifest in earth-eating sometimes had fatal consequences far beyond what might be experienced in simple homesickness. This nostalgia, Fleisner explains, embodied "a 'false appetite'—false presumably in both its object and its ardor, as well as its lethal result." Indeed, nostalgia was aligned with "cachexia Africana, beginning with a generalized lifelessness, and ending as the weakened patient succumbed to 'intercurrent diseases.' In other instances, the nostalgic deliberately sought to end his own life—and, similarly, some argued that earth-eating was consciously practiced by slaves as a means of suicide."[4] As is well known, many slaves held religious beliefs that in death they would return to their homeland in Africa, and suicide among enslaved people often held that promise of freedom. Fleisner notes that many runaways also suffered from nostalgic earth-eating when mourning the separation from family and friends who were left behind in slavery.

The lack of restraint common to alcoholism parallels earth-eating nostalgia, and we can recall Horton's ambiguous position on "home" when he finally disappears after leaving North Carolina slavery. Horton's poetry echoes a critical nostalgia for his "Southern home," and he is presumed to have once again taken to drink—or flight back to a new settlement in Liberia. Ironically, Horton's life and interest in classical Greek and Roman cultures is similar to Chesnutt's cultural creolizations. Like Horton, Chesnutt came from North Carolina and was preoccupied with aspects of classicism that suggest a republican model of "home" and public exchange for the recognition of genius.[5] His emphasis on transformations in the conjure tales resonates for most readers with Ovid's *Metamorphosis*.[6] Why the preoccupation with classical culture by Chesnutt, Horton, and many slaves and former slaves of the South? As I discussed above, Latin and Greek were common in Southern education, and many slaveholders justified chattel slavery by referencing the republican agrarian dignity and leisure of ancient Roman and Greek cultures.[7]

The ideal of a republic with an elite aristocracy capable of genius, rational or oratorical and creative, enticed some in the post-Reconstruction environment. In *The Souls of Black Folk*, W. E. B. Du Bois defended Latin and Greek learning against the agricultural and technical education promoted by Booker T. Washington. And, drawing on Alexander Crummell, Du Bois developed the notion of a "talented tenth" to lead African Americans. Though often mistaken as a call for upper-middle-class leaders, the "talented tenth" could be drawn from any social class and emphasized the development of public talent and genius for democratic discussion and debate. This "passion for public distinction," "virtue," and "emulation" was a hallmark of the revolutionary (and republican) concept of freedom and was partially derived from models of the Greek polis, elementary republics, and public spaces for exchange. Hannah Arendt elaborated these connections in her book *On Revolution*.[8]

The pursuit of virtue and distinction converges with the temperate disposition and character to which many African American reformers aspired. While the connections of Latin and Greek to slaveholding culture were more pervasive, classical models were also essential to the earliest proponents of democratic freedom and to the founding of the United States and its novus ordo seclorum, as Arendt argues. Despite the hint of aristocratic sensibility in the concepts of virtue and talent, Chesnutt, like Brown, witnessed the racism of those who promoted democratic "equality," progress, and the Protestant work ethic.

While the white Northern, middle-class John narrates Chesnutt's conjure tales, the implied author-narrator does not always share John's views.[9] The story of "Lonesome Ben" follows the model of the other conjure tales: Chesnutt's character Uncle Julius relays the story to his new employers, John and Annie, Northerners who have purchased the old plantation after slavery and keep Julius on for employment. In this case, John inquires whether the clay on the land is strong enough to make bricks, which leads Julius to launch into the story of lonesome Ben to prove the strength of the bricks. In most of the stories, Julius has an economic objective or con(jure) as subtext, and this story is no exception; after telling the haunting story of clay-eating, Julius notes that for ten dollars his nephew could remove the clay.[10] As many have noted, an interpretation emphasizing economic gain falls short of explaining Julius's motives for telling the tales. The stories of transformation are enmeshed in an economic system of retribution and diasporic history. For instance, John ironically characterizes Julius's stories while patronizing him: "Old Julius often beguiled our leisure with stories of plantation life, some of them folk-lore stories, which we found to be in general circulation among the colored people. . . . The most striking were purely imaginary, or so colored by old Julius's fancy as to make us speculate at times upon how many original minds, which might have added to the world's wealth of literature and art, had been buried in the ocean of slavery."[11] The "ocean of slavery" situates the story as part of a tragic transatlantic and diasporic network. Certainly, Chesnutt would not agree with John's dismissal of genius on the part of Africans as "purely imaginary" or "fancy."

Thus, while the stories use conjure to challenge the history of slavery and then Northern exploitation, they also reveal conjure as a consumptive process demanding an ethics of reciprocity—the land itself consumes Ben, as it does Henry in "The Goophered Grapevine" and Sandy in "Po' Sandy." "Lonesome Ben" begins with Ben as an inebriate; he gets drunk whenever he can and disobeys his master by drinking whisky and forgetting his errands. Mars Marrabo threatens him, and Ben reflects on his oppression and decides to run away. While hiding in the woods, afraid to return to the plantation and knowing his master will make an example of him, Ben begins eating the clay to survive. The clay and riverbank is a peculiar color, which foreshadows Ben's transformation: "The water . . . had an amber tint to which the sand and clay background of the bed of the stream imparted an even yellower hue."[12] At first, the clay is all Ben can find to eat and it keeps him alive, but he stays too long (a month) and eats too much. By the time he decides to return to the plantation, thinking that perhaps he can persuade his family to escape with him, he is unrecognizable to everyone—including his son, wife, and master—because he has become the yellow color of the clay. The suggestion of racial intermixture (his friend Primus calls him a "merlatter") ends tragically—"neither this, nor that"—and the folktale seems to suggest that liminality as racial ambiguity ends in isolation and death.[13] Yet, Ben's decision to run away on his own—the idea of bringing his family only comes after a month in the woods—and his excessive consumption of the earth, rather than the consumption itself, also contributes to his alienation and death.

Chesnutt's literary mode is one of creolization. The story intermingles allusions and revisions of Ovid, Virgil, and even Shakespeare. Uncle Julius becomes the creolized trickster figure telling the story. Indeed, in the first story of *The Conjure Woman*, "The Goophered Grapevine," John describes Julius as "not entirely black" and the "shrewdness in his eyes" as "not entirely African."[14] In "Lonesome Ben," when Ben confronts his master, claiming he is indeed Ben, Mars Marrabo replies, "No, I doan know yer, yer yaller rascal! W'at de debbil yer mean by tellin me sich a lie? Ben wuz black ez a coal an' straight er an arrer. Youer yaller ez dat clay-bank, an' crooked ez a bair'l hoop."[15] In despair and lonely, alienated from family, friends, and even his master, Ben goes to the stream to look at his reflection in the water. Unlike Narcissus, he does not fall in love with himself, but he can no longer recognize himself: "He didn eben hab his own se'f ter 'so'ciate wid."[16] The story of Echo and Narcissus appears as the bullfrogs echo in the woods, "Turnt ter clay! Turnt ter clay! Turnt ter clay!"[17] Ben begins to turn to clay and is paralyzed, lying on the bank "as a brick" when the wind comes and "smashed im all ter pieces," and he washes away in the water.[18] John also echoes *Hamlet* by muttering "Imperious Caesar, turned to clay." Julius replies that no, this was Ben, though master had another slave "named Caesar."[19] The ironic reference to Southern slaveholders' condescending naming of slaves as Roman emperors and classical figures revises classical mythology as neoclassical *créolité* in slavery. Chesnutt was well versed in and admired European and classical texts.[20] He does not present a simple opposition in the texts but rather a combination, copresence, and transformation of stories characteristic of creolized writing. Taken on its own, without deriving allusive meaning from Ovid, Virgil, or Shakespeare, Chesnutt's story is one of alienation from home and land.

"Lonesome Ben" is a creolized text, and that creolization is connected with an excessive attachment to the land. Relationships to the land can play an important role in literature, as Edouard Glissant notes in his analysis of Gabriel García Marquez's magic realism: "The relationship with the land, one that is even more threatened because the community is alienated from the land, becomes so fundamental in this discourse that landscape in the work stops being merely decorative or supportive and emerges as a full character."[21] In creole folktales, Glissant explains, there are "two conditions, absence or excess." A castle, for instance, may be described with "two hundred and ten toilets." The descriptions are excessive because "'true wealth' is absent from the world of the plantation."[22] In "Dave's Neckliss," the excessive descriptions pertain to food. The punishment meted out to the enslaved Dave for stealing a pig is to wear a ham around his neck, which leads to his presumably imaginary transformation into a pig that commits suicide by hanging himself in the smokehouse. Consumption of food results in the gruesome consequences of commodification, emphasized further when Julius smacks his lips, relishing a slice of ham, after relaying the story of Dave's tragic transformation. Like Kafka, Chesnutt takes the metamorphosis of Ovid to absurdity.[23] Chesnutt's tale of lonesome Ben is also excessive and opaque in its combination of cross-cultural texts, which could stem from the impenetrable character of the land and its ability to consume those who have been displaced when its limitations and transformations are not understood or revered.

Characters are also transformed into the land in "The Goophered Grapevine" and "Po' Sandy." In the latter story, Sandy is transformed into a tree and brutally butchered. The transformation in "The Goophered Grapevine" is more relevant to the issue of addiction and temperance. Aunt Peggy the conjure woman "goophers" the grapevines as part of a deal with slave master "Mars Dugal" so that the slaves become ill or die when they eat from the grapevines; in return for doing so she receives "a basket er chick'n en poun' cake, en a bottle er scuppernon' wine."[24] Henry visits Aunt Peggy because he ate the goophered grapes without knowing the "conseq'ences," and she gives him a potion that tastes like "whisky" to drink. She also tells him he will have to return in spring when the "sap commence," at which time he has to rub the sap on his bald head and can then "eat all the scuppernon' he want."[25] Aunt Peggy is able to help Henry, in exchange for a ham, but Henry is never completely restored. Henry's body and hair assume the character of the grapevines: his hair grows lush in spring and summer and he is "des spry en libely" that he almost gets whipped, but in late summer through the winter he stiffens, withers, and almost dies.

On the one hand, the transformations allegorically show the domination of the land and the body of the enslaved by the slaveholder and then by Northern capitalism. On the other, economic and ecological readings of the stories fall short of understanding the land as an "other" and as the basis for Chesnutt's cosmology of conjure. Reciprocal relationships to the land in voodoo and conjure require exchange and sacrifice. Chesnutt seems equally engaged in the syncretic and creolized force of conjure through its Christian interminglings, which also call for an understanding of limit and sacrifice. Henry's transformation into a grapevine also echoes the myth of Ampelos, a young beautiful satyr boy whom Dionysus loved.[26] In Nonnus's version of the story, one of the fates, Atropus, is moved by Dionysus's suffering and turns Ampelos into the eponymous fruit of the vine. Nonnus's version can resonate with Christian suffering as well: Dionysus's tears suggest weeping for humanity, and Atropos's intervention suggests "solace" in the transformation of Ampelos into the comforting fruit of the vine.[27] Aunt Peggy seems to act as Atropus in transforming Henry into the vine to relieve his personal suffering. Henry's initial transformation is not simply one of "dehumanization" in being connected to the product of the land; rather, it is a gift of salvation from Aunt Peggy that, like all relations to nature, has certain limits.[28]

Henry's master exploits Henry's symbiotic relation to the grapevines and "dehumanizes" him by selling him for thousands of dollars every spring when he is blooming; he then purchases Henry back at a much lower cost in winter when his new masters think Henry's death is at hand. One spring Mars Dugal does not sell him because a "Yankee" has come to show how to cultivate the grapes so he can "make mo' d'n twice't ez many gallons of wine."[29] However, he cuts the vines too close to the roots and the entire crop, including Henry, dies. Uncle Julius tells John this story to warn him that there are still remnants of those goophered grapes and that John should not act as the initial Northern speculator did, but John dismisses Julius's story as a con: "I found, when I bought the vineyard, that Uncle Julius had occupied a cabin on the place for several years, and derived a respectable revenue from the product of the neglected grapes. This, doubtless, accounted for his advice for me not to buy the vineyard, though whether it inspired the goopher story I am unable to state."[30] While John feels he has more than compensated Julius for his lost wine business by employing him as "coachman," the master's profiting from Henry's body grounds Julius's tale.[31] Henry is finally killed by the actions of

Northern capitalist greed, but his status as blooming and wilting grapevine was the price he paid for consuming as much as he wanted, even if he was unaware of Peggy's goopher. In other words, the element of conjure here shows that all exchanges and excesses involve an element of sacrifice. A temperate relation to the land is needed for healing.

Although African Americans may have an intimate relationship with the land, clay-eating—and we could substitute drinking alcohol—is associated with a displaced identity; if not done in moderation, one must pay the price for excessive consumption. The displaced relationship to the land becomes an excessive attachment because home, place, and sustenance are absent. Ben's identity is not whitened so much as miscegenated, creolized, and then consumed by the land itself in his efforts to escape from slavery, from "home." Nostalgia often accompanied clay-eating, but it was a practice shared by members of the African diaspora and poor whites. In Chesnutt's story, we are first introduced to clay-eating when Uncle Julius's white auditors John and Annie ask what the poor white woman suddenly hid in her pocket when she saw them looking at her by the river. We are told that "she hid the lump of clay in her pocket with a shamefaced look." When Annie asks what the woman is doing with the clay, Uncle Julius responds, "She's gwineter eat it, Miss Annie," to which Annie gives an "Ugh!"[32] Uncle Julius notes that he "doan nebber lak ter see no black folks eat'n it" because of the story of Ben.[33] This implies that black people are perhaps more susceptible to the deleterious effects of the clay, such as changes in skin color. Why does Julius suggest that these effects are more prominent with black people? Arguably, because the relationship with the land and clay suggests an in-between, displaced identity that needs community and tradition to impose limits on the consumption of and relation to materiality. The imagined relation to land, home, wealth, and sustenance is either excessive or scarce.

Fleisner perceptively reclaims lonesome Ben's story as one that depicts the dilemmas of "diasporic regional" identity and attachments to the land in the phenomenon of clay-eating.[34] Writing after Reconstruction as a "local color" or regional writer, Chesnutt has often been received ambiguously as romanticizing aspects of plantation life or offering caricatures of former slaves. Others have viewed *The Conjure Tales* as responding to Joel Chandler Harris's Uncle Remus stories in an effort to grant integrity to African American slave culture and dialect. Chesnutt had mixed feelings about aspects of Southern slave culture and, like William Wells Brown, criticized the "superstitious" elements of "conjure" and folklore, but he also used conjure to ironize, subvert, and creolize aspects of white European culture.³⁵ In his essay "Superstitions and Folklore of the South," Chesnutt's position on conjure is ambivalent. Indeed, Chesnutt ends the piece by noting that while a belief in goopher shows a "lack of enlightenment," he himself is carrying a rabbit's foot, a "charm," and a "small bag of roots and herbs."³⁶ In "Lonesome Ben" a creolized cosmology is connected to an excessive attachment to the land.

At another level, "Lonesome Ben" is about temperance and even prohibition. "The Goophered Grapevine" shows the need for moderation and reminds readers that excessive symbiosis with the land also comes with inevitable decay and death. But Ben's clay appetite subsumes his desire for alcohol, with similar deleterious effects. As with Harper's creoles, Ben is not darkened but lightened—and the lightening is associated with excess. Ben becomes yellow from the clay, which evokes racial transformations but also the yellow of jaundice from alcoholism. He loses his home, his family, and his stable identity. When Annie, who comes from "a family of reformers," tells John that Uncle Julius's nephew could remove the clay, John gives an antiprohibition response, but one that still promotes a form of temperance: "As I had no desire to add another permanent member to my household, I told her it would be useless; that if people did not get clay they would find it anywhere, and perhaps an inferior quality, which might do greater harm, and that the best way to stop them from eating it was to teach them self-respect, when she had the opportunity, and those habits of industry and thrift whereby they could get their living from the soil in a manner less direct but more commendable."³⁷ Ben, the former whisky drinker turned clay eater, is consumed by the land, which also points to the postbellum fears of an insatiable appetite for alcohol from which African Americans presumably suffered. Somewhere in the woods of Ben's attempted escape there must be a way to make the periphery a new temperate and creolized source of sustenance and meaning for an inclusive community that acknowledges the restraints imposed by the land itself. There must be a rooted and creole cosmopolitanism that would not sublimate the pursuit of a public freedom and civil space.

Why was temperance the common goal and meaning of freedom for many African American abolitionist and postbellum reformers? The five figures I have examined did not invest themselves passionately in temperance reform only because temperance movements were some of the most common modalities of reform in the nineteenth-century United States. Nor were their commitments to sobriety simply assimilationist goals of racial uplift and progressivism. Rather, temperance encouraged a creolized in-between time that allowed for the imaginative refounding of civil space and freedom for the diaspora. Brown, Delany, Horton, Harper, and Smith express a temperate cosmopolitanism emerging from their confrontations with the myriad disjunctions and conjunctions, paradoxes and parallelisms of addiction, creolization, slavery, and temperance coincidental with the formation of the Atlantic world.

Alcohol, tobacco, indigo, cotton, gold, and the bodies of Africans formed a cycle of material exchange at the root of the transatlantic trade. While a prominent abolitionist and temperance reformer, Frances Harper was also active in movements to oppose the sale of commodities created by slave labor. No other commodity, however, captured the imaginative relation between slavery and freedom, passion and rationality, as did alcohol and the experience of sublimity often associated with it by creative minds of the romantic period. Through the transatlantic trade the nature of matter shifted; through the bodies of slaves as transactable chattel goods an intrinsic value was altered.

Most American temperance movements were nationalistic and often became quests for racial purity. African American reformers, however, viewed themselves as part of a broader diaspora initiated in the transatlantic trade. While the history of alcoholism and addiction in the United States is racialized and bound to slavery, as well as to colonialism, the reformers analyzed here were not simply complicit with the ethnic nationalist and often racist agendas of temperance and, later, prohibition. Temperance for these authors was not a movement that promoted African whitening or the inculcation of the Protestant virtues recommended by Chesnutt's John. Rather, we witness the conviction that restraint is required in the creolized positions created through the excesses of the modern world's founding. In Brown's work and travels to imagine and found a creolized and cosmopolitan civilization, a Southern home was ultimately recognized as a necessary if ambiguous homeland. For Horton, a space of exchange and genius emerged amid efforts to reform his own appearance as "buffoon." In Harper's fiction, a creolized and cosmopolitan hemispheric imagination of American beginnings was created in Louisiana territory. In Smith's missionary travels, she sought freedom in the cosmopolitan religious exchanges among the colonized, and she finally made the periphery her home. Chesnutt's conjure tales are also stories of transformation, liminality, and *créolité*, but "Lonesome Ben" echoes Harper's sense that a cosmopolitan and creole recovery must remain rooted in the land and must acknowledge the excesses of chattel slavery and its compulsive outcomes. All these authors who promoted temperance and confronted the problems with excess at the root of slavery recognized the character of the land. They presented stories of creolization and cosmopolitan exchange open to healing. Temperance provided African American reformers an opportunity to enter the cosmopolitan discourses of the black Atlantic by capturing the imaginative root of excess and enabling them to resist having their identities consumed as commodities.

Notes

INTRODUCTION

1. See Kant, "Idea for a Universal History from a Cosmopolitan Perspective."
2. Werbner, *Anthropology and the New Cosmopolitanism*, 2.
3. Craig Calhoun is an outspoken critic of contemporary versions of cosmopolitanism that have emerged since the end of the Soviet Union. See, for instance, "The Class Consciousness of Frequent Travelers"; and *Nations Matter*.
4. For a discussion of the Great Exhibition within this context, see Burris, *Exhibiting Religion*, esp. chaps. 1–3.
5. Green, "Hiram Powers's 'Greek Slave,'" 35.
6. Brown, *Three Years in Europe*.
7. Farmer, extract from letter to William Lloyd Garrison, June 26, 1851, 81. The "Virginian Slave," as Vivien M. Green comments, is a comic of a "partially clothed" African slave with "an American flag draped over the support [with] the pedestal's inscription 'E Pluribus Unum'": "Punch imagined 'Sambo's' response to the white hostage: 'But though you am a lubly gal, I say you no correct; You not at all de kind ob slave a nigger would expect; You never did no workee wid such hands and feet as dose; You different from SUSANNAH, dere,—you not like coal-black ROSE. Dere's not a mark dat I see ob de cow-hide on your back; No slave hab skin so smooth as youm-dat is, if slavee black.'" Green, "Hiram Powers's 'Greek Slave,'" 37.
8. Farmer, 82.
9. See Greenspan, *William Wells Brown*, 203–67.
10. Brown, *Description of William Wells Brown's Original Panoramic Views of the Scenes in the Life of an American Slave*.
11. Berlin, *Many Thousands Gone*, 7–9.
12. Patterson, *Slavery and Social Death*.
13. See Long, "Indigenous People, Materialities, and Religion," 178.
14. Long, 170.
15. Joe Coker clarifies the "deteriorating racial attitudes" during prohibition and the "black beast" depiction used to degrade black men. A "white hysteria" swept the South at the beginning of the twentieth century, and "evangelical prohibitionists capitalized on this renewed public concern over alcohol and successfully pushed prohibition as the solution to black savagery." *Liquor in the Land of the Lost Cause*, 124.
16. Jefferson, *Notes on the State of Virginia*, query 14, 264–70.
17. See Nott and Gliddon, excerpt from *Types of Mankind*; and Cartwright, *Diseases and Peculiarities of the Negro Race*.
18. Benjamin Rush was one of the main proponents of temperance in the revolutionary period with his scientific approach and the publication of his 1784 tract, *An Inquiry into the Effects of Ardent Spirits upon the Human Body and Mind*. Moderation and a ban on ardent spirits contributed to the development of temperance societies. See Rumbarger, *Profits, Power, and Prohibition*, 5. Rumbarger's aim is to show how "wealthy capitalists" considered temperance as necessary and integral to the development of their social order (xix), a point also made in Rorabaugh, *Alcoholic Republic*.
19. See Tait, *Poisoned Chalice*, 7–8.
20. Tyrell, *Woman's World / Woman's Empire*, 19.
21. See Finkelman, *Imperfect Union*.
22. As Patricia Bradley points out, "In a colonial world that daily saw the existence of the institution, it is difficult to see how the use of the language of slavery could not *but* bring to the political metaphor common beliefs about the people who occupied that status." *Slavery, Propaganda, and the American Revolution*, 5.

23. Kern, *Ordered Love*, 27–28.

24. Levine, *Martin Delany, Frederick Douglass, and the Politics of Representative Identity*, 104.

25. Quarles, *Black Abolitionists*, 93. For a discussion of black temperance's shift from a moral approach similar to that of the white temperance movement toward a political focus, see Yacovene, "Transformation of the Black Temperance Movement."

26. A recent study is Thompson, *Most Stirring and Significant Episode*. While this book is restricted in scope, it discusses the religious and evangelical basis of black temperance in Atlanta following the Civil War. David Fahey also discusses the significance of the AME Church in the promotion of black temperance in *Temperance and Racism*.

27. Beecher, *Six Sermons on Intemperance*, 21–22. Cynthia S. Hamilton also cites this passage when discussing Harriet Beecher Stowe's 1856 novel, which directly connects slaveholding and inebriety, in "'Dred.'"

28. Tait, *Poisoned Chalice*, 9.

29. American temperance corresponded to evangelism in many respects, though the "Puritans," even with their asceticism, did not exclude alcohol from their diet. The widespread individualized context of consumption would not occur until the further development of mercantilism. See Blocker, *American Temperance Movements*, 4.

30. Cook, *Alcohol, Addiction, and Christian Ethics*, 77.

31. Blocker discusses the development of temperance from the revolutionary period to the first organized society in Massachusetts that surpassed the "local scale." The desire for reform was aided by "the perfectionist impulse that emerged from the revivals of the Second Great Awakening (1800–1835), a belief that, with God's grace, human beings could speed the coming of the millennium by improving themselves and their society on earth." Most discussions of temperance address revolutionaries like Benjamin Rush, then consider the development of societies such as the Washingtonians and evangelical and revivalist manifestations of temperance. See Blocker, *American Temperance Movements*, 8, 11, 22.

32. Blocker, 7.

33. See Glaude, *Exodus!* 68, for mention of Rush's scientific observations in "Observations Intended to Favor a Supposition That the Black Color (as It Is Called) of the Negroes Is Caused by Leprosy."

34. James and Johnson, *Doin' Drugs*, 8.

35. Davis, *In the Image of God*, 9. In this chapter, Davis discusses, at some length, the etymology of the word "slave" and its historical association with Africans and blackness.

36. Douglass, *Narrative of the Life of Frederick Douglass*, 395.

37. Douglass, 402.

38. These points about Douglass's internal and masculine locus of freedom have been made by many others, beginning at least with Eric Sundquist's attention to the Hegelian dialectic, "social death," and "conversion to mastery" that Douglass gains when he resists the overseer's (Covey's) whip. See *To Wake the Nations*, 122.

39. Douglass, *Narrative*, 396, 397.

40. Christmon, "Historical Overview of Alcohol in the African American Community," 327.

41. Smallwood, *Saltwater Slavery*, 68.

42. Smallwood, 69.

43. Christmon, "Historical Overview," 325.

44. Malcolm Cowley, introduction to *Adventures of an African Slaver*, xv.

45. Mintz, *Sweetness and Power*, 43.

46. Baucom, *Specters of the Atlantic*, 53.

47. Baucom.

48. Baucom, 62.

49. John Ernest writes, "In his travel narratives . . . Brown transforms himself into a 'fugitive tourist,' presenting a strategic cultural critique and challenging readers' assumptions while seeming to imitate the behaviour and attitudes of a conventional type of cultured American tourist in Europe." *Liberation Historiography*, 334. He furthers this argument in *Chaotic Justice*, 246. See also Baraw, "William Wells Brown, Three Years in Europe, and Fugitive Tourism."

50. Harvey, *Cosmopolitanism and the Geographies of Freedom*, 532.

51. Proposition 7 in Kant, "Idea for a Universal History with a Cosmopolitan Aim," 16.

52. Martha Nussbaum and Anthony Appiah have written extensively on these issues. For

discussions that develop notions of contemporary liberal cosmopolitanism, see Nussbaum, *For Love of Country*. Appiah begins developing the concept of "rooted cosmopolitanism" by reflecting on his father's Ghanaian identity in *Cosmopolitanism*, xv.

53. Werbner, "Introduction," 2.

54. Werbner, 17–18.

55. Many contemporary political theorists, including Bhabha, have discussed the subject position of the refugee as bringing forth a different understanding of cosmopolitanism. Daniel Levy and Nathan Sznaider have also used the term "cosmopolitan memory" to describe the Holocaust as a global event that affected aspects of universal human rights. See Levy and Sznaider, *Holocaust and Memory in the Global Age*.

56. Kant, "An Old Question Raised Again," quoted in Baucom, *Specters of the Atlantic*, 290.

57. Baucom, 252.

58. Klein, *Cigarettes Are Sublime*, 77.

59. Tait, *Poisoned Chalice*, 42, 46.

60. Quoted in Tait, 53.

61. Gilroy, *Black Atlantic*, 187.

62. Baucom discusses Glissant's meaning of "errancy" in *Specters of the Atlantic*, 314.

63. Bhabha, *Location of Culture*, 93.

64. Elias, *Civilizing Process*.

CHAPTER 1

1. Hendler, *Public Sentiments*, 53.

2. Levine, *Martin Delany, Frederick Douglass, and the Politics of Representative Identity*, 108.

3. Delany, "Report of the Niger Valley Exploring Party," 340, 341.

4. Nwankwo, *Black Cosmopolitanism*, 9; she discusses Delany's black cosmopolitanism in chap. 2.

5. Notably, Delany was enrolled in medical school at Harvard for at least a few months until he was expelled because of racial segregation (Levine, *Martin R. Delany*, 1); Brown also took up an interest in practicing medicine around 1865, when, after some study, he started writing "'M.D.' after his name." Though Brown's training is less prestigious, the medical profession likely appealed to both men's sense of healing the collective body. See Farrison, *William Wells Brown*, 400.

6. Delany, *Blake*, 93.

7. Delany, 16–17.

8. Gilroy, *Black Atlantic*, 20.

9. Gilroy, 21.

10. Miller, introduction to Delany, *Blake*, xiii.

11. Delany, *Blake*, 143, 144.

12. Delany, 150, 151.

13. Hendler, *Public Sentiments*, 63.

14. Davis, *Problem of Slavery in the Era of Emancipation*, 211.

15. Albanese, *Republic of Mind and Spirit*, 126.

16. Albanese, 126–27.

17. Jacob, *Strangers Nowhere in the World*, 106.

18. Walker, *Noble Fight*, 20.

19. Delany, "Origin and Objects of Ancient Freemasonry."

20. Delany, 58.

21. Delany, 57.

22. Albanese, *Republic of Mind and Spirit*, 127.

23. Walker, *Noble Fight*, 58.

24. Delany, "Origin and Objects of Ancient Freemasonry," 55, 56.

25. Levine, *Martin R. Delany*, 49.

26. Levine, 67.

27. Levine, 57, 67.

28. Jacob, *Strangers Nowhere in the World*, 99.

29. Jacob, 102.

30. Walker, *Noble Fight*, 103, 101–2.

31. Walker, 111.

32. Delany, *Blake*, 40.

33. Floyd Miller presented Delany as a black nationalist and black capitalist. While recent criticism has created a more complex conception of black nationalism, Delany's black capitalism remains less malleable. Miller views Delany's project to purchase land for settlement in the Niger as "his most serious attempt at 'black capitalism'" (introduction to Delany, xviii).

34. Delany, 142.

35. Chiles, "Within and Without Raced Nations," 337.

36. Quoted in Chiles, 342, from Delany's "Report of the Niger Valley Exploring Party."

37. Hendler, *Public Sentiments*, 60–61.

38. Delany, *Blake*, 109.

39. Nwankwo, *Black Cosmopolitanism*, 57.

40. Delany, *Blake*, 249.

41. Delany, 83, 293.

42. McGann, "Rethinking Delany's *Blake*," 88.
43. Delany, *Blake*, 284.
44. Delany, 285.
45. Delany, 136.
46. Delany, 300, 301.
47. Clymer, "Martin Delany's *Blake* and the Transnational Politics of Property," 723.
48. Delany, *Blake*, 258.
49. Delany, 262.
50. Delany, *Principia of Ethnology*, 481.
51. Levine, *Martin R. Delany*, 468.
52. Delany, *Condition, Elevation, Emigration, and Destiny of the Colored People of the United States*, chap. 9.
53. Washington, *Up from Slavery*, 122.
54. Du Bois, *Souls of Black Folk*, 81.
55. Delany, *Condition, Elevation, Emigration, and Destiny of the Colored People of the United States*, chap. 11.
56. Brown, *Three Years in Europe*, 206.
57. Brown, "Colored People of Canada," 472.
58. Levine, *Martin R. Delany*, 369.
59. Farrison, *William Wells Brown*, 72.
60. See Farrison, "William Wells Brown in Buffalo," 299.
61. Farrison comments in his biography, "In 1840 Brown visited Haiti and Cuba and possibly other islands in the West Indies." Given that Brown had remarked that he was looking for a place to raise his two daughters where they would not experience discrimination, "Haiti was probably his principal objective. He had doubtless heard of the successful revolution of the Haitian Negroes and was interested in the possibilities of life." After this trip, which does not have extensive documentation, Brown returned to Buffalo to continue his work as a conductor for the Underground Railroad. See Farrison, *William Wells Brown*, 74.
62. Farrison, 72.
63. Farrison.
64. Farrison, 423.
65. Blocker, *American Temperance Movements*, 48.
66. Farrison, *William Wells Brown*, 424.
67. Fahey, *Temperance and Racism*, 59.
68. See Fahey, 5. The origin of IOGT is associated with a "Wesleyan minister who had been a Freemason and combined something of the features of Freemasonry and Methodism in the order" (Parker, "Good Templar Coming of Age in England," 78).
69. For instance, David Fahey gives an example of an African American Templar thanking the AME Church leaders for the success of the IOGT, though he was not a Methodist. See *Temperance and Racism*, 106.
70. Fahey, 105.
71. Fahey, 2.
72. Quarles, *Black Abolitionists*, 93.
73. Fahey, *Temperance and Racism*, 11.
74. Fahey.
75. Farrison, *William Wells Brown*, 18.
76. Farmer, "Memoir of William Wells Brown," xv.
77. Brown, *Narrative of William Wells Brown*, 40.
78. Levine, "Whiskey, Blacking, and All," 108.
79. Brown, *Clotel*, 149.
80. Brown, 191.
81. Levine, "Whiskey, Blacking, and All," 109.
82. Levine, 94, 93.
83. Brown, *Three Years in Europe*, 272.
84. Brown, 223.
85. Delany, *Condition, Elevation, Emigration, and Destiny of the Colored People of the United States*, chap. 19.
86. Martin Delany, "The Political Aspect of the Colored People," in Levine, *Martin R. Delany*, 289.
87. Delany, *Blake*, 153. Winnifred Siemerling has recently interpreted Delany's time in Chatham as part of a more positive countercultural black Canadian hemispheric identity. See *Black Atlantic Reconsidered*, 8. Southern Ontario is a strategic location for Delany and others (like Harriet Tubman and John Brown), as well as for the development of distinct traditions. Nevertheless, the civil orderings of community and population were not ideal for Delany or Brown for a critical cosmopolitan resettling.
88. Before the Act of Union in 1841, Ontario was known as Upper Canada and Quebec as Lower Canada. After the act and until 1867 they became known as Canada West and Canada East, respectively. They were still British colonies, or "provinces," during this period. The term Upper Canada is still commonly used, however, to refer to English-speaking parts of Quebec and Ontario.

89. Brown, "Colored People of Canada," 466.
90. Shadd Cary, "Editorial by Mary Ann Shadd Cary," 352.
91. Drew, *The Refugee*, 269.
92. Drew, 294.
93. Bibb, "Editorial by Henry Bibb, 21 May 1851," 136.
94. Ward, "Samuel Ringgold Ward to Henry Bibb, 16 October 1851," 179.
95. Brown, *The Escape*, 45, 47.
96. Ernest, "Reconstruction of Whiteness," 1118.
97. Gikandi, *Slavery and the Culture of Taste*, 100.
98. Arendt, *On Revolution*, 249.
99. Shea, *Cynic Enlightenment*, 299.
100. Shea notes that Rousseau's *Second Discourse* contains a passage that "slides seamlessly from Diogenes to Cato, as if placing both men in the same category, that of untimely men. But the juxtaposition of Diogenes and Cato implies something else as well, that the true object of Diogenes's quest is a man who came after him and whom he could therefore not find: Cato, a man both virtuous and patriotic, a symbol of political liberty" (103).
101. Brown, *The Escape*, 47.
102. Brown, 25.
103. Gikandi, *Slavery and the Culture of Taste*, 216.
104. Gikandi, 264.
105. See Gikandi, 246.
106. Brown, *Clotel*, 57.
107. Brown, 61.
108. Brown, 80, 79.
109. Brown, 66.
110. Lucasi, "William Wells Brown's *Narrative* and Traveling Subjectivity," 523.
111. Brown, "Colored People of Canada," 461.
112. Brown, 462.
113. Brown.
114. Churches were segregated, and the Common School Act of 1850 would be passed to legislate segregated schools in St. Catharines. Fewer black people immigrated prior to the Fugitive Slave Law, which encouraged greater integration than after 1850. In some areas, increasing segregation in various parts of Canada West is a result of all-black settlements organized by white philanthropy (such as Elgin). However, in some cases, segregation resulted from white fear of crime and ethnic civil associations, and worsened as time passed. For example, in the towns of Amherstburg, Colchester, and Sandwich, the census data do not indicate segregation prior to 1851. See Winks, *Blacks in Canada*, 153, 145.
115. Brown, *Clotel*, 214.
116. Brown, 216.
117. Drew writes, "Of the population of about six thousand, it is estimated that eight hundred are of African descent. Nearly all the adult coloured people have at some time been slaves" (*The Refugee*, 41). Michael Wayne points out that these numbers are somewhat exaggerated, the census indicates a population of 601, and Samuel Gridley Howe in 1863 estimates seven hundred (Wayne, 470) for St. Catharines. Wayne also contends that persons of African descent had been more widely "dispersed" throughout the province than either Brown or Drew consider. See Wayne, "Black Population of Canada West on the Eve of the American Civil War," 469.
118. Brown, "Colored People of Canada," 464.
119. Brown, 479. Peter Ripley and colleagues point out in their opening to Brown's document written for James Redpath's Haytian Emigration Bureau, "His personal ambiguity reflected the debate between those who wished to build a model black community in Canada West and those who wanted to create a black nation in the Caribbean." Ripley, *Black Abolitionist Papers*, vol. 2, 461.
120. Brown, "Narrative of the Life and Escape of William Wells Brown," in *Clotel*, 77.
121. See Robert S. Levine's editorial remarks, "Narrative of the Life and Escape of William Wells Brown," in Brown, 77n40.
122. Martha Schoolman discusses Brown's letter promoting West Indian immigration and his criticism of Thomas Carlyle's position on the West Indies. See Schoolman, "Violent Places," 13–16.
123. Brown, "Narrative of the Life and Escape of William Wells Brown," in *Clotel*, 77.
124. Brown, *Clotel*, 216.
125. Brown, 217.
126. Brown, 225.
127. Brown, "Colored People of Canada," 496.
128. Winks, *Blacks in Canada*, 179, 180.

129. Winks, 204, 219.

130. Brown uses the word "amalgamation" to indicate a time when race will not limit association and intermingling will occur. See *My Southern Home*, 183.

131. Brown, "Colored People of Canada," 496.

132. Brown, *Black Man, His Antecedents, His Genius, and His Achievements*, 47.

133. Brown, "Colored People of Canada," 467, 469.

134. Farrison, *William Wells Brown*, 424. Fahey notes that the Sons' efforts were "half-hearted," and Brown would eventually abandon the Sons in favor of the more cosmopolitan Good Templars (*Temperance and Racism*, 58).

135. It is not my purpose to denigrate the significant achievement of those African Canadians who escaped from American slavery to Canada (or those who found better opportunities and legal protection in Canada in earlier periods). Nonetheless, myths about the Underground Railroad and the destination of new Canaan as "Canada" often oversimplify both U.S. and Canadian history. See Sayers, "Underground Railroad Reconsidered," 436.

CHAPTER 2

1. Nwankwo, *Black Cosmopolitanism*, 9.
2. Schoolman, "Violent Places," 7. Schoolman expands this argument in her book *Abolitionist Geographies*.
3. Schoolman, "Violent Places," 8. Tamarkin's representation of Brown's travel narrative and admiration of European culture and literature elides the possibility of self-conscious uses or subtleties in Brown's thoughts on Europe and the history of violence and excess that accompanies the founding of civilizations and modern nation-states.
4. Baraw, "William Wells Brown, *Three Years in Europe*, and Fugitive Tourism," 456.
5. Schoolman, "Violent Places," 8.
6. Schoolman, 26.
7. Schoolman, 24.
8. Schoolman, 20.
9. Joshua Scodel discusses the emphasis on the mean and temperance for the Roman Catholic and Protestant traditions in the early modern period, particularly through John Donne, Ben Johnson, and John Milton. In his postscript he considers some contemporary uses of the sublime in postmodernism and among liberal opponents arguing for a temperate mean. Scodel, *Excess and the Mean in Early Modern English Literature*, 286.
10. Brown, *Three Years in Europe*, 108.
11. Brown, *American Fugitive in Europe*, 196.
12. Tait, *Poisoned Chalice*, 11.
13. Tait, 52.
14. Tait, 46.
15. Levine, "Whiskey, Blacking, and All," 107.
16. Levine, 108.
17. For a reassessment of the "hemispheric" histories of transcultural and creole identities that have been excluded in stories of American nationhood, see Levander and Levine, *Hemispheric American Studies*.
18. Levine, "Whiskey, Blacking, and All," 101.
19. Oftentimes, women were able to reimagine relations to home, work, and their bodies, though they seemed to model this independence on masculine constructions of self-reliance. See chaps. 6 and 7 of Carol Mattingly's discussion of women's temperance fiction in *Well-Tempered Women*.
20. Brown, *Three Years in Europe*, 29–30.
21. Brown, 30.
22. Long, "Primitive / Civilized: The Locus of a Problem," in *Significations*, 90.
23. Brown, *Three Years in Europe*, 235.
24. Brown, 236.
25. Hughes-Warrington, "Coloring Universal History," 126–27.
26. While amalgamation has sometimes been understood as suggesting assimilation, Brown uses it in reference to the world's fair in London simply as cross-cultural and cosmopolitan exchange (*American Fugitive in Europe*, 211).
27. See Farrison, *William Wells Brown*, 14, 433.
28. Farrison, 13. The account of Brown's name change occurs in Brown's *Narrative of William Wells Brown*, 40, 74.
29. Brown, 17, 78.
30. John Ernest sees Brown's trickster identity as connected to the figure of the confidence man in *Resistance and Reformation in Nineteenth-Century African-American Literature*, 22–23. See also Ernest, *Liberation Historiography*, 334.
31. Glissant, *Caribbean Discourse*, 20.

32. Ernest, *Liberation Historiography*, 339.
33. Ernest, Introduction to *My Southern Home* by William Wells Brown, xv.
34. See Baucom, *Specters of the Atlantic*, 213; and Glissant, *Caribbean Discourse*, 101.
35. Glissant, *Caribbean Discourse*, 93.
36. Long, "Primitive / Civilized," in *Significations*, 94.
37. Elias, *Civilizing Process*, 7.
38. David Brion Davis notes, "During the first third of the nineteenth century, Haiti stood as the single decisive example of mass emancipation. . . . Abolitionists in both England and American made remarkably few references to the Northern states' emancipation acts and their consequences. For a time, however, they did pin their hopes on Haiti" (*Problem of Slavery in the Era of Emancipation*, 81).
39. Bethel, "Images of Hayti," 827. Bethel notes the shift in the *lieux de memoire* from Africa to Haiti: "Unlike Africa, Hayti was not a mysterious and removed place for Afro-Americans living in the cities along the eastern seaboard of the United States during the early years of the nineteenth century. For many, one of those islands had been their first stop in the New World, their terminus of the middle passage, the site of their earliest New World experiences and memories" (832).
40. Ripley, *Black Abolitionist Papers*, vol. 2, 449.
41. Alexander, "Black Republic," 210.
42. Ripley, *Black Abolitionists*, vol. 2, 449.
43. Brown, *Rising Son*, 238, 239.
44. Elizabeth Fox-Genovese and Eugene Genovese have outlined some of the ideological Southern uses of Greek and Roman examples, as well as arguments over the racial character of ancient slavery and disputes over the Egyptian association with "black" Africa, or Ethiopia. See *Mind of the Master Class*, 287.
45. Pagden, *Fall of Natural Man*, 42.
46. Pagden, 43.
47. Brown, *Rising Son*, 171; Brown, *Black Man, His Antecedents, His Genius, and His Achievements*, 102.
48. Levine, "Whisky, Blacking, and All," 104.
49. Brown, *Rising Son*, 171.
50. Brown, 118.
51. Brown, 91.
52. Brown, 92.
53. Quoted in Brown.
54. Brown, 102, 100, 134.
55. This observation is taken from E. H. Sears, "The Christian Examiner," July 1846, in Brown, 44.
56. See Andrews, introduction to *From Fugitive Slave to Free Man*, 6.
57. Andrews, 5.
58. Brown, *American Fugitive in Europe*, 95.
59. See Ernest, introduction to *The Escape*, xx–xxi.
60. Andrews, introduction to *From Fugitive Slave to Free Man*, 6, 7.
61. Brown, *Black Man*, 278–84. This tale seems to be autobiographical. In regard to what many have viewed as the trickster-like aspects of Brown's antiheroism, Robert D. Pelton explains that the Ashanti trickster Ananse is "neither a mythic nor a social entrepreneur whose self-determination determines the world under the guidance of some invisible hand [and is] far more ambiguous" (*Trickster in West Africa*, 225).
62. Fanuzzi, "Taste, Manners, and Miscegenation," 577.
63. Fanuzzi, 590.
64. Fanuzzi, 596.
65. Quoted in Garrett and Robbins, introduction to *The Works of William Wells Brown*, xxvii.
66. Brown, *Clotel*, 316.
67. Farrison, *William Wells Brown*, 421.
68. Fahey, *Temperance and Racism*, 113.
69. Schoolman, "Violent Places," 7.
70. Farrison, *William Wells Brown*, 446.
71. Schoolman follows Ezra Greenspan in noting that no particular "place" is associated with Brown, and he has few attachments to "home" ("Violent Places," 8). While Brown was always actively traveling as a reformer, he does recommend farming for local African American communities (*My Southern Home*, 181).
72. Brown, 182.
73. Brown, *Clotel*, 160.
74. Brown, 180, 177.
75. Brown, *Three Years in Europe*, 38, 67.
76. Brown, *American Fugitive in Europe*, 193–94.
77. Brown, 194.

78. Brown, *Three Years in Europe*, 46.

79. Brown, 159.

80. While Brown often pays tribute to British authors like Walter Scott, Wordsworth, and Byron, at the Crystal Palace he is critical of Carlyle and especially his concept of "hero worship." Brown points to Carlyle's criticism of West Indian emancipation and his structure of heroism, which "holds no communion with his kind, but stands alone without mate or fellow. He is like a solitary peak, all access to which is cut off" (218). Carlyle, like Romantics before, had located freedom in the self, working against what Brown found attractive in British "civilization."

81. Brown, 160.

82. Brown, 166.

83. Hendler, *Public Sentiments*, 34.

84. Hendler, 32.

85. Ernest, *Resistance and Reformation*, 24.

86. Ernest, 28 (quoting Farrison).

87. As Ernest also notes, plagiarism was more common in Brown's time, as there were fewer copyright laws. Nonetheless, American romanticism, following the British romanticism of Wordsworth and Coleridge, desired the immediacy of "genius" and transcendental access to truth through the passionate connection of the poet as a type of secular prophet. This went against the Enlightenment focus on reason, instead emphasizing a highly subjectivist sense of sublimity. See Samuel Coleridge's distinction between "imagination" and "fancy" in *Biographia Literaria*, 1:295.

88. Baucom, *Specters of the Atlantic*, 312.

89. Fahey, *Temperance and Racism*, 58. See also Farrison, *William Wells Brown*, 423–36.

90. Yacovone, "Transformation of the Black Temperance Movement," 294.

91. Brown, *Three Years in Europe*, 117.

92. Fahey, *Temperance and Racism*, 30.

93. Fahey, 11.

94. Farrison, *William Wells Brown*, 435.

95. Quoted in Fahey, *Temperance and Racism*, 101.

96. Brown, *Three Years in Europe*, 116.

97. Brown, 117.

98. Brown, *My Southern Home*, 232.

99. Brown, *Three Years in Europe*, 50.

100. Tamarkin, *Anglophilia*, 178. Tamarkin is referring to Alexander Crummell's use of this phrase in arguing for the superiority of British education. She extends the phrase to claim a generalized idealization of English culture by black abolitionists as "anglophilia" (182). While Brown does devote a chapter to Byron, among other poets, this can be viewed as part of Brown's reflections on what it means to found modern "civilization" rather than as an uncritical Eurocentrism.

101. Quoted in Fahey, *Temperance and Racism*, 120.

102. Brown, *My Southern Home*, 263.

103. Brown, 152.

104. Brown, 155.

105. Brown.

106. Kohn, "Other America," 186, 187.

107. Pagden, "Europe," 37–38.

108. Brown, *My Southern Home*, 173.

109. Brown, *Three Years in Europe*, 141–42.

110. Victor Turner and Edith Turner define communitas or "social antistructure" as the basis of an "undifferentiated, egalitarian" bond that "strains toward universalism and openness," often dangerously surrounded by uncertain taboos, rife with possibilities for potential novel forms structure (*Image and Pilgrimage in Christian Culture*, 250–51).

111. Brown, *My Southern Home*, 177.

112. Brown, 171.

113. Brown, 287.

114. Brown, 13.

115. Brown, 173.

116. Brown, 177.

117. Brown, 178.

118. Brown, 182.

119. Brown, 186.

120. Brown, 95.

121. Brown, *Description of William Wells Brown's Original Panoramic Views of the Scenes in the Life of an American Slave*, 213–14.

CHAPTER 3

1. Andrews, *North Carolina Roots of African American Literature*, 2.

2. Andrews, 3.

3. Andrews, 4.

4. Horton, preface to "Life of George Moses Horton," vi.

5. Horton, xiv.

6. See Sherman, *Black Bard of North Carolina*, 2–3; and Richmond, *Bid the Vassal Soar*, 85–91. Sherman's book has an introduction to Horton's life and poetry, and contains selections of his poems.

7. Sherman, 3, 14–16.

8. Sherman, 9.

9. Sherman, 10.

10. William Andrews notes that this declared goal of moving to Liberia was perhaps not Horton's idea, given that many Southerners who supported manumission also supported colonization, often as a result of their racism (*North Carolina Roots*, 5).

11. For a full discussion of these early publications, see Sherman, *Black Bard of North Carolina*, 9–14.

12. See Sherman, 16. Walker supported Horton's bid for freedom, though, as Andrews notes, Walker was opposed to colonization and would have had problems with the proviso that Horton move to Liberia (*North Carolina Roots*, 6).

13. Sherman, 20.

14. Sherman, 29.

15. See Mason, "To Be an Author," 717.

16. Schuman, "UNC Dedicates Dorm to Chatham Slave, Poet."

17. DeSimone and Louis, *Voices Beyond Bondage*, vii.

18. Franklin, *From Slavery to Freedom*, 172.

19. Walser, *Black Poet*, 28.

20. Walser, 55.

21. Sherman, *Black Bard of North Carolina*, 14.

22. Sherman, 34.

23. Sherman, 40.

24. Elizabeth Fox-Genovese and Eugene Genovese point out that classical learning "distinguished the Southern gentleman" during this time. David Swain's library may have contributed to his veneration of Homer. See Fox-Genovese and Genovese, *Mind of the Master Class*, 250, 255.

25. Leonard's commentary is sympathetic but also dismissive. He concludes that Horton's poetic "innovations" were "narrow" because of his limited environment, which did not allow him the same access to "mainstream culture" (*Fettered Genius*, 17–18).

26. Sherman, *Black Bard of North Carolina*, 23.

27. Quoted in Sherman, 62. Line numbers for all poetry hereafter cited in the text parenthetically.

28. Leonard, *Fettered Genius of North Carolina*, 20.

29. Walser, *Black Poet*, 39.

30. Richmond, *Bid the Vassal Soar*, 156.

31. Most of the autobiographical information on Horton can be found in his preface to *The Poetical Works*. Richard Walser (*Black Poet*, 3) notes that the 1800 census credits William Horton with eight slaves; Joan Sherman also provides much biographical and contextual information in her introduction to Horton's selected poems. The address is difficult to read, as Sherman notes, because each page seems to have been transcribed by a different hand and small parts are illegible. When I cite the address I am referring to my own deciphering of that handwriting. Unfortunately, there is no official published version or transcription of this address, and it is only available at University of North Carolina Special Collections. See Horton, "An Address."

32. Pitts, "Let Us Desert This Friendless Place," 147.

33. Berlin, *Generations of Captivity*; Pitts, 148.

34. Pitts, 151.

35. Walser, *Black Poet*, 106.

36. Richmond, *Bid the Vassal Soar*, 175.

37. Quoted in Jackson and Rubin, *Black Poetry in America*, 7.

38. Crowley, "Slaves to the Bottle," 129.

39. Crowley, 122.

40. Levine, "Whiskey, Blacking, and All."

41. Levine, *Martin Delany, Frederick Douglass, and the Politics of Representative Identity*; and Levine, "Disturbing Boundaries." The latter also addresses the dominant rhetoric of temperance in Philadelphia in the 1840s.

42. Douglas W. Carlson argues that temperance reformers in the North and South used similar rhetoric ("Drinks He to His Own Undoing").

43. Douglass, *My Bondage and My Freedom*, 256.

44. Quoted in Davis, *Problem of Slavery in the Age of Emancipation*, 35.

45. Davis, 40.

46. Douglass, *Narrative of the Life of Frederick Douglass*, 351.

47. Douglass, 359.
48. Horton, "Division of an Estate," 87.
49. Sherman, *Black Bard of North Carolina*, 40.
50. Fahey, *Temperance and Racism*, 69.
51. Sherman, *Black Bard of North Carolina*, 18.
52. Frey, *Water from the Rock*, 327.
53. Critics have depicted *The Poetical Works* as more reserved and conservative about opposing slavery than was Horton's first book, *In Hope of Liberty*. This is because of the series of laws passed following slave rebellions and the generally bleak prospect of obtaining legal freedom during this time. See Farrison, "George Moses Horton," 238. Nonetheless, Horton's dialogue with temperance continues in a similar manner long after the publication of the 1845 book, as the quoted poems suggest.
54. Horton, "Life of George Moses Horton," xvi.
55. Sherman, *Black Bard of North Carolina*, 7–8.
56. Horton, "Intemperance Club," 154.
57. On the claims of contemporaries that Poe plagiarized parts of "The Raven," see Richards, "Outsourcing 'The Raven.'" "The Raven" was published in January 1845 and Horton's *The Poetical Works* was published later that same year, though Horton would have been reciting many of these poems prior to 1845. While not wanting to add to the speculation regarding from whom Poe may have plagiarized, it is worth noting that Poe is said to have composed "The Raven" on the Virginia–North Carolina state line at a stagecoach stop called "the Halfway House," a gambling establishment where dueling occurred and runaway slaves from Virginia often hid. Federal Writers Project, *North Carolina*, 277. Given that Raleigh is not too far from Virginia and that Horton's poems circulated among University of North Carolina and University of Virginia students, one might speculate that Poe had heard some of his works before. Indeed, Poe was an editor for the *Southern Literary Messenger* and published in the journal regularly. Two of Horton's poems were published in that journal, and the entire manuscript of *The Poetical Works* seems to have been circulating prior to 1843. Sherman, *Black Bard of North Carolina*, 15.
58. Poe, "The Raven," 58–61.
59. Sherman, 7.
60. Horton, "Life of George Moses Horton," xiv.
61. Horton, xvii.
62. See Levine, *Martin R. Delany*, 117, for a discussion of Douglass's use of the "safety valve" analogy in his autobiographies in an effort to contain the slaves' "revolutionary energies."
63. Horton, "Life of George Moses Horton," xii.
64. Horton, xi–xii.
65. Levine, *Martin R. Delany*, 122.
66. Sherman, *Black Bard of North Carolina*, 38.
67. Quoted in Sherman, 10.
68. Horton, "An Address," 6.
69. Horton, 8.
70. Sherman, *Black Bard of North Carolina*, 22.
71. See the letter petitioning the president of the university, David Swain, for his freedom in 1852, quoted in Sherman, 23.
72. Horton, "Art of a Poet," 147.
73. See Jefferson, *Notes on the State of Virginia*.
74. Anonymous, introduction to *The Poetical Works*, xxi.
75. Sherman, *Black Bard of North Carolina*, 6.
76. Horton, "Life of George Moses Horton," xiii.
77. Sherman notes the stricter laws against slave literacy and hiring out in North Carolina following Turner's rebellion (*Black Bard of North Carolina*, 17). Revolts, especially the Haitian Revolution, "Gabriel's Revolt of 1800 in Virginia and the great Vesey Plot of 1822 in South Carolina," led to fears about the potentially revolutionary insights that could be mobilized during the Second Great Awakening (Frey, *Water from the Rock*, 58). Sherman also notes the emergence of temperance movements at the university in Raleigh during this period (7–8).
78. Horton, preface to "Life of George Moses Horton," xiv.
79. A. Leon Higginbotham makes this point in various ways by analyzing how the law deals with race and color in forming its early sense of freedom in the colonial period (*In the Matter of Color*).
80. Richmond, *Bid the Vassal Soar*, 83.

81. Horton, "Life of George Moses Horton," xiv.
82. Pratt, *Imperial Eyes*, 6–7.
83. Horton, "Life of George Moses Horton," v.
84. Horton, "An Address" 4.
85. Horton, 5.
86. Horton, 6.
87. Horton, 22.
88. Horton, 15.
89. Horton, 23.
90. Turner, *Anthropology of Performance*, 107.
91. Quoted in Richmond, *Bid the Vassal Soar*, 148.
92. Horton, "Imploring to Be Resigned at Death," 102.
93. Horton, "One Generation Passeth Away and Another Cometh," 133.
94. Horton.
95. Arendt, *Human Condition*, 55.
96. Horton, "One Generation Passeth Away and Another Cometh," 133.
97. See Jacob, *Strangers Nowhere in the World*, 1. The title of her book is taken from Denis Diderot's 1751 encyclopedia definition of cosmopolitanism.
98. Sherman, *Black Bard of North Carolina*, 30.
99. Horton, "Southern Refugee," 124.
100. Faith Barrett argues that Horton's poems, particularly from *Naked Genius*, should be read in light of the more traditional Southern romanticism of Henry Timrod in order to understand the ambivalence expressed toward the Southern national, and indeed national, "we." She furthermore dismisses the notion that Horton expresses a simple Southern "nostalgia" in *Naked Genius*. See *To Fight Aloud Is Very Brave*, 230–32.

CHAPTER 4

1. Harper, *Iola Leroy*, 219.
2. Harper, *Minnie's Sacrifice, Sowing and Reaping, Trial and Triumph*, 67.
3. Foreman, "Reading Aright," 335; Foster, *Brighter Coming Day*, 19–21.
4. Fulton, "Sowing Seeds in an Untilled Field," 208.
5. In 2015, Johanna Ornter discovered a copy of *Forest Leaves* while researching at the Maryland Historical Society. A copy of that early manuscript and Ortner's account of her discovery can be found in "Lost No More." See also Foster, *Brighter Coming Day*, 8.
6. Foster, 9. Foster also notes that Harper's father may have been white (6).
7. Foster, 6–7.
8. Foster, 5. See also William Still's entry on Harper in *Underground Railroad*.
9. Foster, 13.
10. Foster, 9.
11. See Peterson, "Frances Harper, Charlotte Forten, and African American Literary Reconstruction."
12. Peterson, 46.
13. Peterson, 49.
14. Peterson, 47.
15. See Ryan and McCullough, *Cosmopolitan Twain*.
16. Jennifer Rae Greeson renames "local color" as "global color" in her discussion of the publication of travel literature during the Reconstruction period and the "exportable" nature of the literature of local color authors like George Washington Cable ("Expropriating the Great South and Exporting 'Local Color,'" 117). Susan Gilman also points out that the fiction of Cable, Chopin, and Twain was set during the antebellum period though they were writing in the 1880s. She also mentions Harper's efforts to link the time periods through flashbacks to the antebellum period but argues that the slave past overwhelms the "narrative present" (*Blood Talk*, 38).
17. Harper, *Iola Leroy*, 279.
18. Harper.
19. Harper.
20. Pagden, *Worlds at War*, 112.
21. My interpretation of Harper's "communities of interest" approximates Anthony Appiah's "rooted cosmopolitanism" (*Cosmopolitanism*, 91), even if Appiah's contemplations seem, according to Harvey, too similar to liberal individualism, "still grounded in the abstracted liberal and Kantian concept of the individual person as an actor" (*Cosmopolitanism and the Geographies of Freedom*, 259). For a discussion of the recurrence and the treatment of the phrase

"community of interest" in Harper's speeches, see Logan, *We Are Coming*.

22. Harper, *Iola Leroy*, 219.

23. Harvey, *Cosmopolitanism and the Geographies of Freedom*, 163–64.

24. Harvey, 164.

25. Peterson, "Literary Transnationalism and Diasporic History," 206.

26. Lewis, "Biracial Promise and the New South in *Minnie's Sacrifice*," 759.

27. See Nerad, "Slippery Language and False Dilemmas," 816. She argues that the insight into recognizing "passing" as an aspect of performativity draws on the "tragic mulatta" stereotype, and the commitment to "one-drop" racial categories prevents makes passing an effort to deny one's true identity.

28. Fabi, "Reconstructing Literary Genealogies," 59. Jessica Wells Cantiello reads this "geographical vagueness" as facilitating a "double-voiced discourse" in the novel that also suggests the way in which "African American texts talk to each other"; however, she situates Harper's *Iola Leroy* within the context of discourses on Indian education ("Frances E. W. Harper's Educational Reservations," 576).

29. Glissant, *Caribbean Discourse*, 14.

30. Bauer, "Hemispheric Genealogies of 'Race,'" 40.

31. Bauer.

32. Bauer, 41.

33. Stewart, "Spirituality and Resistance Among African-Creoles," 176.

34. Bauer, "Hemispheric Genealogies of 'Race,'" 41.

35. Harper, *Minnie's Sacrifice, Sowing and Reaping, Trial and Triumph*, 9.

36. Quoted in Lewis, "Biracial Promise and the New South in *Minnie's Sacrifice*," 758.

37. This point regarding a new episteme of creolization is the burden of Charles H. Long's essay on New Orleans, "New Orleans as an American City."

38. Clearly this is the case for both Iola and Doctor Latimer, with Iola desiring to "do something of lasting service for the race" (*Iola Leroy*, 262), and both working for the new dawn of freedom. Earlier, *Minnie's Sacrifice* had expressed the intimate commitment clearly: "that future in which they should clasp hands again and find their duty and their pleasure in living for the welfare and happiness of *our* race, as Minnie would often say" (67).

39. Nerad, "Slippery Language and False Dilemmas," 834.

40. According to Nerad, "Passers—including the fictional ones under examination here—are raised and raced as white. These individuals can choose to become black, but they cannot return to the black race because they have never been black" (817). Though the logic makes sense here, the context of the one-drop racial law and enslavement seems to be diminished in this account.

41. Bauer, "Hemispheric Genealogies of 'Race,'" 53. Bauer also notes that ideas about equality among whites in the United States were contingent on the existence of slavery and race, thus tinging the structure of nationalist democracy in the United States with this ethnos, though Craig Calhoun notes that the process of nationalism need not be framed with such negativity ("Cosmopolitanism and Nationalism," 444).

42. Long, "New Orleans as an American City," 215.

43. Long, 219.

44. Cable, *Grandissimes*, 24.

45. Cable, 283.

46. Greeson, "Expropriating the Great South," 131.

47. Greeson.

48. Greeson, 132.

49. Guterl, "American Mediterranean," 103.

50. Harper, *Minnie's Sacrifice, Sowing and Reaping, Trial and Triumph*, 278.

51. Harper.

52. It seems that Harper's speeches and essays approximate a "Unitarian and utilitarian" perspective (Foster, *Brighter Coming Day*, 95), and the AME Church also figures prominently in most of her fiction. In *Minnie's Sacrifice*, the Northern couple with antiracist sentiments who adopt her are Quakers (29), and there is a reference to the Catholic Church's openness in *Iola Leroy* (124).

53. Harper, *Iola Leroy*, 99.

54. Harper, 61.

55. Harper, 113, 124.

56. Harper, 62.

57. Harper, 65.

58. Harper, 61.
59. Harper, *Minnie's Sacrifice*, 7.
60. Harper, 11.
61. Harper, 7.
62. Harper, 21.
63. Harper, 9.
64. Harper.
65. Harper.
66. Bauer, "Hemispheric Genealogies of 'Race,'" 51.
67. Bauer, 53.
68. Greeson, "Expropriating the Great South," 128.
69. Harper, *Iola Leroy*, 49.
70. Harper, *Minnie's Sacrifice, Sowing and Reaping, Trial and Triumph*, 9.
71. Harper, 3.
72. Harper, 11.
73. Harper, *Iola Leroy*, 84–85.
74. Harper, 85.
75. Harper, *Minnie's Sacrifice, Sowing and Reaping, Trial and Triumph*, 10.
76. Harper, 22.
77. Lewis, "Biracial Promise and the New South in *Minnie's Sacrifice*," 763.
78. Harper, *Minnie's Sacrifice, Sowing and Reaping, Trial and Triumph*, 10.
79. Harper, 15.
80. Harper, 81.
81. Harper, 80.
82. Harper, "Woman's Christian Temperance Union and the Colored Woman," 283.
83. Harper, *Minnie's Sacrifice, Sowing and Reaping, Trial and Triumph*, 80.
84. Harper, *Iola Leroy*, 243.
85. Harper, 247.
86. In many respects, Delany's post-Reconstruction work, particularly *Principia of Ethnology: The Origin of Races and Color, with an Archeological Compendium of Ethiopian and Egyptian Civilization, from Years of Careful Examination and Enquiry* (1879), parallels the "*conversatione*" at the end of *Iola Leroy* about the nature of civilization, immigration to Africa, and spiritual, national, and racial pride.
87. Lucy A. Delaney's *From the Darkness Cometh the Light; or, Struggles for Freedom* was first published in 1891. Gabrielle P. Foreman makes this connection in "Reading Aright."
88. Harper, *Iola Leroy*, 247.

89. Harper, 247–48.
90. See Harper, *Minnie's Sacrifice, Sowing and Reaping, Trial and Triumph*, 220.
91. Hildegaard Hoeller argues that Harper's discourse draws on but varies from the Emersonian focus on self-reliance in masculinist and individualist terms ("Self-Reliant Women in Frances Harper's Writings," 214). A link might equally be made to her desire for a Christian cosmopolitan civilization and her awareness of the tyranny of public opinion in nurturing nationalist, masculinist, and racist self-conceptions.
92. Wallerstein, "Neither Patriotism nor Cosmopolitanism," 124. See also Calhoun, "Cosmopolitanism and Nationalism," 440.
93. According to William Still's biography, Harper was conversant with all popular magazines and issues (Foster, *Brighter Coming Day*, 20). Harper waged a type of rhetorical war on the "tyranny of public opinion" throughout most of her work. Harper, *Minnie's Sacrifice, Sowing and Reaping, Trial and Triumph*, 214–15.
94. Harper, 73.
95. Harper, "We Are All Bound Up Together," 219.
96. For a good discussion of Harper's challenge to the focus on sex (rather than race) within the women's suffrage movement, see O'Brien, "White Women All Go for Sex."
97. Harper, *Iola Leroy*, 217.
98. Harper, 250.
99. Harper, 254.
100. Elias, *Civilizing Process*, 27, 43.
101. Castiglia and Hendler, introduction to *Franklin Evans*, xxxi.
102. Rosenthal, *Race Mixture in Nineteenth-Century U.S. and Spanish American Fictions*, 68.
103. Castiglia and Hendler, introduction to *Franklin Evans*, ivi.
104. Whitman, *Franklin Evans*, 80.
105. Whitman, 83.
106. Castiglia and Hendler, introduction to *Franklin Evans*, li; Whitman, *Franklin Evans*, 78.
107. Castiglia and Hendler, li.
108. Castiglia and Hendler, iv.
109. Castiglia and Hendler, lvii.
110. Harper, *Iola Leroy*, 159.
111. Harper, 160.

112. Harper, *Minnie's Sacrifice, Sowing and Reaping, Trial and Triumph*, 144.
113. Harper, 146.
114. Harper, 147–48.
115. Harper, 99.
116. Harper, 110.
117. Harper, 134.
118. Harper, "Woman's Christian Temperance Union and the Colored Woman," 281.
119. See Wells, *Crusade for Justice*, 204–12; and Foreman, "Reading Aright," 340.
120. Frances Willard describes this shift in emphasis from Moody's evangelism quite early in the life of the WCTU (*Glimpses of Fifty Years*, 401). See also Ruth Bordin, who explains that the shift away from "gospel temperance" for Willard meant less of a concern with helping alcoholics and more of a concern with influencing politics (*Frances Willard*, 82).
121. Gilmore, *Gender and Jim Crow*, 49.
122. Peterson, "Literary Transnationalism and Diasporic History," 197.
123. Harper, *Minnie's Sacrifice, Sowing and Reaping, Trial and Triumph*, 100.
124. Harper, "We Are All Bound Up Together," 218.
125. Rosenthal, "Deracialized Discourse," 154.
126. As Debra Rosenthal notes "Publication of these novels in the Afro-Protestant press evidences a substantial African American reading population: 86 percent of black Bostonians were literate in 1850, and 92 percent by 1860" (155).
127. Rosenthal, 154.
128. Rosenthal, 157.
129. Fulton, "Sowing Seeds in an Untilled Field," 212.
130. Foreman, "Reading Aright," 331.
131. Fulton, "Sowing Seeds in an Untilled Field," 215.
132. Harper, *Minnie's Sacrifice, Sowing and Reaping, Trial and Triumph*, 99.
133. Harper, 165, 109.
134. Harper, 100.
135. As Hoeller puts it, "Harper provokes women into becoming radically independent of public opinion and of the institution (but not the ideal) of marriage that may hold them in shackles and destroy them; she celebrates the role of the 'old maid' as one viable option of female self-reliance" ("Self-Reliant Women in Frances Harper's Writings," 208).

136. Harper, *Minnie's Sacrifice, Sowing and Reaping, Trial and Triumph*, 173.
137. Harper, 161.
138. Foster, *Brighter Coming Day*, 105; Harper, "Two Offers," 107, 106.
139. Foster, 6. See also the original letter in Boyd, *Discarded Legacy*, 43.
140. Stewart, "Spirituality and Resistance Among African-Creoles," 181.
141. Harper, *Iola Leroy*, 282.

CHAPTER 5

The title of this chapter is drawn from Smith's famous observation, "I think some people would understand the quintessence of sanctifying grace if they could be black about twenty-four hours" (*An Autobiography*, 116–17). Hereafter cited parenthetically in the text and notes.

1. Ruth Bordin discusses the WCTU's break with evangelism and its movement toward more ostensibly political goals (*Frances Willard*, 126–30).
2. William Andrews notes that "sanctification" was "a second experience of divine grace in the soul following conversion." In the Holiness strain of Methodism, "To be sanctified was to experience full freedom from 'intentional sin'" (*Sisters of the Spirit*, 5). Smith's experience of sanctification begins while attending Tuesday night Holiness meetings led by Phoebe Palmer, one of the founders of the Holiness movement. After these meetings, Smith begins to argue that conversion does not entail works but faith, "enduring grace" derived from the directly felt experience of conversion, and "heart purity" (62).
3. Katherine Clay Bassard notes that, "as Julia A. Foote and Amanda Berry Smith testify, their belief in the doctrine of sanctification placed them far outside the circle of power relations in the AME Church, itself formed from the schism between the black and white members of St. George's Episcopal in Philadelphia because of racial prejudice" ("Gender and Genre," 121). The Holiness movement "was largely a women's movement," and many African American Holiness women "were directly embroiled in conflicts of gender

through the debate over women's place in the church" (122).

4. Inskip was the founder of the National Camp Meeting Association for the Promotion of Holiness. See Elkin Grammer, *Some Wild Visions*, 13.

5. Israel, *Amanda Berry Smith*, 54.

6. Dodson, introduction to *An Autobiography*, xxviii.

7. As Dodson notes, women were licensed as evangelists in an 1884 decision, while Smith was abroad (xxxvi). She continues, "Amanda and her work would represent the force that caused her Church to expand its structure to include women in such positions as stewardess, conference evangelist, and denomination deaconess" (xxviii).

8. Israel, *Amanda Berry Smith*, 91–93

9. Israel, 98–100.

10. Women like Smith, Jarena Lee, Zilpha Elaw, and Rebecca Jackson also come from the tradition of the AME Church, and they helped pave the way for the organization's subsequent expansion of public roles for women (see Dodson, introduction to *An Autobiography*, xxxi). Many African American women were involved with temperance, including Julia Foote, a member of the AME Zion Church, and Rebecca Cox Jackson, a prominent black female Shaker.

11. Chavigny discusses the different forms of temperance, including gospel temperance, leading to the "disease concept" of alcoholism so prominent in the twentieth century ("Reforming Drunkards in Nineteenth-Century America," 113).

12. Smith addresses the limits of good works and attempts to achieve conversion through mental acts. Smith also accepted aspects of medicine to heal her own illnesses when she was in England and criticized the racial discrimination in the United States that would not allow black people to visit some "sanatoriums." Some American Protestants criticized her outspoken critique of racism, and others accused her of not relying on "faith alone" because she visited a hospital. See Israel, *Amanda Berry Smith*, 104.

13. See Smith, *Autobiography*, 353; and Israel, 92.

14. Israel, 87.

15. Richard J. Douglass-Chin refers to her as "bourgeois-aspiring" in *Preacher Woman Sings the Blues*, 158, 146.

16. Smith was at pains to rid herself of the burden of fashion and dress especially prominent in some clubs and churches. See Klassen, "Robes of Womanhood," 56.

17. Klassen, 69.

18. Smith consistently attributes acts of charity toward her as the "Lord's doing" and rarely gives any special credit to the doer of the act. See, for instance, the account of a Father Bummel giving her five dollars (134).

19. Douglass-Chin, *Preacher Woman Sings the Blues*, 123.

20. Israel, *Amanda Berry Smith*, 73–74.

21. Foster, *Witnessing Slavery*, 150.

22. Foster, "In Respect to Females," 69; Smith, *Autobiography*, 155.

23. Douglass-Chin argues that there are aspects of "signifying" and doubling present in Smith's autobiography, but he favors Julia Foote's more direct style and comfort with the vernacular tradition. He tends to miss some of the subtleties in Smith's text, however, and often presents her as a conforming mind who even romanticized slavery. I disagree with the sense that Smith's prose is "genteel," and she clearly describes the slave owners through what others said. See Douglass-Chin, *Preacher Woman Sings the Blues*, 126.

24. Clay Bassard comments on this scene and concludes "that spiritual autobiographers go beyond the ideology of literacy . . . to contemplate the limits of language itself. For women evangelicals, the misuse of language is a sin" ("Gender and Genre," 126).

25. Clay Bassard.

26. Mendiola, "Hand of a Woman," 268.

27. Douglass-Chin, *Preacher Woman Sings the Blues*, 151.

28. Edouard Glissant contends that diversion and parallelism are used in creole discourse to suggest simultaneous histories and stories rather than the single history of the West (*Caribbean Discourse*, 93).

29. See Mendiola, "Hand of a Woman," 139, chap. 1.

30. Berlin, *Generations of Captivity*, 261.

31. Just prior to deciding to depart for India, and after the devil accuses her of not "providing

for her own household," Smith says that her greatest sense of home occurred in the house in New York with her daughter Mazie, perhaps because it was the first home she had as a single mother-evangelist, supporting her child (175).

32. Csordas, introduction to *Transnational Transcendence*, 1.

33. Haynes, *Divine Destiny*, 122.

34. Haynes, 118.

35. Elkin Grammer notes, "James Smith was devoted neither to God—his religious profession, she discovered, was entirely fraudulent—nor to his family." Smith portrays his death without much emotion and a "dry irony" (*Some Wild Visions*, 28).

36. See Elkin Grammer, 66–68.

37. Quoted in Elkin Grammer, 68.

38. Elkin Grammer, 49.

39. Elkin Grammer.

40. In 1893 an infamous interview appeared in Britain's *Westminster Gazette* in which Ida B. Wells criticized Willard, who then attempted to modify her seemingly lukewarm stance on the antilynching campaign. Willard, as the more powerful associate of Lady Henry Somerset, was supported in British papers, with Somerset, according to Wells, attempting to tarnish Wells's public reputation. Wells comments in her autobiography, "There is not a single colored woman admitted to the Southern WCTU, but still Miss Willard blames the Negro for the defeat of prohibition in the South!'" (*Crusade for Justice*, 209, 210).

41. See Israel, *Amanda Berry Smith*, 58.

42. As Mendiola notes, Willard recalls the "romantic racialism" employed by Harriet Beecher Stowe in her 1863 description of Sojourner Truth as "The Libyan Sybil," whom Stowe ironically thought was dead. White female camp meeting participants commonly allude to popular mammy-type characters, rendering Smith as a manifestation of the plantation-derived stereotype, "the idea of the simple, humble and forgiving black saint" ("Hand of a Woman," 232). Quoted in Israel, 61.

43. Israel, 113.

44. Smith criticizes the African American colonization of Liberia for the lack of funds to immigrants and because of the lack of knowledge of the region and unwillingness to learn from the natives (461).

45. Harvey, *Cosmopolitanism and the Geographies of Freedom*, 104.

46. Walters, *Black Americans and the Evangelization of Africa*, 3.

47. See Walters, 136, 91–92. Walters notes Smith's conviction that she was called to partake in the missionary redemption of Africa.

48. Smith was sometimes ambiguous about whether circumstances modified the requirement to abstain from certain substances, such as medicine. See Israel, *Amanda Berry Smith*, 104.

49. Quoted in Israel, 80.

50. Israel, 76.

51. Walters, *Black Americans and the Evangelization of Africa*, 113.

52. This is also the most common view given by missionaries in accounts from the American Colonization Society. For example, the Reverend A. D. Philips from the Southern Baptist Board of Missions in 1871 views the Bassa's conception of God and the devil as adaptable to his version of Christianity, though "they are idolaters but would perhaps more properly be called fetish worshippers." *African Repository and Colonial Journal*, 264. Smith also refers to the Basso and Grebo (as well as Catholics) as fetish worshippers.

53. I have adapted this point from Thomas Csordas's "Oxymorons and Short-Circuits in the Re-enchantment of the World," 22.

54. Notably, though Smith was a WCTU evangelist later in life, those years and travels were not without racial tensions. According to Israel, when Smith was in England working for the WCTU on a planned evangelist tour in 1894, she suffered from severe arthritis and could not keep up her public appearances. In doing so, "Smith also became embroiled in a debate about racism in the United States. When forced to get medical treatment, she wrote John Thompson that she was glad to be in Britain since she could not have received the same level of treatment in the United States because of her race" (*Amanda Berry Smith*, 104).

55. Elkin Grammer, *Some Wild Visions*, 34.

56. Kant, "Idea for a Universal History from a Cosmopolitan Perspective."

57. See Turner, "Center Out There."

58. Israel, *Amanda Berry Smith*, 5.

59. Smith, *Autobiography*, 197.
60. See Israel, *Amanda Berry Smith*, 142.

EPILOGUE

1. Fleisner, "Earth-Eating, Addiction, Nostalgia," 331.
2. Chesnutt's "Lonesome Ben" was written and submitted to the *Atlantic Monthly* in 1897, though it was rejected. It was published by the *Southern Workman* in 1900; see Stepto and Greeson, *Conjure Stories*, 50n1. Fleisner provides evidence that earth-eating was a form of suicide for many slaves and a major cause for concern for slaveholders (322).
3. Chireau traces what she calls the multiple forms of conjure that could be called "religion" (*Black Magic*, 17).
4. Fleisner, "Earth-Eating, Addiction, Nostalgia," 324.
5. Chesnutt was proud of his knowledge of Latin and Greek, particularly because he was excluded from an education that offered advanced study of the classics. Sarah Wagner-McCoy convincingly juxtaposes Virgil's treatment of nature with the pastoral visions prominent in antebellum aristocratic culture ("Virgilian Chesnutt," 200).
6. In many of the conjure tales and in lonesome Ben's transformation to clay, Ovid's (or Virgil's) metamorphoses and creation myths loom in the background. See, for example, Myers, "Mythic Patterns in Charles Waddel Chesnutt's *The Conjure Woman* and Ovid's *Metamorphoses*"; and Sollors, "Goopher in Charles Chesnutt's Conjure Tales."
7. Of course, there were differences in the forms of slavery, but in ancient slavery racial differences did not qualify one as a "natural slave," even in Aristotle's definition. See David Brion Davis's early discussion of different forms of slavery in *The Problem of Slavery in Western Culture*, esp. chap. 3.
8. I have made this argument on the "talented tenth" and the relation of Du Bois to Arendt elsewhere; see "Challenging Liberal Justice"; and *Strange Jeremiahs*, 243. See also Arendt, *On Revolution*, esp. "The Pursuit of Happiness" and "Foundation I: *Constitutio Liberatis*."

9. Sundquist, *To Wake the Nations*, 295.
10. Chesnutt, "Lonesome Ben," 59.
11. Chesnutt, 52.
12. Chesnutt, 55.
13. Chesnutt, 56.
14. Chesnutt, "Goophered Grapevine," 6. John seems to be following the romantic racialist stereotypes that attribute critical thought to whiteness. Critics have also commented on the trickster aspects of Uncle Julius. See Montgomery, "Testing and Tricking."
15. Chesnutt, "Lonesome Ben," 57.
16. Chesnutt, 58.
17. Chesnutt.
18. Chesnutt, 59.
19. Chesnutt, 58.
20. In the tale "A Deep Sleeper," Uncle Julius parodies the use of classical and biblical names for slaves with four names: "Skundus," "Tushus," "Cottus," and "Squinchus." Julius comments that their mother wanted to call them something more ordinary, like "'Rastus' er 'Caesar' er 'George Wash'n'ton';" but the master wanted to be able to tell them apart ("Deep Sleeper," 45).
21. Glissant, *Caribbean Discourse*, 105.
22. Glissant, 131.
23. Eric Sundquist comments that "Dave's Neckliss" is a "brilliant, grisly tale, which Frances Keller rightly compares to Kafka's story 'The Metamorphosis.' Dave's madness, love over a woman, and punishment by his master for stealing a ham, leads to his transformation into a ham who hangs himself" (*To Wake the Nations*, 379).
24. Chesnutt, "Goophered Grapevine," 8.
25. Chesnutt, 9.
26. See Myers, "Other Nature."
27. This interpretation of Dionysus and Atropus is pre-Christian, and there are debates over whether Dionysus's tears are simply expressions of personal loss or tears for the whole of humanity (as with Christ's tears). Robert Shorrock argues that, in either case, it is Atropus who is moved for humanity's sake (*Myth of Paganism*, 103).
28. I generally agree with Jeffrey Myers's interpretation of Chesnutt's *Conjure Woman* as showing that "African Americans and the land they have worked, as well as the surviving tracts of uncultivated and undeveloped land, have

a symbiosis that the slave-owning plantation owners—and the Northern capitalists who replaced them as landowners—lack" ("Other Nature," 10). However, the representation of the land is also excessive and irreducible—given that the transformations result not only from domination but also from conjure and indigenous traditions. This opaqueness suggests a relationship of reverence and temperance that allows for a dependence and mutuality.

29. Chesnutt, "Goophered Grapevine," 12.
30. Chesnutt, 13, 14.
31. Chesnutt, 14.
32. Chesnutt, "Lonesome Ben," 52.
33. Chesnutt, 59.
34. Fleisner, "Earth-Eating, Addiction, Nostalgia," 320.
35. Sundquist, *To Wake the Nations*, 294. Sundquist elaborates on Chesnutt's duplicity and sympathies with the trickster figure.
36. For a discussion of Chesnutt's modification of African religions and seriousness about conjure, see Murray, *Matter, Magic, and Spirit*. See also Chesnutt, "Superstitions and Folk-Lore of the South," 204.
37. Chesnutt, "Lonesome Ben," 59.

Bibliography

Albanese, Catherine L. *A Republic of Mind and Spirit: A Cultural History of American Metaphysical Religion.* New Haven, CT: Yale University Press, 2007.

Alexander, Leslie M. "'The Black Republic': The Influence of the Haitian Revolution on Northern Black Political Consciousness, 1816–1862." In *Haitian History: New Perspectives: Rewriting Histories,* edited by Alyssa Goldstein Sepinwall, 197–214. New York: Routledge, 2012.

Andrews, William L. Introduction to *From Fugitive Slave to Free Man: The Autobiographies of William Wells Brown,* edited by William L. Andrews, 1–12. Columbia: University of Missouri Press, 1993.

———, ed. *The North Carolina Roots of African American Literature: An Anthology.* Chapel Hill: University of North Carolina Press, 2006.

———, ed. *Sisters of the Spirit: Three Black Women's Autobiographies of the Nineteenth Century.* Bloomington: Indiana University Press, 1986.

Anonymous. Introduction to *The Poetical Works,* by George Moses Horton, xxi–xxii.

Appiah, Kwame Anthony. *Cosmopolitanism: Ethics in a World of Strangers.* New York: Norton, 2006.

———. "Cosmopolitan Patriots." In *Cosmopolitics: Thinking and Feeling Beyond the Nation,* edited by Pheng Cheah and Bruce Robbins, 81–114. Minneapolis: University of Minnesota Press, 1998.

Arendt, Hannah. *The Human Condition.* 2nd ed. Chicago: University of Chicago Press, 1998.

———. *On Revolution.* New York: Penguin, 1990.

Baraw, Charles. "William Wells Brown, *Three Years in Europe,* and Fugitive Tourism." *African American Review* 44, no. 3 (Fall 2011): 453–70.

Barrett, Faith. *To Fight Aloud Is Very Brave: American Poetry and the Civil War.* Amherst: University of Massachusetts Press, 2012.

Baucom, Ian. *Specters of the Atlantic: Finance Capital, Slavery, and the Philosophy of History.* Durham, NC: Duke University Press, 2005.

Bauer, Ralph. "The Hemispheric Genealogies of 'Race': Creolization and the Cultural Geography of Colonial Difference Across the Eighteenth-Century Americas." In Levander and Levine, *Hemispheric American Studies,* 36–56.

Beecher, Lyman. *Six Sermons on Intemperance. Delineating Its Nature, Occasions, Signs, Evils, and Remedy.* Edinburgh: Scottish Temperance Society, 1846.

Berlin, Ira. *Generations of Captivity: A History of African-American Slaves.* Cambridge, MA: Harvard University Press, 2003.

———. *Many Thousands Gone: The First Two Centuries of Slavery in North America.* Cambridge, MA: Harvard University Press, 1998.

Berman, Jessica. *Modernist Fiction, Cosmopolitanism and the Politics of Community.* Cambridge, UK: Cambridge University Press, 2001.

Bethel, Elizabeth Rauh. "Images of Hayti: The Construction of An Afro-American *Lieu De Mémoire.*" In "Haitian Literature and Culture, Part 2," special issue of *Callaloo* 15, no. 3 (Summer 1992): 827–41.

Bhabha, Homi K. *The Location of Culture*. New York: Routledge, 1994.

Bibb, Henry. "Editorial by Henry Bibb, 21 May 1851: Color-Phobia in Canada." In Ripley, *Black Abolitionist Papers*, vol. 2, 136–41.

Birnbaum, Michele. "Racial Hysteria: Female Pathology and Race Politics in France Harper's 'Iola Leroy' and W. D. Howells's 'An Imperative Duty.'" *African American Review* 33, no. 1 (1999): 7–23.

Blocker, Jack S., Jr. *American Temperance Movements: Cycles of Reform*. Boston: Twayne, 1989.

Bordin, Ruth. *Frances Willard: A Biography*. Chapel Hill: University of North Carolina Press, 1986.

Borgstrom, Michael. "Face Value: Ambivalent Citizenship in *Iola Leroy*." *African American Review* 40, no. 4 (2006): 779–92.

Boyd, Melba Joyce. *Discarded Legacy: Politics and Poetics in the Life of Frances E. W. Harper, 1825–1911*. Detroit: Wayne State University Press, 1994.

Bradley, Patricia. *Slavery, Propaganda, and the American Revolution*. Jackson: University Press of Mississippi, 1998.

Brown, William Wells. *The American Fugitive in Europe: Sketches of Places and People Abroad*. 1854. In Jefferson, *Travels of William Wells Brown*.

———. *The Black Man, His Antecedents, His Genius, and His Achievements*. 1863. New York: Thomas Hamilton, Johnson Reprint, 1968.

———. *Clotel; or, The President's Daughter: A Narrative of Slave Life in the United States*. 1853. Edited by Robert S. Levine. Boston: Bedford / St. Martin's, 2000.

———. "The Colored People of Canada." 1861. In Ripley, *Black Abolitionist Papers*, vol. 2, 458–98.

———. *A Description of William Wells Brown's Original Panoramic Views of the Scenes in the Life of an American Slave, from His Birth in Slavery to His Death, or His Escape to His First Home of Freedom on British Soil*. 1852. In Ripley, *Black Abolitionist Papers*, vol. 1, 191–224.

———. *The Escape; or, A Leap for Freedom: A Drama in Five Acts*. Edited by John Ernest. Knoxville: University of Tennessee Press, 2001.

———. *My Southern Home; The South and Its People*. Edited by John Ernest. Chapel Hill: University of North Carolina Press, 2011.

———. *Narrative of William Wells Brown a Fugitive Slave*. 1847. 2nd ed. In Jefferson, *Travels of William Wells Brown*, 21–70.

———. *The Rising Son; or, The Antecedents of the Advancement of the Colored Race*. Boston: A. J. Brown, 1874.

———. *Three Years in Europe; or, Places I Have Seen and People I Have Met*. London: Gilpin, 1852. Documenting the American South. University Library, University of North Carolina at Chapel Hill. http://docsouth.unc.edu/.

Burris, John. *Exhibiting Religion: Colonialism and Spectacle at International Expositions, 1851–1893*. Charlottesville: University of Virginia Press, 2001.

Cable, George Washington. *The Grandissimes: A Story of Creole Life*. New York: Penguin, 1988.

Calhoun, Craig. "The Class Consciousness of Frequent Travelers: Toward a Critique of Actually Existing Cosmopolitanism." *South Atlantic Quarterly* 101, no. 4 (2002): 869–97.

———. "Cosmopolitanism and Nationalism." *Nations and Nationalism* 14, no. 3 (2008): 427–48.

———. *Nations Matter: Culture, History, and the Cosmopolitan Dream*. New York: Routledge, 2007.

Callahan, Richard J., Jr., ed. *New Territories, New Perspectives: The Religious Impact of the Louisiana Purchase*. Columbia: University of Missouri Press, 2008.

Cantiello, Jessica Wells. "Frances E. W. Harper's Educational Reservations: The Indian Question in *Iola Leroy*." *African American Review* 45, no. 4 (2012): 575–92.

Carlson, Douglas W. "'Drinks He to His Own Undoing': Temperance Ideology in the Deep South." *Journal of the Early Republic* 18, no. 4 (Winter 1998): 659–91.

Cartwright, Samuel A. *Diseases and Peculiarities of the Negro Race*. In Brown, *Clotel*, 390–94.

Castiglia, Christopher, and Glenn Hendler. Introduction to *Franklin Evans; or, The Inebriate: A Tale of the Times*, by Walt Whitman, ix–lvii. Edited by Christopher Castiglia and Glenn Hendler. Durham, NC: Duke University Press, 2007.

Chavigny, Katherine A. "Reforming Drunkards in Nineteenth-Century America: Religion, Medicine, Therapy." In *Altering American Consciousness: The History of Alcohol and Drug Use in the United States, 1800–2000*, edited by Sarah W. Tracy and Caroline Jean Acker, 108–25. Amherst: University of Massachusetts Press, 2004.

Chesnutt, Charles W. "A Deep Sleeper." In Stepto and Greeson, *Conjure Stories*, 42–50.

———. "The Goophered Grapevine." In Stepto and Greeson, *Conjure Stories*, 3–14.

———. "Lonesome Ben." In Stepto and Greeson, *Conjure Stories*, 50–59.

———. "Superstitions and Folk-Lore of the South." In Stepto and Greeson, *Conjure Stories*, 199–205.

Chiles, Katy. "Within and Without Raced Nations: Intratextuality, Martin Delany, and *Blake; or the Huts of America*." *American Literature* 80, no. 2 (2008): 323–52.

Chireau, Yvonne P. *Black Magic: Religion and the African American Conjuring Tradition*. Berkeley: University of California Press, 2003.

Christmon, Kenneth. "Historical Overview of Alcohol in the African American Community." *Journal of Black Studies* 25, no. 3 (January 1995): 318–30.

Clay Bassard, Katherine. "Gender and Genre: Black Women's Autobiography and the Ideology of Literacy." *African American Review* 26, no. 1 (Spring 1992): 119–29.

Clymer, Jeffory A. "Martin Delany's *Blake* and the Transnational Politics of Property." *American Literary History* 15, no. 4 (2003): 709–31.

Coker, Joe. *Liquor in the Land of the Lost Cause: Southern White Evangelicals and the Prohibition Movement, 1880–1915*. Lexington: University Press of Kentucky, 2007.

Coleridge, Samuel. *Biographia Literaria; or, Biographical Sketches of My Literary Life and Opinions*. 2 vols. London, 1817.

Cook, Christopher. *Alcohol, Addiction, and Christian Ethics*. New York: Cambridge University Press, 2006.

Cowley, Malcolm. Introduction to *Adventures of an African Slaver: Being a True Account of the Life of Captain Theodore Canot, Trader in Gold, Ivory and Slaves on the Coast of Guinea*, by Theodore Canot. New York: Albert & Charles Boni, 1928.

Crowley, John W. "Slaves to the Bottle: Gough's Autobiography and Douglass's Narrative." In Reynolds and Rosenthal, *Serpent in the Cup*, 115–35.

Csordas, Thomas J. Introduction to *Transnational Transcendence: Essays on Religion and Globalization*, 1–29. Edited by Thomas J. Csordas. Berkeley: University of California Press, 2009.

———. "Oxymorons and Short-Circuits in the Re-enchantment of the World: The Case of the Catholic Charismatic Renewal." In "Debetorverde Wereld," special issue of *Etnofoor* 8, no. 1 (1995): 5–26.

Darwin, John. *After Tamerlane: The Global History of Empire Since 1405*. New York: Bloomsbury, 2008.

Davis, David Brion. *In the Image of God: Religion, Moral Values, and Our Heritage of Slavery*. New Haven, CT: Yale University Press, 2001.

———. *The Problem of Slavery in the Age of Emancipation*. New York: Knopf, 2014.

———. *The Problem of Slavery in an Age of Revolution, 1770–1823*. Ithaca, NY: Cornell University Press, 1975.

———. *The Problem of Slavery in Western Culture*. New York: Oxford University Press, 1966.

Delaney, Lucy A. *From the Darkness Cometh the Light; or, Struggles for Freedom*. St. Louis: Publishing House of J. T. Smith, 1891.

Delany, Martin. *Blake; or, The Huts of America*. 1859–62. Boston: Beacon, 1971.

———. *The Condition, Elevation, Emigration, and Destiny of the Colored People of the United States*. 1852. Project Gutenberg, 2005. http://ia802300.us.archive.org/7/items/theconditionelev17154gut/17154-8.txt.

———. "The Origin and Objects of Ancient Freemasonry: Its Introduction into the United States, and Legitimacy Among Colored Men. A Treatise Delivered Before St Cyprian Lodge, No. 13, June 24th, A.D. 1853–A.L. 5853." In Levine, *Martin R. Delany*, 49–67.

———. *Principia of Ethnology: The Origins of Races and Color, with an Archaeological Compendium of Ethiopian and Egyptian Civilization, from Years of Careful Examination and Enquiry*. 1879. In Levine, *Martin R. Delany*, 468–83.

———. "Report of the Niger Valley Exploring Party." 1861. In Levine, *Martin R. Delany*, 336–57.

DeSimone, Erika, and Louis Fidel, eds. *Voices Beyond Bondage: An Anthology of Verse by African Americans of the 19th Century*. Montgomery, AL: NewSouth Books, 2014.

Dodson, Julyanne. Introduction to *An Autobiography: The Story of the Lord's Dealings with Mrs. Amanda Smith the Colored Evangelist*, by Amanda Smith. 1893. Schomburg Library of Nineteenth-Century Black Women Writers. New York: Oxford University Press, 1988.

Douglass, Frederick. *My Bondage and My Freedom*. New York: Arno, 1968.

———. *Narrative of the Life of Frederick Douglass*. In *The Classic Slave Narratives*, edited by Henry Louis Gates Jr., 323–436. New York: Penguin, 2002.

Douglass-Chin, Richard J. *Preacher Woman Sings the Blues: The Autobiographies of Nineteenth-Century African American Evangelists*. Columbia: University of Missouri Press, 2001.

Drew, Benjamin, ed. *The Refugee; or, The Narratives of Fugitive Slaves in Canada Related by Themselves, with an Account of the History and Condition of the Colored Populations of Upper Canada*. 1856. Toronto: Prospero, 2000.

Du Bois, W. E. B. *The Souls of Black Folk*. New York: Penguin, 1995.

Elias, Norbert. *The Civilizing Process: Sociogenetic and Psychogenetic Investigations*. Rev. ed. Malden, MA: Blackwell, 2000.

Elkin Grammer, Elizabeth. *Some Wild Visions: Autobiographies by Female Itinerant Evangelists in Nineteenth-Century America*. New York: Oxford University Press, 2003.

Ernest, John. *Chaotic Justice: Rethinking African American Literary History*. Chapel Hill: University of North Carolina Press, 2009.

———. Introduction to *The Escape; or, a Leap for Freedom*, by William Wells Brown, xx–xxi. Edited by John Ernest. Knoxville: University of Tennessee Press, 2001.

———. *Liberation Historiography: African American Writers and the Challenge of History, 1794–1861*. Chapel Hill: University of North Carolina Press, 2004.

———. "The Reconstruction of Whiteness: William Wells Brown's *The Escape; or, A Leap for Freedom*." *PMLA* 113, no. 5 (October 1998): 1108–21.

———. *Resistance and Reformation in Nineteenth-Century African-American Literature: Brown, Wilson, Jacobs, Delany, Douglass, and Harper*. Jackson: University Press of Mississippi, 1995.

Fabi, M. Giulia. "Reconstructing Literary Genealogies: Frances E. W. Harper's and William Dean Howells's Race Novels." In *Soft Canons: American Women Writers and the Masculine

Tradition, edited by Karen L. Kilcup, 48–67. Iowa City: University of Iowa Press, 1999.

Fahey, David M. *Temperance and Racism: John Bull, Johnny Reb, and the Good Templars*. Lexington: University of Kentucky Press, 1996.

Fanuzzi, Robert. "Taste, Manners, and Miscegenation: French Racial Politics in the U.S." *American Literary History* 19, no. 3 (2007): 573–602.

Farmer, William. Extract from letter to William Lloyd Garrison, June 26, 1851. In *Running a Thousand Miles for Freedom*, by William Craft and Ellen Craft, 79–82. Athens: University of Georgia Press, 1999. [Full letter found in Still, *Underground Railroad*.]

———. "Memoir of William Wells Brown." In Brown, *Three Years in Europe*, x–xxxii.

Farrison, William E. "George Moses Horton: Poet for Freedom." *CLA Journal* 14, no. 3 (March 1971): 227–41.

———. *William Wells Brown: Author and Reformer*. Chicago: University of Chicago Press, 1969.

———. "William Wells Brown in Buffalo." *Journal of Negro History* 39, no. 4 (October 1954): 298–314.

Federal Writers Project. *North Carolina: A Guide to the Old North States*. Chapel Hill: University of North Carolina Press, 1939.

Finkelman, Paul. *An Imperfect Union: Slavery, Federalism, and Comity*. Chapel Hill: University of North Carolina Press, 1981.

Fleisner, Jennifer L. "Earth-Eating, Addiction, Nostalgia: Charles Chesnutt's Diasporic Regionalism." In "Nostalgia, Melancholy, Anxiety: Discursive Mobility and the Circulation of Bodies," special issue of *Studies in Romanticism* 49, no. 2 (Summer 2010): 313–36.

Foreman, P. Gabrielle. "'Reading Aright': White Slavery, Black Referents, and the Strategy of Histotextuality in *Iola Leroy*." *Yale Journal of Criticism* 10, no. 2 (1997): 327–54.

Foster, Frances Smith, ed. *A Brighter Coming Day: A Frances Ellen Watkins Harper Reader*. New York: Feminist Press, 1990.

———. "'In Respect to Females . . .': Differences in the Portrayals of Women by Male and Female Narrators." *Black American Literature Forum* 15, no. 2 (Summer 1981): 66–70.

———. *Witnessing Slavery: The Development of Ante-Bellum Slave Narratives*. Madison: University of Wisconsin Press, 1994.

Fox-Genovese, Elizabeth, and Eugene D. Genovese. *The Mind of the Master Class: History and Faith in the Southern Slaveholders' Worldview*. New York: Cambridge University Press, 2005.

Franklin, John Hope. *From Slavery to Freedom: A History of Negro Americans*. 5th ed. New York: Knopf, 1980.

Frey, Sylvia R. *Water from the Rock: Black Resistance in a Revolutionary Age*. Princeton, NJ: Princeton University Press, 1991.

Fulton, DoVeanna S. "Sowing Seeds in an Untilled Field: Temperance and Race, Indeterminacy and Recovery in Frances E. W. Harper's *Sowing and Reaping*." *Legacy: A Journal of American Women Writers* 24, no. 2 (2007): 207–24.

Garrett, Paula, and Hollis Robbins. Introduction to *The Works of William Wells Brown: Using His "Strong, Manly Voice,"* edited by Paula Garrett and Hollis Robbins, xvii–xxxviii. New York: Oxford University Press, 2006.

Gikandi, Simon. *Slavery and the Culture of Taste*. Princeton, NJ: Princeton University Press, 2011.

Gilman, Susan. *Blood Talk: American Race Melodrama and the Culture of the Occult*. Chicago: University of Chicago Press, 2003.

Gilmore, Glenda Elizabeth. *Gender and Jim Crow: Women and the Politics of White Supremacy in North Carolina, 1896–1920*. Chapel Hill: University of North Carolina Press, 1996.

Gilroy, Paul. *The Black Atlantic: Modernity and Double Consciousness.* Cambridge, MA: Harvard University Press, 1993.

Glaude, Eddie S. *Exodus! Religion, Race, and Nation in Early Nineteenth-Century Black America.* Chicago: University of Chicago Press, 2000.

Glenn, Patrick. *The Cosmopolitan State.* New York: Oxford University Press, 2013.

Glissant, Edouard. *Caribbean Discourse.* Translated by J. Michael Dash. Charlottesville: University Press of Virginia, 1989.

Green, Vivien M. "Hiram Powers's 'Greek Slave': Emblem of Freedom." *American Art Journal* 14, no. 4 (Autumn 1982): 31–39.

Greenspan, Ezra. *William Wells Brown. An African American Life.* New York: Norton, 2014.

Greeson, Jennifer Rae. "Expropriating the Great South and Exporting 'Local Color': Global and Hemispheric Imaginaries of the First Reconstruction." In Levander and Levine, *Hemispheric American Studies*, 116–39.

Gruesz, Kirsten Silva. "The Mercurial Space of 'Central' America: New Orleans, Honduras, and the Writing of the Banana Republic." In Levander and Levine, *Hemispheric American Studies*, 140–65.

Guterl, Matthew Pratt. "An American Mediterranean: Haiti, Cuba, and the American South." In Levander and Levine, *Hemispheric American Studies*, 96–115.

Hamilton, Cynthia S. "'Dred': Intemperate Slavery." *Journal of American Studies* 34, no. 2 (2000): 257–77.

Harper, Frances E. W. "The Great Problem to be Solved." 1875. In Foster, *Brighter Coming Day*, 219–22.

———. *Iola Leroy; or, Shadow's Uplifted.* 1892. New York: Oxford University Press, 1990.

———. "Letter." September 28, 1854. In Foster, *Brighter Coming Day*, 44.

———. *Minnie's Sacrifice, Sowing and Reaping, Trial and Triumph: Three Rediscovered Novels by Frances E. W. Harper.* Edited by Frances Smith Foster. Boston: Beacon, 1994.

———. "The Two Offers." 1859. In Foster, *Brighter Coming Day*, 105–14.

———. "We Are All Bound Up Together." 1866. In Foster, *Brighter Coming Day*, 217–19.

———. "The Woman's Christian Temperance Union and the Colored Woman." 1888. In Foster, *Brighter Coming Day*, 281–85.

Harvey, David. *Cosmopolitanism and the Geographies of Freedom.* New York: Columbia University Press, 2009.

Haynes, Carolyn A. *Divine Destiny: Gender and Race in Nineteenth-Century Protestantism.* Jackson: University Press of Mississippi, 1998.

Hendler, Glenn. *Public Sentiments: Structures of Feeling in Nineteenth-Century American Literature.* Chapel Hill: University of North Carolina Press, 2001.

Higginbotham, A. Leon. *In the Matter of Color: Race and the American Legal Process.* New York: Oxford University Press, 1978.

Hoeller, Hildegard. "Self-Reliant Women in Frances Harper's Writings." *American Transcendental Quarterly* 19, no. 3 (September 2005): 205–20.

Horton, George Moses. "An Address. The Stream of Liberty and Science. To Collegiates of the University of N.C. By George M. Horton The Black Bard." 1859. North Carolina Collection, University of North Carolina at Chapel Hill.

———. "The Art of a Poet." 1865. In Sherman, *Black Bard of North Carolina*, 147.

———. "Division of an Estate." In Horton, *Poetical Works*, 87.

———. "Imploring to Be Resigned at Death." In Horton, *Poetical Works*, 75.

———. "The Intemperance Club." 1865. In Sherman, *Black Bard of North Carolina*, 154.

———. "Life of George Moses Horton: The Colored Bard of North Carolina." 1845. In Horton, *Poetical Works*, iii–xx.

———. "One Generation Passeth Away and Another Cometh." 1865. In Sherman, *Black Bard of North Carolina*, 133.

———. "On Liberty and Slavery." 1829. In Sherman, *Black Bard of North Carolina*, 75.

———. *The Poetical Works*. 1845. Documenting the American South. University Library, University of North Carolina at Chapel Hill. http://docsouth.unc.edu/.

———. "The Southern Refugee." In Sherman, *Black Bard of North Carolina*, 124.

———. "The Tippler to His Bottle." In Horton, *Poetical Works*, 55.

Hughes-Warrington, Marnie. "Coloring Universal History: Robert Benjamin Lewis's *Light and Truth* (1843) and William Wells Brown's *The Black Man* (1863)." *Journal of World History* 20, no. 1 (2009): 99–130.

Israel, Adrienne M. *Amanda Berry Smith: From Washerwoman to Evangelist*. Lanham, MD: Scarecrow, 1998.

Jackson, Blyden, and Louis D. Rubin Jr. *Black Poetry in America: Two Essays in Historical Interpretation*. Baton Rouge: Louisiana State University Press, 1974.

Jacob, Margaret C. *Strangers Nowhere in the World: The Rise of Cosmopolitanism in Early Modern Europe*. Chicago: University of Chicago Press, 2007.

James, William H., and Stephen L. Johnson. *Doin' Drugs: Patterns of African American Addiction*. Austin: University of Texas Press, 1996.

Jefferson, Paul, ed. *The Travels of William Wells Brown*. New York: Markus Wiener, 1991.

Jefferson, Thomas. *Notes on the State of Virginia*. In *Thomas Jefferson: Writings*, edited by Merrill D. Peterson. New York: Library of America, 1984.

Kant, Immanuel, "Idea for a Universal History from a Cosmopolitan Perspective." 1784. Translated by David L. Colclasure. In *Toward Perpetual Peace and Other Writings on Politics, Peace, and History*, edited by Pauline Kleingeld, 3–16. New Haven, CT: Yale University Press, 2006.

———. "Idea for a Universal History with a Cosmopolitan Aim." 1784. Translated by Allen W. Wood. In *Kant's Idea for a Universal History with a Cosmopolitan Aim: A Critical Guide*, edited by Amélie Oksenberg Rorty and James Schmidt, 10–23. Cambridge, UK: Cambridge University Press, 2009.

Kern, Louis J. *An Ordered Love: Sex Roles and Sexuality in Victorian Utopias—the Shakers, the Mormons, and the Oneida Community*. Chapel Hill: University of North Carolina Press, 1981.

Klassen, Pamela E. "The Robes of Womanhood: Dress and Authenticity Among African American Methodist Women in the Nineteenth Century." *Religion and American Culture* 14, no. 1 (2004): 39–82.

Klein, Richard. *Cigarettes Are Sublime*. Durham, NC: Duke University Press, 1993.

Kohn, Margaret. "The Other America: Tocqueville and Beaumont on Race." *Polity* 35, no. 2 (2002): 169–87.

Leonard, Keith. *Fettered Genius: The African American Bardic Poet from Slavery to Civil Rights*. Charlottesville: University of Virginia Press, 2005.

Levander, Caroline F., and Robert S. Levine, eds. *Hemispheric American Studies*. New Brunswick, NJ: Rutgers University Press, 2008.

Levine, Robert S. "Disturbing Boundaries: Temperance, Black Elevation, and Violence in Frank J. Webb's *The Garies and Their Friends*." *Prospects* 19 (1994): 349–74.

———. "Introduction: Cultural and Historical Background." In Brown, *Clotel*, 3–27.

———. *Martin Delany, Frederick Douglass, and the Politics of Representative Identity*. Chapel Hill: University of North Carolina Press, 1997.

———, ed. *Martin R. Delany: A Documentary Reader*. Chapel Hill: University of North Carolina Press, 2003.

———. "'Whiskey, Blacking, and All': Temperance and Race in William Wells Brown's *Clotel*." In Reynolds and Rosenthal, *Serpent in the Cup*, 93–114.

Levy, Daniel, and Nathan Sznaider. *The Holocaust and Memory in the Global Age*. Philadelphia: Temple University Press, 2006.

Lewis, Leslie W. "Biracial Promise and the New South in *Minnie's Sacrifice*: A Protocol for Reading *The Curse of Caste; or, The Slave Bride*." *African American Review* 40, no. 4 (2006): 755–67.

Lincoln, Abraham. "An Address Delivered Before the Springfield Washingtonian Temperance Society at the Second Presbyterian Church, Springfield, Illinois, on the 22nd Day of February, 1842." In Whitman, *Franklin Evans*, 135–43.

Logan, Shirley Wilson. *We Are Coming: The Persuasive Discourse of Nineteenth Century Black Women*. Carbondale: Southern Illinois University Press, 1999.

Long, Charles H. "Indigenous People, Materialities, and Religion." In *Religion and Global Cultures: New Terrain in the Study of Religion and the Work of Charles H. Long*, edited by Jennifer I. M. Reid, 167–80. Lanham, MD: Lexington Books, 2003.

———. "New Orleans as an American City: Origins, Exchanges, Materialities, and Religion." In *New Territories, New Perspectives: The Religious Impact of the Louisiana Purchase*, edited by Richard J. Callahan Jr., 203–22. Columbia: University of Missouri Press, 2008.

———. *Significations: Signs, Symbols, and Images in the Interpretation of Religion*. Aurora, CO: Davies Group, 1995.

Lucasi, Stephan. "William Wells Brown's Narrative and Traveling Subjectivity." *African American Review* 41, no. 3 (2007): 521–40.

Mason, Julian. "'To Be an Author': Letters of Charles W. Chesnutt, 1889–1905." *Mississippi Quarterly* 51, no. 4 (1998): 717.

Mattingly, Carol. *Well-Tempered Women: Nineteenth-Century Temperance Rhetoric*. Carbondale: Southern Illinois University Press, 2000.

McGann, Jerome. "Rethinking Delany's *Blake*." *Callaloo* 39, no. 1 (2016): 80–95.

Mendiola, Kelly Willis. "The Hand of a Woman: Four Holiness-Pentecostal Evangelists and American Culture, 1840–1930." PhD diss., University of Texas at Austin, 2002.

Miller, Floyd. Introduction to Delany, *Blake*, xi–xxv.

Mintz, Sidney. *Sweetness and Power: The Place of Sugar in Modern History*. New York: Penguin, 1985.

Montgomery, Georgene Bess. "Testing and Tricking: Elegba in Charles Chesnutt's 'The Goophered Grapevine' and 'The Passing of Grandison.'" *Studies in the Literary Imagination* 43, no. 2 (Fall 2010): 5–14.

Murray, David. *Matter, Magic, and Spirit: Representing Indian and African American Belief*. Philadelphia: University of Pennsylvania Press, 2013.

Myers, Jeffrey. "Other Nature: Resistance to Ecological Hegemony in Charles Chesnutt's *The Conjure Woman*." *African American Review* 37, no. 1 (2003): 5–20.

Myers, Karen Magee. "Mythic Patterns in Charles Waddel Chesnutt's *The Conjure Woman* and Ovid's *Metamorphoses*." *Black American Literature Forum* 13 (1979): 13–17.

Nerad, Julie Cary. "Slippery Language and False Dilemmas: The Passing Novels of Child, Howells, and Harper." *American Literature* 75, no. 4 (December 2003): 813–40.

Nott, Josiah C., and George R. Gliddon. Excerpt from *Types of Mankind*. In Brown, *Clotel*, 386–90.

Nussbaum, Martha. *For Love of Country: Debating the Limits of Patriotism*. Edited by Joshua Cohen. Boston: Beacon, 2002.

Nwankwo, Ifeoma Kiddoe. *Black Cosmopolitanism: Racial Consciousness and Transnational Identity in the Nineteenth-Century Americas*. Philadelphia: University of Pennsylvania Press, 2005.

O'Brien, C. C. "'The White Women All Go for Sex': Frances Harper on Suffrage,

Citizenship, and the Reconstruction South." *African American Review* 43, no. 4 (Winter 2009): 605–20.

O'Malley, Michael. "Species and Specie: Race and the Money Question in Nineteenth-Century America." *American Historical Review* 99 (1994): 369–95.

Ornter, Johanna. "Lost No More: Recovering Frances Ellen Watkins Harper's *Forest Leaves*." *Common Place* 15, no. 4 (Summer 2015): http://common-place.org/book/lost-no-more-recovering-frances-ellen-watkins-harpers-forest-leaves.

Pagden, Anthony. "Europe: Conceptualizing a Continent." In *The Idea of Europe: From Antiquity to the European Union*, edited by Anthony Pagden, 33–54. New York: Cambridge University Press, 2002.

———. *The Fall of Natural Man*. New York: Cambridge University Press, 1982.

———. *Worlds at War: The 2,500-Year Struggle Between East and West*. New York: Random House, 2008.

Parker, B. F. "The 'Good Templar Coming of Age in England.'" In *The International Good Templar*, vol. 6. n.p., 1893. Google Books, 2012. http://books.google.ca/books?id=9UA2AQAAMAAJ.

Patterson, Orlando. *Slavery and Social Death: A Comparative Study*. Cambridge, MA: Harvard University Press, 1982.

Pelton, Robert D. *The Trickster in West Africa: A Study of Mythic Irony and Sacred Delight*. Berkeley: University of California Press, 1980.

Peterson, Carla. "Frances Harper, Charlotte Forten, and African American Literary Reconstruction." In *Challenging Boundaries: Gender and Periodization*, edited by Joyce W. Warren and Margaret Dickie, 39–61. Athens: University of Georgia Press, 2012.

———. "Literary Transnationalism and Diasporic History: Frances Watkins Harper's 'Fancy Sketches,' 1859–60." In *Women's Rights and Transatlantic Antislavery in the Era of Emancipation*, edited by Kathryn Kish Sklar and James Brewer Stewart, 189–207. New Haven, CT: Yale University Press, 2007.

Philips, Rev. A. D. *The African Repository and Colonial Journal* 47 (1871): https://catalog.hathitrust.org/Record/004565311.

Pitts, Reginald. "'Let Us Desert This Friendless Place': George Moses Horton in Philadelphia, 1866." *Journal of Negro History* 80, no. 4 (Fall 1995): 145–56.

Poe, Edgar Allan. "The Raven." 1845. In *The Selected Writings of Edgar Allan Poe*, edited by G. R. Thompson, 58–61. New York: Norton, 2004.

Pratt, Mary Louise. *Imperial Eyes: Travel Writing and Transculturation*. London: Routledge, 1992.

Provine, Doris Marie. *Unequal Under Law: Race in the War on Drugs*. Chicago: University of Chicago Press, 2007.

Quarles, Benjamin. *Black Abolitionists*. New York: Oxford University Press, 1969.

Remond, Charles Lenox. "Paisley Temperance Society Soiree, in Honor of Mr. Charles Lenox." *Liberator*, October 30, 1840, 1. Black Abolitionist Archives, University of Detroit Mercy. http://research.udmercy.edu/digital_collections/baa/Remond_05127spe.pdf.

Reynolds, David S., and Debra J. Rosenthal, eds. *The Serpent in the Cup: Temperance in American Literature*. Amherst: University of Massachusetts Press, 1997.

Richards, Eliza. "Outsourcing 'The Raven': Retroactive Origins." *Victorian Poetry* 43, no. 2 (2005): 205–21.

Richmond, Merle A. *Bid the Vassal Soar: Interpretative Essays on the Life and Poetry of Phillis Wheatley (ca. 1753–1784) and George Moses Horton (ca. 1797–1883)*. Washington, DC: Howard University Press, 1974.

Ripley, Peter, et al., eds. *The Black Abolitionist Papers*. Vol. 1, *The British Isles, 1830–1865*. Chapel Hill: University of North Carolina Press, 1985.

———. *The Black Abolitionist Papers*. Vol. 2, *Canada, 1830–1865*. Chapel Hill: University of North Carolina Press, 1986.

Rorabaugh, W. J. *The Alcoholic Republic: An American Tradition*. New York: Oxford University Press, 1979.

Rosenthal, Debra J. "Deracialized Discourse: Temperance and Racial Ambiguity in Harper's 'The Two Offers' and Sowing and Reaping." In Reynolds and Rosenthal, *Serpent in the Cup*, 153–64.

———. *Race Mixture in Nineteenth-Century U.S. and Spanish American Fictions*. Chapel Hill: University of North Carolina Press, 2004.

Rumbarger, John. *Profits, Power, and Prohibition: Alcohol Reform and the Industrializing of America, 1800–1930*. Albany: State University of New York Press, 1989.

Rush, Benjamin. "Observations Intended to Favor a Supposition that the Black Color (as It Is Called) of the Negroes Is Caused by Leprosy: Read at a Special Meeting July 14, 1797." *Transactions of the American Philosophical Association* 4 (1797): 289–97.

Ryan, Ann M., and Joseph B. McCullough, eds. *Cosmopolitan Twain*. Columbia: University of Missouri Press, 2008.

Sayers, Daniel O. "The Underground Railroad Reconsidered." *Western Journal of Black Studies* 28, no. 3 (2004): 435–43.

Schoolman, Martha. *Abolitionist Geographies*. Minneapolis: University of Minnesota Press, 2014.

———. "Violent Places: Three Years in Europe and the Question of William Wells Brown's Cosmopolitanism." *ESQ: A Journal of the American Renaissance* 58, no. 1 (2012): iv–35.

Schuman, Jamie. "UNC Dedicates Dorm to Chatham Slave, Poet." *Chapel Hill Herald*, February 11, 2007.

Scodel, Joshua. *Excess and the Mean in Early Modern English Literature*. Princeton, NJ: Princeton University Press, 2002.

Shadd Cary, Mary Ann. "Editorial by Mary Ann Shadd Cary, 6 December 1856." In Ripley, *Black Abolitionist Papers*, vol. 2, 352.

Shea, Louisa. *The Cynic Enlightenment: Diogenes in the Salon*. Baltimore: Johns Hopkins University Press, 2010.

Sherman, Joan R. *The Black Bard of North Carolina: George Moses Horton and His Poetry*. Chapel Hill: University of North Carolina Press, 1997.

Shorrock, Robert. *The Myth of Paganism: Nonnus, Dionysus and the World of Late Antiquity*. London: Bristol Classical Press, 2011.

Siemerling, Winnifred. *The Black Atlantic Reconsidered: Black Canadian Writing, Cultural History, and the Presence of the Past*. Montreal: McGill-Queen's University Press, 2015.

Smallwood, Stephanie. *Saltwater Slavery: A Middle Passage from Africa to American Diaspora*. Cambridge, MA: Harvard University Press, 2007.

Smith, Amanda Berry. *An Autobiography: The Story of the Lord's Dealings with Mrs. Amanda Smith the Colored Evangelist*. 1893. Schomburg Library of Nineteenth-Century Black Women Writers. New York: Oxford University Press, 1988.

Sollors, Werner. "The Goopher in Charles Chesnutt's Conjure Tales: Superstition, Ethnicity, and Modern Metamorphosis." *Letterature d'America* 6 (1986): 107–29.

Stepto, Robert B., and Jennifer Rae Greeson, eds. *The Conjure Stories*. New York: Norton, 2012.

Stewart, Carole Lynn. "Challenging Liberal Justice: The Talented Tenth Revisited." In *Recognizing W. E. B. Du Bois in the Twenty-First Century*, edited by Chester Fontenot Jr., and Mary Keller, 112–41. Macon, GA: Mercer University Press, 2007.

———. *Strange Jeremiahs: Civil Religion and the Literary Imaginations of Jonathan Edwards, Herman Melville, and W. E. B. Du Bois*. Albuquerque: University of New Mexico Press, 2010.

Stewart, John. "Spirituality and Resistance Among African-Creoles." In *New Territories, New Perspectives: The Religious Impact of the Louisiana Purchase*, edited by Richard J. Callahan Jr., 168–202. Columbia: University of Missouri Press, 2008.

Still, William. *The Underground Railroad: A Record of Facts, Authentic Narratives, Letters, &c.* Philadelphia: Porter & Coates, 1872. http://www.gutenberg.org/ebooks/15263.

Stowe, Harriet Beecher. *Uncle Tom's Cabin*. New York: Norton, 1994.

Sundquist, Eric. *To Wake the Nations*. Cambridge, MA: Harvard University Press, 1993.

Tait, Jennifer L. Woodruff. *The Poisoned Chalice: Eucharistic Grape Juice and Common-Sense Realism in Victorian Methodism*. Tuscaloosa: University of Alabama Press, 2011.

Tamarkin, Elisa. *Anglophilia: Deference, Devotion, and Antebellum America*. Chicago: University of Chicago Press, 2008.

Thompson, Paul, Jr. *A Most Stirring and Significant Episode: Religion and the Rise of Fall of Prohibition in Black Atlanta, 1865–1887*. DeKalb: Northern Illinois University Press, 2013.

Tocqueville, Alexis de. *Democracy in America*. 1862. 2 vols. The Henry Reeve text, revised by Frances Bowen. New York: Vintage Books, 1990.

Turner, Victor. *The Anthropology of Performance*. New York: PAJ Publications, 1987.

———. "The Center Out There: Pilgrim's Goal." *History of Religions* 12, no. 6 (1973): 191–230.

Turner, Victor, and Edith Turner. *Image and Pilgrimage in Christian Culture*. New York: Columbia University Press, 1978.

Tyrell, Ian. *Woman's World / Woman's Empire: The Woman's Christian Temperance Union in International Perspective, 1880–1930*. Chapel Hill: University of North Carolina Press, 1991.

Vice, Sue. "Intemperate Climate: Drinking, Sobriety, and the American Literary Myth." *American Literary History* 11, no. 4 (Winter 1999): 699–709.

Vinson, Synan. *The Holiness-Pentecostal Tradition: Charismatic Movements in the Twentieth Century*. Grand Rapids, MI: Eerdmans, 1997.

Wagner-McCoy, Sarah. "Virgilian Chesnutt: Eclogues of Slavery and Georgics of Reconstruction in the *Conjure Tales*." *ELH* 80, no. 1 (Spring 2013): 199–220.

Walker, Corey. *A Noble Fight: African American Freemasonry and the Struggle for Democracy in America*. Urbana: University of Illinois Press. 2008.

Wallerstein, Immanuel. "Neither Patriotism nor Cosmopolitanism." In *For Love of Country: Debating the Limits of Patriotism*, by Martha C. Nussbaum, edited by Joshua Cohen, 122–24. Boston: Beacon, 2002.

Walser, Richard. *The Black Poet: Being the Remarkable Story (Partly Told My [sic] Himself) of George Moses Horton a North Carolina Slave*. New York: Philosophical Library, 1966.

Walters, William L. *Black Americans and the Evangelization of Africa, 1877–1900*. Madison: University of Wisconsin Press 1982.

Ward, Samuel Ringgold. "Samuel Ringgold Ward to Henry Bibb, 16 October 1851." In Ripley, *Black Abolitionist Papers*, vol. 2, 177–81.

Washington, Booker T. *Up from Slavery: An Autobiography*. New York: Doubleday, Page, 1902.

Wayne, "The Black Population of Canada West on the Eve of the American Civil War: A Reassessment Based on the Manuscript Census of 1861." *Social History / Histoire Sociale* 28, no. 56 (1995): 465–85.

Wells, Ida B. *Crusade for Justice: The Autobiography of Ida B. Wells*. Edited by Alfreda M. Duster. Chicago: University of Chicago Press, 1991.

Werbner, Pnina, ed. *Anthropology and the New Cosmopolitanism: Rooted, Feminist and*

Vernacular Perspectives. Oxford, U.K.: Berg, 2008.

Whitman, Walt. *Franklin Evans; or, The Inebriate: A Tale of the Times*. Edited by Christopher Castiglia and Glenn Hendler. Durham, NC: Duke University Press, 2007.

Willard, Frances. *Glimpses of Fifty Years: The Autobiography of an American Woman*. Boston: G. M. Smith, 1889.

Winks, Robin. *The Blacks in Canada: A History*. Montreal: McGill-Queen's University, 1997.

Yacovene, Donald. "The Transformation of the Black Temperance Movement, 1827–1854: An Interpretation." *Journal of the Early Republic* 8 (1988): 281–97.

Index

abstinence, 10, 41, 78, 163
addiction, 18, 146, 169, 178
African American Freemasonry, 30
African Methodist Episcopal (AME) Church, 144–45, 195n10. *see also* Holiness movement; Methodist Church
Albanese, Catharine, 29
alcohol/alcoholism. *see also* inebriety/intemperance; stereotypes
    as anodyne, 41, 42
    class and, 44
    disease of, 133
    entertainment and, 134
    Inquiry into the Effect of Ardent Spirits Upon the Human Body and the Mind, An (Rush), 10
    master race/master class and, 27, 42, 99
    race and, 94, 132
    recovery and, 135
    slave holding states and, 12
    slavery and, 6, 178
    suffering/sublime and, 18, 19
    triangular slave trade and, 14–15
    in the United States, 9
amalgamation, 63–64, 186n26
American Fugitive in Europe: Sketches of Places and People Abroad (Brown), 59, 65, 69, 74–75. *see also* Brown, William Wells
Andrews, William, 85
appetite, 139, 169, 170
Appiah, Anthony, 17, 183n52
Arendt, Hannah, 48, 108, 110, 171–172, 197n8
Aristotle, 68, 93, 197n7
"Art of the Poet, The" (Horton), 101. *see also* Horton, George Moses
autobiographies, 153, 195n24
Autobiography: The Story of the Lord's Dealings with Mrs. Amanda Smith, the Colored Evangelist; Containing an Account of Her Life Work of Faith, and Her Travels in America, England, Ireland, Scotland, *India, and Africa, as Independent Missionary* (Smith), 141–42. *see also* Smith, Amanda Berry

Baraw, Charles, 58, 61–62
Barrett, Faith, 110, 191n100
Bassard, Katherine Clay, 152–53
Baucom, Ian, 15–18, 22, 65, 76
Bauer, Ralph, 118, 125–26
Beaumont, Gustave de, 71–72, 80
Beecher, Lyman, 9
Berlin, Ira, 4–5, 91, 153
Bibb, Henry, 47
Black Man, His Antecedents, His Genius, and His Achievements, The (Brown), 55, 67, 187n61. *see also* Brown, William Wells
Blake; or, The Huts of America (Delany). *see under* Delany, Martin
Blassingame, John W., 119
"body of time," 103–4, 107–8
Brown, William Wells, 57-84
    alcohol and class, 43–44
    alcohol use, personal, 42
    amalgamation and, 63–64, 186n26
    American Fugitive in Europe: Sketches of Places and People Abroad (Brown), 59, 65, 69, 74–75
    Black Man, His Antecedents, His Genius, and His Achievements, The (Brown), 55, 67, 187n61
    on Canada, 45, 47, 49, 51–54
    civilization and, 61–64, 70, 83
    Clotel; or, the President's Daughter (Brown): "blacking" in, 43; Canada in, 49, 51–53; "passing" as white in, 51, 54; "patiche" in, 76; revised ending of, 72; "tragic mulatta," 43, 72; Underground Railroad and, 52
    "Colored People of Canada, The" (Brown), 45, 55
    cosmopolitanism and, 23–24, 40, 57, 83

Brown, William Wells (*continued*)
    creolization/creolized aesthetics, 76
    culture and "civilization," 82
    on democracy/democratic values, 60–61, 79, 80, 84
    duplication in writing, 76
    elevation and, 44
    elitism and, 37–38
    emigration and, 38–40, 67
    Escape; or, A Leap for Freedom, The (Brown), 19, 47–49, 68
    escape/Underground Railroad and, 50
    as a fugitive, 182n49
    Great Exhibition and, 3–4, 22
    Haiti and, 58, 184n61
    heroism/antiheroism and, 71, 187n61
    historiography in writings, 63
    home and, 50, 72–74, 83
    identity and, 49, 66, 83, 186n30, 187n61
    Independent Order of Good Templars and, 40–41, 73
    on John B. Gough, 75–76
    on manners, 66, 72, 74, 80–81, 84
    on Martin Delany, 39
    My Southern Home (Brown): aristocratic culture in, 78–79; Catholicism and, 79–80; civil societies, 73; communitas/communities in, 81–82; cosmopolitan exchange, 63–64; discussions in, 71; home/sacred spaces, 83; Poplar Farms in, 72; rooted cosmopolitanism in, 57; temperance organizations and, 58; temperance/self-control in, 60
    Narrative (Brown), 42
    narrative strategies/voice of, 22, 60, 65
    on "passing" as white, 51, 54, 56
    on restraint, 69–70, 75, 81, 147–48
    Rising Son; or the Antecedents of the Advancement of the Colored Race, The (Brown), 58, 65, 67–70
    on slavery, 82
    on soil, 50, 56, 83–84
    Sons of Temperance, 40–41, 73
    the sublime and, 22
    on sympathy, 76
    temperance and, 23, 43
    temperance societies and, 77–78
    Three Years in Europe; or, Places I Have Seen and People I Have Met (Brown): civilization in, 62–63; civil societies, 81; cosmopolitan alternative/cultural position in, 59; culture/nobility in, 79; Edinburgh Temperance Society, 77; on Elihu Burritt, 44; manners/restraint in, 74–75; relationship to surroundings in, 61–62; St. Catharines and, 51
    on Toussaint L'Ouverture, 67–69
    transnational structures, 61
    travel narratives of, 16, 19, 39
    on Washingtonians, 40

Cable, George Washington, 121–22, 126
Canada
    dry communities in, 46–47
    Martin Delany on, 44–45
    racism in, 46–47
    segregation in, 51, 54, 56, 185n114
    William Wells Brown on, 45, 47, 51–54
capitalism
    black capitalism, 28, 183n33
    in *Blake; or, The Huts of America* (Delany), 32–33
    in Charles Chesnutt's writing, 175–76, 198n28
    Frances Harper on, 111–12, 115–16
    Protestantism and, 5
Catholicism, 79–80, 120, 164, 166
chattel slavery. *see* slaves/slavery
Chavigny, Katherine A., 147
Chesnutt, Charles
    classicism and, 171, 197n5
    conjure and, 170, 175–76
    Conjure Woman, The (Chesnutt), 170
    "Dave's Neckliss" (Chesnutt), 174
    economic subtext in writing, 172
    "Goophered Grapevine, The" (Chesnutt), 174–75, 177, 197n14
    as "local color," 176
    "Lonesome Ben" (Chesnutt): as creolized text, 174; earth-eating and, 169, 173, 197n2; racial ambiguity in, 173; relation to the land, 170; temperance and, 177
    metamorphosis/transformations and, 174–75, 197n6
    "Superstitions and Folklore of the South" (Chesnutt), 177
Chiles, Katy, 33
Chireau, Yvonne, 170

civilization
    creolized civilization, 64, 119
    Frances Harper on, 130–33
    locus of, 31, 70
    William Wells Brown on, 61–63, 83
civil space, 23–24, 92. see also space
clay-eating. see "earth-eating"
Clotel; or, the President's Daughter (Brown). see under Brown, William Wells
Clymer, Jeffory, 35
"Colored People of Canada, The" (Brown), 45, 55. see also Brown, William Wells
"Color-Phobia in Canada" (Bibb), 47
communitas, 82, 160, 164–65, 188n110
Condition, Elevation, Emigration and Destiny of the Colored People of the United States, The (Delany), 36–38, 45. see also Delany, Martin
conjure, 35, 170, 172, 175–76
conjure tales, 169, 172, 178, 197n6
Conjure Woman, The (Chesnutt), 170. see also Chesnutt, Charles
cosmopolitan exchange
    amalgamation and, 64, 71–72, 186n26
    Delany and Brown on, 28
    George Moses Horton and, 89, 91, 108
    William Wells Brown and, 83–84
cosmopolitan identity, 130
cosmopolitanism. see also Kant, Immanuel; rooted cosmopolitanism
    Amanda Berry Smith and, 166
    "from below," 25, 57, 63
    bourgeois cosmopolitanism, 116
    communities of interest and, 115
    creole cosmopolitanism, 114, 127, 177
    critical cosmopolitanism, 59
    definition of, 2
    Diogenes the Cynic and, 2, 115
    formative site for, 140
    Frances Harper and, 114, 119, 127, 130
    Haitian cosmopolites, 120–21
    "Idea for a Universal History with a Cosmopolitan Perspective" (Kant, 1784), 165
    Martin Delany and, 23, 37
    racial nationalism and, 27
    refugees and, 27–28, 183n55
    temperance and, 59
    versions of, 16–17
    William Wells Brown and, 23

cosmopolitan memory, 183n55
cosmopolitan space, 20–21, 86. see also space
creole/Creoles. see also mulattos; one-drop racism; quadroons
    appetite and, 139
    definition/meaning of, 114, 118, 140, 177
    deracialized fiction and, 138
    Martin Delany on, 34
    racial ambiguity and, 122–23
creole folktales, 174
créolité, 60, 114, 117, 140
creolization
    assimilation and, 28
    in Charles Chesnutt's writing, 173
    cultural/linguistic process, 118–19
    diversion and, 65
    in Frances Harper's writing, 113
    liminality and, 128
    temperance and, 20
    transnational creolization, 140
creolized civilization, 64, 119
creolized style, 152
Crowley, John W., 92, 189n38-39
Crystal Palace Exhibition. see Great Exhibition
Csordas, Thomas J., 157

"Dave's Neckliss" (Chesnutt), 174. see also Chesnutt, Charles
Davis, David Brion, 29
Delany, Martin
    1853 lectures on Masonry, 30–31
    black nationalism, 26, 28, 37, 183n33
    Blake; or, The Huts of America (Delany): capitalism in, 32–33; "Divine Providence"/religion in, 34–35; hierarchy in, 28, 35–36; internal purity in, 26; Masonry in, 32; racism in, 34, 45; on Canada, 44–45
    Condition, Elevation, Emigration and Destiny of the Colored People of the United States, The (Delany), 36–38, 45
    cosmopolitanism and, 23, 27, 37
    elitism and, 37–38
    emigration and, 24, 33, 38, 45
    Frederick Douglass and, 25
    hierarchy and, 27–28, 35–36
    "Political Aspect of the Colored People, The" (Delaney), 45
    Political Destiny of the Colored Race on the American Continent (Delany), 33

Delany, Martin (*continued*)
   Principia of Ethnology (Delany), 36, 193n86
   racial identity and, 34
   racial/masculine purity, 27
   "Report of the Niger Valley Exploring Party" (Delany), 25
   temperance and, 23–25, 37
   transnationalism and, 26
   on William Wells Brown, 39
democratic civilization/values, 60–61, 79–80, 84
dialect, 152. *see also* language
diaspora, 8, 28, 178
Diogenes the Cynic, 2, 48, 115, 185n100
diversion, 22, 64–65, 142, 196n23
"Division of an Estate" (Horton), 95. *see also* Horton, George Moses
Douglass, Frederick
   alcohol and, 93
   animalization and, 94
   freedom and, 10–11, 182n38
   intemperance and, 12, 99–100
   Narrative of the Life of Frederick Douglass (Douglass), 11–12
Douglass-Chin, Richard, 150–52
Dred Scott decision (1857), 67
Drew, Benjamin, 52, 185n117
drunkenness. *see* inebriety/intemperance
Du Bois, W.E.B., 37–38, 171

"earth-eating," 169, 171, 176
Elias, Norbert, 22, 66, 132
elitism, 27, 37–38, 94
emigration, 24–25, 33, 39, 45, 67
Enlightenment, 2, 6
Ernest, John, 16, 48, 58, 65, 76
Escape; or, A Leap for Freedom, The (Brown), 19, 47–49, 68. *see also* Brown, William Wells
ethnology, 36, 133

Fahey, David, 41, 73, 77, 182n26, 184n68-69, 186n34
faith, 149, 161–62. *see also* Smith, Amanda Berry
"Fancy Sketches" (Harper), 116. *see also* Harper, Frances
Farmer, William, 4, 42–43
Fleisner, Jennifer L., 169–71, 176
Foreman, Gabrielle P., 138
Franklin, John Hope, 88

Franklin Evans; or The Inebriate: A Tale of the Times (Whitman), 132–33. *see also* Whitman, Walt
freedom
   community and, 143
   elements of, 5–6
   Frederick Douglass and, 10–11, 182n38
   George Moses Horton and, 105–7, 109
   holiness/sanctification as, 152
   of the land, 84
   public memory/recognition as, 89, 108
   "the pursuit of happiness" and, 92
   temperance as, 97, 142, 177–78
   temperate public space and, 91, 101
Freemasonry
   Amanda Berry Smith and, 148
   Martin Delany and, 28–32, 37
Fugitive Slave Law (1851), 67, 84
Fulton, DoVeanna S., 137–38

Gabriel Prosser's Rebellion (1800), 32
genius
   animalization and, 93
   Charles Chesnutt and, 172
   George Moses Horton and, 86, 89–90, 101–3
   Thomas Jefferson on, 125
Gemeinschaft/Gesellschaft, 115
Gikandi, Simon, 48–49
Gilmore, Glenda Elizabeth, 136
Gilroy, Paul, 16, 22, 26, 34
Glissant, Eduard, 64–66, 77, 118, 174
"Goophered Grapevine, The" (Chesnutt), 174–75, 177, 197n14. *see also* Chesnutt, Charles
Grandissimes, The (Cable), 121–22. *see also* Cable, George Washington
Great Exhibition, 1–3
Greeson, Jennifer Rae, 122, 191n16, 197n2

Haiti
   emigration and, 33, 66–67
   in Frances Harper's writing, 114
   Haitian cosmopolites, 120–21
   Haitian/Haytian Revolution, 187n38
   lieux de mémoire and, 187n39
   as modern black republic, 125
   William Wells Brown on, 39, 58, 68, 184n61
Hall, Prince, 30
Harper, Frances, 111-140

on capitalism, 111
civilization and, 130–33
communities of interest and, 115–16, 135
cosmopolitanism and, 114, 119, 127, 130
creoles in writing, 122, 138–39
on creolization, 133
on domesticity, 138–39
early life, 112
excess and, 124
"Fancy Sketches" (Harper), 116
Haiti and, 114, 133
histotextuality and, 138
on inebriety/intemperance, 21, 132–33, 135
Iola Leroy (Harper): "conversazione" in, 129; cosmopolitanism in, 114–15; excess and, 116; geographic setting of, 117, 192n28; "passing" as white, 120; racial ambiguity in, 123–24
Minnie's Sacrifice (Harper): Anglo asceticism and, 126; excess and, 116, 127; Haitian Revolution and, 113–14; New Orleans and, 117; "passing" as white, 124–25; privilege in, 128; racial ambiguity in, 124; self-discipline in, 113
on natural history, 129
New Orleans in writings, 119
on Northern racism, 126, 134
"passing" as white in writing, 117, 120, 124–25
poetry of, 112
public opinion and, 131, 137, 193n91, 194n135
racial ambiguity in writing, 119–20, 123, 137
racial identity, personal, 140
racial uplift and, 116–17, 120
readership and, 124
on self-discipline, 113
Sowing and Reaping: A Temperance Tale (Harper), 112–13, 134–35, 138–39
support groups and, 134
temperance and, 111–13, 136
"tragic mulatta" in writing, 117
transnationalism, 120, 127
Trial and Triumph (Harper), 123, 130
"Two Offers, The" (Harper), 112, 139
"We Are All Bound Up Together" (Harper), 131, 137
Women's Christian Temperance Union and, 111–12, 128–29, 131

"Women's Christian Temperance Union and the Colored Woman, The" (Harper), 135
Harvey, David, 16, 116, 161, 191n21
Hendler, Glenn, 24, 27, 76
hiring out, 85
Holiness movement, 142, 145, 155, 194n2, 194n3
home
    Amanda Berry Smith and, 157–59, 196n31
    in Charles Chesnutt's writing, 171, 176
    George Moses Horton and, 90, 109–10
    lieux de mémoire and, 49–50
    pilgrimages and, 167
    William Wells Brown and, 61, 73, 83
homelessness, 48, 165
Hope of Liberty, The (Horton), 87–88. see also Horton, George Moses
Horton, George Moses, 85–110
    alcohol and, 97, 99
    animalization and, 94–95, 103
    "Art of the Poet, The" (Horton), 101
    background/characterization of, 86–87, 96
    body of time, 103–4, 107, 108
    Caroline Lee Hentz and, 87, 100
    cosmopolitanism and, 21
    "Division of an Estate" (Horton), 95
    and Edgar Allan Poe, 97–98
    egotism and, 91
    elitism and, 94, 107
    freedom (inner), 97, 99
    freedom (literal), 87, 89–91, 102, 109
    freedom (performative), 93, 105–7
    genius and, 101–3, 107
    home and, 90, 109–10
    "In Hope of Liberty" (Horton), 95
    Hope of Liberty, The (Horton), 87–88
    inebriety/sobriety and, 88–89, 98, 100
    "Intemperance Club" (Horton), 96–97
    "On Liberty and Slavery" (Horton), 95, 103
    Naked Genius (Horton), 88, 109–10
    Neoclassical tradition, 100–101, 106
    nostalgia in poetry, 171
    "One Generation Passeth Away and Another Cometh" (Horton), 107
    as an orator, 104
    Poetical Works, The (Horton), 86, 88, 96, 102, 190n53
    "Poet's Feeble Petition, The" (Horton), 90

Horton, George Moses (*continued*)
    public fame, 102, 107–8
    public space and, 100–101, 105, 107–8
    rhyme/meter/style and, 87, 100
    "Southern Refugee, The" (Horton), 109
    sublimity and, 98
    themes in writing, 89, 95–97, 106
    "Tippler to His Bottle, The" (Horton), 97–98
    University of North Carolina and, 86, 91, 103–5
Hughes-Warrington, Marnie, 63

"Idea for a Universal History with a Cosmopolitan Perspective" (Kant), 2, 165. *see also* Kant, Immanuel
identity. *see also* racial ambiguity/identity
    authentic identity, 48
    cosmopolitan identity, 130
    displaced, 176
    and homeland, 83
    immigrants and, 56
    positive sources of, 120
    primitive/civilized, 64
    transnational identity, 66, 120
    trickster identity, 82, 173, 186n30, 187n61, 197n14
Independent Order of Good Templars, 40–41, 73, 77–79
Industrial Revolution, 3–5
inebriety/intemperance
    Benjamin Rush on, 10
    as character defect, 147
    in *Clotel; or, the President's Daughter* (Brown), 92
    excess of power and, 92
    George Moses Horton and, 88, 96, 104
    Lyman Beecher on, 9
    master race/class and, 27, 42, 99
    risk for, 44
    slavery and, 7, 69
    Walt Whitman on, 132
"In Hope of Liberty" (Horton), 95. *see also* Horton, George Moses
Inquiry into the Effect of Ardent Spirits Upon the Human Body and the Mind, An (Rush), 10. *see also* Rush, Benjamin
"Intemperance Club" (Horton), 96–97. *see also* Horton, George Moses
Iola Leroy (Harper). *see under* Harper, Frances

Islam, 64, 69–70
Israel, Adrienne, 196n42, 196n48, 196n54

Jacob, Margaret, 29, 31
Jefferson, Thomas, 7, 48, 125

Kant, Immanuel
    alliances and, 57
    citizen of the world, 19
    on cosmopolitanism, 16–17, 116
    human affairs/society and, 166
    "Idea for a Universal History with a Cosmopolitan Perspective" (Kant), 2, 165
    sublime and, 76

language, 153, 195n24. *see also* dialect
Leonard, Keith, 89–90
Levine, Robert
    on Frederick Douglass, 10
    on Martin Delany, 25–26, 31, 36
    on temperance, 8
    on William Wells Brown, 43, 60, 69
Lewis, Leslie 117, 128
liberal cosmopolitanism, 16–17, 22
lieux de mémoire, 49–50, 187n39
liminality, 105, 128, 173
literacy, 87, 102, 190n77
local color, 114, 176, 191n16
"Lonesome Ben" (Chesnutt). *see under* Chesnutt, Charles
Long, Charles H., 6, 62, 66, 121, 192n37
Louisiana, 119, 121–22, 125, 130

Masonry. *see* Freemasonry
McGann, Jerome, 35
Mendiola, Kelly Willis, 154
metaphors
    "blacking" as, 43, 92
    intoxication as, 44
    slavery as, 8–10, 13, 130
    "slave to the bottle" as, 99
Methodist Church, 142, 144, 151. *see also* African Methodist Episcopal (AME) Church; Holiness movement
Middle Passage, 9, 14
Minnie's Sacrifice (Harper). *see under* Harper, Frances
mulattos, 34, 122. *see also* "passing" as white; "tragic mulatta"

My Southern Home (Brown). *see* under Brown, William Wells

Naked Genius (Horton), 88, 109–10. *see also* Horton, George Moses
Narrative (Brown), 42. *see also* Brown, William Wells
Narrative of the Life of Frederick Douglass (Douglass), 11–12. *see also* Douglass, Frederick
natural history, 125–26, 128–29
Nerad, Julie Cary, 119–20
New Orleans. *see under* Harper, Frances; Louisiana
nostalgia, 169–71
Notes on the State of Virginia (Jefferson), 7. *see also* Jefferson, Thomas
Nwankwo, Ifeoma Kiddoe, 25, 34, 57

one-drop racism, 117–20, 121, 192n27
"One Generation Passeth Away and Another Cometh" (Horton), 107. *see also* Horton, George Moses
"On Liberty and Slavery" (Horton), 95, 103. *see also* Horton, George Moses

Pagden, Anthony, 68, 81, 187n45-46, 188n107, 191n20,
parallelism, 65, 154, 196n23
Park, Mungo, 70
"passing" as white, 51, 117, 124-25, 192n40. *see also* "tragic mulatta"
performance, 93, 105–7, 192n27
Peterson, Carla, 113, 116, 119
pilgrimages, 50, 166–67
plagiarism, 188n87, 190n57
Poetical Works, The (Horton), 86, 88, 96, 102, 190n53. *see also* Horton, George Moses
"Poet's Feeble Petition, The" (Horton), 90. *see also* Horton, George Moses
"Political Aspect of the Colored People, The" (Delany), 45. *see also* Delany, Martin
Political Destiny of the Colored Race on the American Continent (Delany), 33. *see also* Delany, Martin
poverty, 41–42, 44, 149
Powers, Hiram and "The Greek Slave," 3–4
Principia of Ethnology (Delany), 36, 193n86. *see also* Delany, Martin
Prohibition, 181n15

Protestantism, 5, 7, 29, 80–81
psychogenesis/sociogenesis, 66, 132
public space, 100–101, 105, 107–8. *see also* space
purity, 26, 96

quadroons, 122, 128

racial ambiguity/identity
  "creole" as, 122, 138, 140
  in Frances Harper's writing, 116–17, 119, 123
  liminality, 173
  Martin Delany and, 34
racial uplift, 116–17
racism, 7, 47, 55, 126, 131, 136. *see also* one-drop racism; white supremacy
Redding, Saunders, 91
religion. *see* African Methodist Episcopal (AME) Church; Catholicism; conjure; Holiness movement; Islam; Methodist Church; Protestantism
"Report of the Niger Valley Exploring Party" (Delany), 25. *see also* Delany, Martin
restraint
  creolized positions and, 178
  temperate practices and, 116
  William Wells Brown on, 69–70, 74–75, 81, 146
rhetorical devices/strategies, 95, 105, 154
Rising Son; or the Antecedents of the Advancement of the Colored Race, The (Brown), 58, 65, 67–70. *see also* Brown, William Wells
romanticism, 98, 188n87
rooted cosmopolitanism
  Anthony Appiah and, 17, 183n52
  Frances Harper and, 114, 120, 127, 130
  William Wells Brown and, 57, 83
Rorabaugh, W. J., 9
Rosenthal, Debra, 132, 137, 194n126
rum, 14. *see also* alcohol/alcoholism
Rush, Benjamin, 10

sacred space, 50, 83, 161, 166–67. *see also* space
Schoolman, Martha, 58, 61–62
Shadd Cary, Mary Ann, 46, 54
Sherman, Joan, 88–89, 95–96, 101
sin, 134, 144, 147, 155, 194n2
slaves/slavery
  alcoholism and, 6, 134, 178
  animalization of, 93–94

slaves/slavery (*continued*)
    Aristotle on, 68, 93, 197n7
    classical examples of, 100, 171, 197n7
    hiring out and, 85
    Louisiana Purchase and, 121
    meaning of, 93
    as metaphor, 8, 13, 130
    obscurity and, 108
    recovery from, 135
    slave societies and, 5
    sublimity and, 18
    transatlantic trade and, 178
    triangular slave trade, 14–15
    as ungodly, 145
Smith, Amanda Berry, 141–168
    abstinence and, 163
    alcohol/liquor and, 149, 161
    anxieties and, 150, 153
    Autobiography: The Story of the Lord's Dealings with Mrs. Amanda Smith, the Colored Evangelist; Containing an Account of Her Life Work of Faith, and Her Travels in America, England, Ireland, Scotland, India, and Africa, as an Independent Missionary (Smith), 141–42
    charity and, 150–51, 164, 195n18
    communitas and, 160, 164–65
    conversion and, 144, 162
    cosmopolitanism and, 166
    domestic life, 157–58
    faith and, 149, 161–62
    God and, 157–58, 164–65, 167
    gospel temperance and, 21, 146–49
    Great Commission and, 155, 158
    on heathens, 160–62
    home and, 157, 159, 196n31
    identity and, 156
    independence and, 151, 167
    Liberia/West Africa and, 149, 151, 155–56, 160–61, 196n44
    life as antistructure, 167–68
    Masonry and, 148
    pilgrimages/missionary journeys and, 156, 159, 166–67
    on racial categories/equality, 144–45, 162
    racism and, 155
    sanctification and, 143–44, 147, 155, 160, 167
    Satan's voice and, 153, 158, 163
    sense of space, 154–55
    on superstition, 161–64
    temperance and, 142–43, 145, 152
    transnationalism, 156–57, 164
    on Victorian values, 149–50
    Women's Christian Temperance Union and, 142, 146, 159, 196n54
    writing style of, 20, 154
sobriety, 69, 88–89. *see also* inebriety/intemperance
social death, 5, 11
soil, 50, 56, 73, 83–84. *see also* "earth-eating"
Sons of Temperance, 40–41, 56, 73, 77
"Southern Refugee" (Horton), 109. *see also* Horton, George Moses
Sowing and Reaping: A Temperance Tale (Harper), 112–13, 134–35, 138–39. *see also* Harper, Frances
space
    civil space, 23–24, 92
    cosmopolitan space, 20–21, 86
    creolized space, 130
    public space, 100–101, 105, 107–8
    sacred space, 50, 83, 161, 166–67
    transcultural exchange and, 61
St. Catharines. *see* Canada
Still, William, 112, 193n93
stereotypes, 6–7, 124, 139, 196n42, 197n14. *see also* "tragic mulatta"
sublimity, 17–19, 22, 76, 98. *see also* cosmopolitanism; Kant, Immanuel
"Superstitions and Folklore of the South" (Chesnutt), 177. *see also* Chesnutt, Charles

Tait, Jennifer L. Woodruff, 9
temperance
    abstinence and, 163
    alcohol and, 9–10
    antislavery and, 9, 23, 46
    creolized origins of, 70
    development of, 182n31
    diasporic communities and, 12
    diasporic understanding of, 24
    freedom and, 41, 142, 177–78
    gospel temperance, 146–49
    Islam and, 69–70
    meaning of, 6, 59
    Methodism and, 60
    Protestantism and, 7

public culture and, 99
purity and, 96, 133
temperance literature, 19, 92, 96–97, 133
temperance societies, 24, 40, 77, 181n18. *see also* Sons of Temperance; Washingtonians; Women's Christian Temperance Union
Temperance Society of St. Catharines, 46
Templars. *see* Independent Order of Good Templars
Three Years in Europe; or, Places I Have Seen and People I Have Met (Brown). *see under* Brown, William Wells
"Tippler to His Bottle, The" (Horton), 97–98. *see also* Horton, George Moses
Tocqueville, Alexis de, 71, 80–82
"tragic mulatta," 43, 72, 117, 192n27. *see also* mulattos
transatlantic slave trade, 14–15
transformation stories, 172
transnational exchange, 166
transnational identity, 66, 120
transnationalism
    Amanda Berry Smith and, 156–57, 164
    chattel slavery and, 6
    Frances Harper and, 120, 127
    Martin Delany and, 26
    New Orleans and, 122
    William Wells Brown and, 61
"traveling subjectivity," 50
travel literature/narratives, 39, 60
Travels in the Interior Districts of Africa (Park), 70. *see also* Park, Mungo
Trial and Triumph (Harper), 123, 130. *see also* Harper, Frances
triangular slave trade, 14–15, 48
trickster identity, 82, 173, 186n30, 187n61, 197n14
Turner, Victor, 82, 160, 167, 188n110
"Two Offers, The" (Harper), 112, 139. *see also* Harper, Frances
Tyrell, Ian, 7

Underground Railroad,
    William Wells Brown and, 21, 45, 49-50, 52, 184n61
    Frances Harper and, 112
    Amanda Berry Smith and, 152
    Canada and, 186n135
University of North Carolina, 86, 91, 103–5

vernacular cosmopolitanism, 17
"Virginian Slave," 3–4, 181n7

Walker, Corey, 29–30, 32
Walser, Richard, 88–89
Washington, Booker T., 37–38, 152, 171
Washingtonians, 40, 75–76, 78
"We Are All Bound Up Together" (Harper), 131, 137. *see also* Harper, Frances
Wells, Ida B., 13, 136, 159, 196n40
white supremacy, 6, 73, 117, 128, 153
Whitman, Walt, 132–33
Willard, Frances E., 13, 136, 159, 194n120, 196n40, 196n42. *see also* Women's Christian Temperance Union
Women's Christian Temperance Union
    Amanda Berry Smith and, 142, 146, 159, 196n51
    Frances Harper and, 111–12, 128–29, 131, 137
    "Home Protection Movement," 136
    missionizing and, 7–8
    segregation in, 13
"Women's Christian Temperance Union and the Colored Woman, The" (Harper), 135. *see also* Harper, Frances

Zong massacre (1781), 15–16

www.ingramcontent.com/pod-product-compliance
Lightning Source LLC
Chambersburg PA
CBHW021945290426

44108CB00012B/965